C-2061   CAREER EXAMINATION SERIES

This is your PASSBOOK® for...

Supervising Court Office Assistant

Test Preparation Study Guide
Questions & Answers

NATIONAL LEARNING CORPORATION

PASSBOOK®

NOTICE

PASSBOOK SERIES®

THE *PASSBOOK SERIES®* has been created to prepare applicants and candidates for the ultimate academic battlefield – the examination room.

At some time in our lives, each and every one of us may be required to take an examination – for validation, matriculation, admission, qualification, registration, certification, or licensure.

Based on the assumption that every applicant or candidate has met the basic formal educational standards, has taken the required number of courses, and read the necessary texts, the *PASSBOOK SERIES®* furnishes the one special preparation which may assure passing with confidence, instead of failing with insecurity. Examination questions – together with answers – are furnished as the basic vehicle for study so that the mysteries of the examination and its compounding difficulties may be eliminated or diminished by a sure method.

This book is meant to help you pass your examination provided that you qualify and are serious in your objective.

The entire field is reviewed through the huge store of content information which is succinctly presented through a provocative and challenging approach – the question-and-answer method.

A climate of success is established by furnishing the correct answers at the end of each test.

You soon learn to recognize types of questions, forms of questions, and patterns of questioning. You may even begin to anticipate expected outcomes.

You perceive that many questions are repeated or adapted so that you can gain acute insights, which may enable you to score many sure points.

You learn how to confront new questions, or types of questions, and to attack them confidently and work out the correct answers.

You note objectives and emphases, and recognize pitfalls and dangers, so that you may make positive educational adjustments.

Moreover, you are kept fully informed in relation to new concepts, methods, practices, and directions in the field.

You discover that you are actually taking the examination all the time: you are preparing for the examination by "taking" an examination, not by reading extraneous and/or supererogatory textbooks.

In short, this PASSBOOK®, used directedly, should be an important factor in helping you to pass your test.

SUPERVISING COURT OFFICE ASSISTANT

DUTIES

Supervising Court Office Assistants are unit supervisors of a clerical or processing unit staffed by three or more subordinate personnel, or are assistant supervisors within a large unit supervised by higher-level personnel. Supervising Court Office Assistants work with a substantial degree of independence on a variety of office clerical and administrative tasks. Supervising Court Office Assistants may perform incidental keyboarding of information, may work in courts of every jurisdiction as part clerks in those parts that operate on less than a full-time basis, or as supervisors of central jury rooms, and perform other related duties. Supervising Court Office Assistants are located in courts of every jurisdiction, Country Clerks' and Commissioner of Jurors' Offices, law libraries, and administrative offices and auxiliary agencies in the Unified Court System.

SCOPE OF THE EXAMINATION

The <u>written test</u> will cover knowledge, skills and/or abilities in such areas as:

1. Applying facts and information to given situations;
2. Court record keeping;
3. Preparing written material;
4. Legal terminology; and
5. Supervision and office management.

HOW TO TAKE A TEST

I. YOU MUST PASS AN EXAMINATION

A. WHAT EVERY CANDIDATE SHOULD KNOW

Examination applicants often ask us for help in preparing for the written test. What can I study in advance? What kinds of questions will be asked? How will the test be given? How will the papers be graded?

As an applicant for a civil service examination, you may be wondering about some of these things. Our purpose here is to suggest effective methods of advance study and to describe civil service examinations.

Your chances for success on this examination can be increased if you know how to prepare. Those "pre-examination jitters" can be reduced if you know what to expect. You can even experience an adventure in good citizenship if you know why civil service exams are given.

B. WHY ARE CIVIL SERVICE EXAMINATIONS GIVEN?

Civil service examinations are important to you in two ways. As a citizen, you want public jobs filled by employees who know how to do their work. As a job seeker, you want a fair chance to compete for that job on an equal footing with other candidates. The best-known means of accomplishing this two-fold goal is the competitive examination.

Exams are widely publicized throughout the nation. They may be administered for jobs in federal, state, city, municipal, town or village governments or agencies.

Any citizen may apply, with some limitations, such as the age or residence of applicants. Your experience and education may be reviewed to see whether you meet the requirements for the particular examination. When these requirements exist, they are reasonable and applied consistently to all applicants. Thus, a competitive examination may cause you some uneasiness now, but it is your privilege and safeguard.

C. HOW ARE CIVIL SERVICE EXAMS DEVELOPED?

Examinations are carefully written by trained technicians who are specialists in the field known as "psychological measurement," in consultation with recognized authorities in the field of work that the test will cover. These experts recommend the subject matter areas or skills to be tested; only those knowledges or skills important to your success on the job are included. The most reliable books and source materials available are used as references. Together, the experts and technicians judge the difficulty level of the questions.

Test technicians know how to phrase questions so that the problem is clearly stated. Their ethics do not permit "trick" or "catch" questions. Questions may have been tried out on sample groups, or subjected to statistical analysis, to determine their usefulness.

Written tests are often used in combination with performance tests, ratings of training and experience, and oral interviews. All of these measures combine to form the best-known means of finding the right person for the right job.

II. HOW TO PASS THE WRITTEN TEST

A. NATURE OF THE EXAMINATION

To prepare intelligently for civil service examinations, you should know how they differ from school examinations you have taken. In school you were assigned certain definite pages to read or subjects to cover. The examination questions were quite detailed and usually emphasized memory. Civil service exams, on the other hand, try to discover your present ability to perform the duties of a position, plus your potentiality to learn these duties. In other words, a civil service exam attempts to predict how successful you will be. Questions cover such a broad area that they cannot be as minute and detailed as school exam questions.

In the public service similar kinds of work, or positions, are grouped together in one "class." This process is known as *position-classification*. All the positions in a class are paid according to the salary range for that class. One class title covers all of these positions, and they are all tested by the same examination.

B. FOUR BASIC STEPS

1) Study the announcement

How, then, can you know what subjects to study? Our best answer is: "Learn as much as possible about the class of positions for which you've applied." The exam will test the knowledge, skills and abilities needed to do the work.

Your most valuable source of information about the position you want is the official exam announcement. This announcement lists the training and experience qualifications. Check these standards and apply only if you come reasonably close to meeting them.

The brief description of the position in the examination announcement offers some clues to the subjects which will be tested. Think about the job itself. Review the duties in your mind. Can you perform them, or are there some in which you are rusty? Fill in the blank spots in your preparation.

Many jurisdictions preview the written test in the exam announcement by including a section called "Knowledge and Abilities Required," "Scope of the Examination," or some similar heading. Here you will find out specifically what fields will be tested.

2) Review your own background

Once you learn in general what the position is all about, and what you need to know to do the work, ask yourself which subjects you already know fairly well and which need improvement. You may wonder whether to concentrate on improving your strong areas or on building some background in your fields of weakness. When the announcement has specified "some knowledge" or "considerable knowledge," or has used adjectives like "beginning principles of..." or "advanced ... methods," you can get a clue as to the number and difficulty of questions to be asked in any given field. More questions, and hence broader coverage, would be included for those subjects which are more important in the work. Now weigh your strengths and weaknesses against the job requirements and prepare accordingly.

3) Determine the level of the position

Another way to tell how intensively you should prepare is to understand the level of the job for which you are applying. Is it the entering level? In other words, is this the position in which beginners in a field of work are hired? Or is it an intermediate or advanced level? Sometimes this is indicated by such words as "Junior" or "Senior" in the class title. Other jurisdictions use Roman numerals to designate the level – Clerk I, Clerk II, for example. The word "Supervisor" sometimes appears in the title. If the level is not indicated by the title, check the description of duties. Will you be working under very close supervision, or will you have responsibility for independent decisions in this work?

4) Choose appropriate study materials

Now that you know the subjects to be examined and the relative amount of each subject to be covered, you can choose suitable study materials. For beginning level jobs, or even advanced ones, if you have a pronounced weakness in some aspect of your training, read a modern, standard textbook in that field. Be sure it is up to date and has general coverage. Such books are normally available at your library, and the librarian will be glad to help you locate one. For entry-level positions, questions of appropriate difficulty are chosen – neither highly advanced questions, nor those too simple. Such questions require careful thought but not advanced training.

If the position for which you are applying is technical or advanced, you will read more advanced, specialized material. If you are already familiar with the basic principles of your field, elementary textbooks would waste your time. Concentrate on advanced textbooks and technical periodicals. Think through the concepts and review difficult problems in your field.

These are all general sources. You can get more ideas on your own initiative, following these leads. For example, training manuals and publications of the government agency which employs workers in your field can be useful, particularly for technical and professional positions. A letter or visit to the government department involved may result in more specific study suggestions, and certainly will provide you with a more definite idea of the exact nature of the position you are seeking.

III. KINDS OF TESTS

Tests are used for purposes other than measuring knowledge and ability to perform specified duties. For some positions, it is equally important to test ability to make adjustments to new situations or to profit from training. In others, basic mental abilities not dependent on information are essential. Questions which test these things may not appear as pertinent to the duties of the position as those which test for knowledge and information. Yet they are often highly important parts of a fair examination. For very general questions, it is almost impossible to help you direct your study efforts. What we can do is to point out some of the more common of these general abilities needed in public service positions and describe some typical questions.

1) General information

Broad, general information has been found useful for predicting job success in some kinds of work. This is tested in a variety of ways, from vocabulary lists to questions about current events. Basic background in some field of work, such as sociology or economics, may be sampled in a group of questions. Often these are principles which have become familiar to most persons through exposure rather than through formal training. It is difficult to advise you how to study for these questions; being alert to the world around you is our best suggestion.

2) Verbal ability

An example of an ability needed in many positions is verbal or language ability. Verbal ability is, in brief, the ability to use and understand words. Vocabulary and grammar tests are typical measures of this ability. Reading comprehension or paragraph interpretation questions are common in many kinds of civil service tests. You are given a paragraph of written material and asked to find its central meaning.

3) Numerical ability

Number skills can be tested by the familiar arithmetic problem, by checking paired lists of numbers to see which are alike and which are different, or by interpreting charts and graphs. In the latter test, a graph may be printed in the test booklet which you are asked to use as the basis for answering questions.

4) Observation

A popular test for law-enforcement positions is the observation test. A picture is shown to you for several minutes, then taken away. Questions about the picture test your ability to observe both details and larger elements.

5) Following directions

In many positions in the public service, the employee must be able to carry out written instructions dependably and accurately. You may be given a chart with several columns, each column listing a variety of information. The questions require you to carry out directions involving the information given in the chart.

6) Skills and aptitudes

Performance tests effectively measure some manual skills and aptitudes. When the skill is one in which you are trained, such as typing or shorthand, you can practice. These tests are often very much like those given in business school or high school courses. For many of the other skills and aptitudes, however, no short-time preparation can be made. Skills and abilities natural to you or that you have developed throughout your lifetime are being tested.

Many of the general questions just described provide all the data needed to answer the questions and ask you to use your reasoning ability to find the answers. Your best preparation for these tests, as well as for tests of facts and ideas, is to be at your physical and mental best. You, no doubt, have your own methods of getting into an exam-taking mood and keeping "in shape." The next section lists some ideas on this subject.

IV. KINDS OF QUESTIONS

Only rarely is the "essay" question, which you answer in narrative form, used in civil service tests. Civil service tests are usually of the short-answer type. Full instructions for answering these questions will be given to you at the examination. But in case this is your first experience with short-answer questions and separate answer sheets, here is what you need to know:

1) Multiple-choice Questions

Most popular of the short-answer questions is the "multiple choice" or "best answer" question. It can be used, for example, to test for factual knowledge, ability to solve problems or judgment in meeting situations found at work.

A multiple-choice question is normally one of three types—

- It can begin with an incomplete statement followed by several possible endings. You are to find the one ending which *best* completes the statement, although some of the others may not be entirely wrong.
- It can also be a complete statement in the form of a question which is answered by choosing one of the statements listed.
- It can be in the form of a problem – again you select the best answer.

Here is an example of a multiple-choice question with a discussion which should give you some clues as to the method for choosing the right answer:

When an employee has a complaint about his assignment, the action which will *best* help him overcome his difficulty is to
- A. discuss his difficulty with his coworkers
- B. take the problem to the head of the organization
- C. take the problem to the person who gave him the assignment
- D. say nothing to anyone about his complaint

In answering this question, you should study each of the choices to find which is best. Consider choice "A" – Certainly an employee may discuss his complaint with fellow employees, but no change or improvement can result, and the complaint remains unresolved. Choice "B" is a poor choice since the head of the organization probably does not know what assignment you have been given, and taking your problem to him is known as "going over the head" of the supervisor. The supervisor, or person who made the assignment, is the person who can clarify it or correct any injustice. Choice "C" is, therefore, correct. To say nothing, as in choice "D," is unwise. Supervisors have and interest in knowing the problems employees are facing, and the employee is seeking a solution to his problem.

2) True/False Questions

The "true/false" or "right/wrong" form of question is sometimes used. Here a complete statement is given. Your job is to decide whether the statement is right or wrong.

SAMPLE: A person-to-person long-distance telephone call costs less than a station-to-station call to the same city.

This statement is wrong, or false, since person-to-person calls are more expensive.

This is not a complete list of all possible question forms, although most of the others are variations of these common types. You will always get complete directions for answering questions. Be sure you understand *how* to mark your answers – ask questions until you do.

V. RECORDING YOUR ANSWERS

For an examination with very few applicants, you may be told to record your answers in the test booklet itself. Separate answer sheets are much more common. If this separate answer sheet is to be scored by machine – and this is often the case – it is highly important that you mark your answers correctly in order to get credit.

An electric scoring machine is often used in civil service offices because of the speed with which papers can be scored. Machine-scored answer sheets must be marked with a pencil, which will be given to you. This pencil has a high graphite content which responds to the electric scoring machine. As a matter of fact, stray dots may register as answers, so do not let your pencil rest on the answer sheet while you are pondering the correct answer. Also, if your pencil lead breaks or is otherwise defective, ask for another.

Since the answer sheet will be dropped in a slot in the scoring machine, be careful not to bend the corners or get the paper crumpled.

The answer sheet normally has five vertical columns of numbers, with 30 numbers to a column. These numbers correspond to the question numbers in your test booklet. After each number, going across the page are four or five pairs of dotted lines. These short dotted lines have small letters or numbers above them. The first two pairs may also have a "T" or "F" above the letters. This indicates that the first two pairs only are to be used if the questions are of the true-false type. If the questions are multiple choice, disregard the "T" and "F" and pay attention only to the small letters or numbers.

Answer your questions in the manner of the sample that follows:

32. The largest city in the United States is
    A. Washington, D.C.
    B. New York City
    C. Chicago
    D. Detroit
    E. San Francisco

1) Choose the answer you think is best. (New York City is the largest, so "B" is correct.)
2) Find the row of dotted lines numbered the same as the question you are answering. (Find row number 32)
3) Find the pair of dotted lines corresponding to the answer. (Find the pair of lines under the mark "B.")
4) Make a solid black mark between the dotted lines.

VI. BEFORE THE TEST

Common sense will help you find procedures to follow to get ready for an examination. Too many of us, however, overlook these sensible measures. Indeed, nervousness and fatigue have been found to be the most serious reasons why applicants fail to do their best on civil service tests. Here is a list of reminders:

- Begin your preparation early – Don't wait until the last minute to go scurrying around for books and materials or to find out what the position is all about.
- Prepare continuously – An hour a night for a week is better than an all-night cram session. This has been definitely established. What is more, a night a

6

week for a month will return better dividends than crowding your study into a shorter period of time.

- Locate the place of the exam – You have been sent a notice telling you when and where to report for the examination. If the location is in a different town or otherwise unfamiliar to you, it would be well to inquire the best route and learn something about the building.
- Relax the night before the test – Allow your mind to rest. Do not study at all that night. Plan some mild recreation or diversion; then go to bed early and get a good night's sleep.
- Get up early enough to make a leisurely trip to the place for the test – This way unforeseen events, traffic snarls, unfamiliar buildings, etc. will not upset you.
- Dress comfortably – A written test is not a fashion show. You will be known by number and not by name, so wear something comfortable.
- Leave excess paraphernalia at home – Shopping bags and odd bundles will get in your way. You need bring only the items mentioned in the official notice you received; usually everything you need is provided. Do not bring reference books to the exam. They will only confuse those last minutes and be taken away from you when in the test room.
- Arrive somewhat ahead of time – If because of transportation schedules you must get there very early, bring a newspaper or magazine to take your mind off yourself while waiting.
- Locate the examination room – When you have found the proper room, you will be directed to the seat or part of the room where you will sit. Sometimes you are given a sheet of instructions to read while you are waiting. Do not fill out any forms until you are told to do so; just read them and be prepared.
- Relax and prepare to listen to the instructions
- If you have any physical problem that may keep you from doing your best, be sure to tell the test administrator. If you are sick or in poor health, you really cannot do your best on the exam. You can come back and take the test some other time.

VII. AT THE TEST

The day of the test is here and you have the test booklet in your hand. The temptation to get going is very strong. Caution! There is more to success than knowing the right answers. You must know how to identify your papers and understand variations in the type of short-answer question used in this particular examination. Follow these suggestions for maximum results from your efforts:

1) Cooperate with the monitor
The test administrator has a duty to create a situation in which you can be as much at ease as possible. He will give instructions, tell you when to begin, check to see that you are marking your answer sheet correctly, and so on. He is not there to guard you, although he will see that your competitors do not take unfair advantage. He wants to help you do your best.

2) Listen to all instructions
Don't jump the gun! Wait until you understand all directions. In most civil service tests you get more time than you need to answer the questions. So don't be in a hurry.

Read each word of instructions until you clearly understand the meaning. Study the examples, listen to all announcements and follow directions. Ask questions if you do not understand what to do.

3) Identify your papers

Civil service exams are usually identified by number only. You will be assigned a number; you must not put your name on your test papers. Be sure to copy your number correctly. Since more than one exam may be given, copy your exact examination title.

4) Plan your time

Unless you are told that a test is a "speed" or "rate of work" test, speed itself is usually not important. Time enough to answer all the questions will be provided, but this does not mean that you have all day. An overall time limit has been set. Divide the total time (in minutes) by the number of questions to determine the approximate time you have for each question.

5) Do not linger over difficult questions

If you come across a difficult question, mark it with a paper clip (useful to have along) and come back to it when you have been through the booklet. One caution if you do this – be sure to skip a number on your answer sheet as well. Check often to be sure that you have not lost your place and that you are marking in the row numbered the same as the question you are answering.

6) Read the questions

Be sure you know what the question asks! Many capable people are unsuccessful because they failed to *read* the questions correctly.

7) Answer all questions

Unless you have been instructed that a penalty will be deducted for incorrect answers, it is better to guess than to omit a question.

8) Speed tests

It is often better NOT to guess on speed tests. It has been found that on timed tests people are tempted to spend the last few seconds before time is called in marking answers at random – without even reading them – in the hope of picking up a few extra points. To discourage this practice, the instructions may warn you that your score will be "corrected" for guessing. That is, a penalty will be applied. The incorrect answers will be deducted from the correct ones, or some other penalty formula will be used.

9) Review your answers

If you finish before time is called, go back to the questions you guessed or omitted to give them further thought. Review other answers if you have time.

10) Return your test materials

If you are ready to leave before others have finished or time is called, take ALL your materials to the monitor and leave quietly. Never take any test material with you. The monitor can discover whose papers are not complete, and taking a test booklet may be grounds for disqualification.

VIII. EXAMINATION TECHNIQUES

1) Read the general instructions carefully. These are usually printed on the first page of the exam booklet. As a rule, these instructions refer to the timing of the examination; the fact that you should not start work until the signal and must stop work at a signal, etc. If there are any *special* instructions, such as a choice of questions to be answered, make sure that you note this instruction carefully.

2) When you are ready to start work on the examination, that is as soon as the signal has been given, read the instructions to each question booklet, underline any key words or phrases, such as *least, best, outline, describe* and the like. In this way you will tend to answer as requested rather than discover on reviewing your paper that you *listed without describing*, that you selected the *worst* choice rather than the *best* choice, etc.

3) If the examination is of the objective or multiple-choice type – that is, each question will also give a series of possible answers: A, B, C or D, and you are called upon to select the best answer and write the letter next to that answer on your answer paper – it is advisable to start answering each question in turn. There may be anywhere from 50 to 100 such questions in the three or four hours allotted and you can see how much time would be taken if you read through all the questions before beginning to answer any. Furthermore, if you come across a question or group of questions which you know would be difficult to answer, it would undoubtedly affect your handling of all the other questions.

4) If the examination is of the essay type and contains but a few questions, it is a moot point as to whether you should read all the questions before starting to answer any one. Of course, if you are given a choice – say five out of seven and the like – then it is essential to read all the questions so you can eliminate the two that are most difficult. If, however, you are asked to answer all the questions, there may be danger in trying to answer the easiest one first because you may find that you will spend too much time on it. The best technique is to answer the first question, then proceed to the second, etc.

5) Time your answers. Before the exam begins, write down the time it started, then add the time allowed for the examination and write down the time it must be completed, then divide the time available somewhat as follows:
   - If 3-1/2 hours are allowed, that would be 210 minutes. If you have 80 objective-type questions, that would be an average of 2-1/2 minutes per question. Allow yourself no more than 2 minutes per question, or a total of 160 minutes, which will permit about 50 minutes to review.
   - If for the time allotment of 210 minutes there are 7 essay questions to answer, that would average about 30 minutes a question. Give yourself only 25 minutes per question so that you have about 35 minutes to review.

6) The most important instruction is to *read each question* and make sure you know what is wanted. The second most important instruction is to *time yourself properly* so that you answer every question. The third most

9

important instruction is to *answer every question*. Guess if you have to but include something for each question. Remember that you will receive no credit for a blank and will probably receive some credit if you write something in answer to an essay question. If you guess a letter – say "B" for a multiple-choice question – you may have guessed right. If you leave a blank as an answer to a multiple-choice question, the examiners may respect your feelings but it will not add a point to your score. Some exams may penalize you for wrong answers, so in such cases *only*, you may not want to guess unless you have some basis for your answer.

7) Suggestions
   a. Objective-type questions
      1. Examine the question booklet for proper sequence of pages and questions
      2. Read all instructions carefully
      3. Skip any question which seems too difficult; return to it after all other questions have been answered
      4. Apportion your time properly; do not spend too much time on any single question or group of questions
      5. Note and underline key words – *all, most, fewest, least, best, worst, same, opposite*, etc.
      6. Pay particular attention to negatives
      7. Note unusual option, e.g., unduly long, short, complex, different or similar in content to the body of the question
      8. Observe the use of "hedging" words – *probably, may, most likely*, etc.
      9. Make sure that your answer is put next to the same number as the question
      10. Do not second-guess unless you have good reason to believe the second answer is definitely more correct
      11. Cross out original answer if you decide another answer is more accurate; do not erase until you are ready to hand your paper in
      12. Answer all questions; guess unless instructed otherwise
      13. Leave time for review

   b. Essay questions
      1. Read each question carefully
      2. Determine exactly what is wanted. Underline key words or phrases.
      3. Decide on outline or paragraph answer
      4. Include many different points and elements unless asked to develop any one or two points or elements
      5. Show impartiality by giving pros and cons unless directed to select one side only
      6. Make and write down any assumptions you find necessary to answer the questions
      7. Watch your English, grammar, punctuation and choice of words
      8. Time your answers; don't crowd material

8) Answering the essay question

Most essay questions can be answered by framing the specific response around several key words or ideas. Here are a few such key words or ideas:

M's: manpower, materials, methods, money, management
P's: purpose, program, policy, plan, procedure, practice, problems, pitfalls, personnel, public relations
  a. Six basic steps in handling problems:
      1. Preliminary plan and background development
      2. Collect information, data and facts
      3. Analyze and interpret information, data and facts
      4. Analyze and develop solutions as well as make recommendations
      5. Prepare report and sell recommendations
      6. Install recommendations and follow up effectiveness

  b. Pitfalls to avoid
      1. *Taking things for granted* – A statement of the situation does not necessarily imply that each of the elements is necessarily true; for example, a complaint may be invalid and biased so that all that can be taken for granted is that a complaint has been registered
      2. *Considering only one side of a situation* – Wherever possible, indicate several alternatives and then point out the reasons you selected the best one
      3. *Failing to indicate follow up* – Whenever your answer indicates action on your part, make certain that you will take proper follow-up action to see how successful your recommendations, procedures or actions turn out to be
      4. *Taking too long in answering any single question* – Remember to time your answers properly

IX. AFTER THE TEST

Scoring procedures differ in detail among civil service jurisdictions although the general principles are the same. Whether the papers are hand-scored or graded by machine we have described, they are nearly always graded by number. That is, the person who marks the paper knows only the number – never the name – of the applicant. Not until all the papers have been graded will they be matched with names. If other tests, such as training and experience or oral interview ratings have been given, scores will be combined. Different parts of the examination usually have different weights. For example, the written test might count 60 percent of the final grade, and a rating of training and experience 40 percent. In many jurisdictions, veterans will have a certain number of points added to their grades.

After the final grade has been determined, the names are placed in grade order and an eligible list is established. There are various methods for resolving ties between those who get the same final grade – probably the most common is to place first the name of the person whose application was received first. Job offers are made from the eligible list in the order the names appear on it. You will be notified of your grade and your rank as soon as all these computations have been made. This will be done as rapidly as possible.

People who are found to meet the requirements in the announcement are called "eligibles." Their names are put on a list of eligible candidates. An eligible's chances of getting a job depend on how high he stands on this list and how fast agencies are filling jobs from the list.

When a job is to be filled from a list of eligibles, the agency asks for the names of people on the list of eligibles for that job. When the civil service commission receives this request, it sends to the agency the names of the three people highest on this list. Or, if the job to be filled has specialized requirements, the office sends the agency the names of the top three persons who meet these requirements from the general list.

The appointing officer makes a choice from among the three people whose names were sent to him. If the selected person accepts the appointment, the names of the others are put back on the list to be considered for future openings.

That is the rule in hiring from all kinds of eligible lists, whether they are for typist, carpenter, chemist, or something else. For every vacancy, the appointing officer has his choice of any one of the top three eligibles on the list. This explains why the person whose name is on top of the list sometimes does not get an appointment when some of the persons lower on the list do. If the appointing officer chooses the second or third eligible, the No. 1 eligible does not get a job at once, but stays on the list until he is appointed or the list is terminated.

X. HOW TO PASS THE INTERVIEW TEST

The examination for which you applied requires an oral interview test. You have already taken the written test and you are now being called for the interview test – the final part of the formal examination.

You may think that it is not possible to prepare for an interview test and that there are no procedures to follow during an interview. Our purpose is to point out some things you can do in advance that will help you and some good rules to follow and pitfalls to avoid while you are being interviewed.

What is an interview supposed to test?

The written examination is designed to test the technical knowledge and competence of the candidate; the oral is designed to evaluate intangible qualities, not readily measured otherwise, and to establish a list showing the relative fitness of each candidate – as measured against his competitors – for the position sought. Scoring is not on the basis of "right" and "wrong," but on a sliding scale of values ranging from "not passable" to "outstanding." As a matter of fact, it is possible to achieve a relatively low score without a single "incorrect" answer because of evident weakness in the qualities being measured.

Occasionally, an examination may consist entirely of an oral test – either an individual or a group oral. In such cases, information is sought concerning the technical knowledges and abilities of the candidate, since there has been no written examination for this purpose. More commonly, however, an oral test is used to supplement a written examination.

Who conducts interviews?

The composition of oral boards varies among different jurisdictions. In nearly all, a representative of the personnel department serves as chairman. One of the members of the board may be a representative of the department in which the candidate would work. In some cases, "outside experts" are used, and, frequently, a businessman or some other representative of the general public is asked to serve. Labor and management or other special groups may be represented. The aim is to secure the services of experts in the appropriate field.

However the board is composed, it is a good idea (and not at all improper or unethical) to ascertain in advance of the interview who the members are and what groups they represent. When you are introduced to them, you will have some idea of their backgrounds and interests, and at least you will not stutter and stammer over their names.

What should be done before the interview?

While knowledge about the board members is useful and takes some of the surprise element out of the interview, there is other preparation which is more substantive. It *is* possible to prepare for an oral interview – in several ways:

1) Keep a copy of your application and review it carefully before the interview

This may be the only document before the oral board, and the starting point of the interview. Know what education and experience you have listed there, and the sequence and dates of all of it. Sometimes the board will ask you to review the highlights of your experience for them; you should not have to hem and haw doing it.

2) Study the class specification and the examination announcement

Usually, the oral board has one or both of these to guide them. The qualities, characteristics or knowledges required by the position sought are stated in these documents. They offer valuable clues as to the nature of the oral interview. For example, if the job involves supervisory responsibilities, the announcement will usually indicate that knowledge of modern supervisory methods and the qualifications of the candidate as a supervisor will be tested. If so, you can expect such questions, frequently in the form of a hypothetical situation which you are expected to solve. NEVER go into an oral without knowledge of the duties and responsibilities of the job you seek.

3) Think through each qualification required

Try to visualize the kind of questions you would ask if you were a board member. How well could you answer them? Try especially to appraise your own knowledge and background in each area, *measured against the job sought*, and identify any areas in which you are weak. Be critical and realistic – do not flatter yourself.

4) Do some general reading in areas in which you feel you may be weak

For example, if the job involves supervision and your past experience has NOT, some general reading in supervisory methods and practices, particularly in the field of human relations, might be useful. Do NOT study agency procedures or detailed manuals. The oral board will be testing your understanding and capacity, not your memory.

5) Get a good night's sleep and watch your general health and mental attitude

You will want a clear head at the interview. Take care of a cold or any other minor ailment, and of course, no hangovers.

What should be done on the day of the interview?

Now comes the day of the interview itself. Give yourself plenty of time to get there. Plan to arrive somewhat ahead of the scheduled time, particularly if your appointment is in the fore part of the day. If a previous candidate fails to appear, the board might be ready for you a bit early. By early afternoon an oral board is almost invariably behind schedule if there are many candidates, and you may have to wait.

Take along a book or magazine to read, or your application to review, but leave any extraneous material in the waiting room when you go in for your interview. In any event, relax and compose yourself.

The matter of dress is important. The board is forming impressions about you – from your experience, your manners, your attitude, and your appearance. Give your personal appearance careful attention. Dress your best, but not your flashiest. Choose conservative, appropriate clothing, and be sure it is immaculate. This is a business interview, and your appearance should indicate that you regard it as such. Besides, being well groomed and properly dressed will help boost your confidence.

Sooner or later, someone will call your name and escort you into the interview room. *This is it.* From here on you are on your own. It is too late for any more preparation. But remember, you asked for this opportunity to prove your fitness, and you are here because your request was granted.

What happens when you go in?

The usual sequence of events will be as follows: The clerk (who is often the board stenographer) will introduce you to the chairman of the oral board, who will introduce you to the other members of the board. Acknowledge the introductions before you sit down. Do not be surprised if you find a microphone facing you or a stenotypist sitting by. Oral interviews are usually recorded in the event of an appeal or other review.

Usually the chairman of the board will open the interview by reviewing the highlights of your education and work experience from your application – primarily for the benefit of the other members of the board, as well as to get the material into the record. Do not interrupt or comment unless there is an error or significant misinterpretation; if that is the case, do not hesitate. But do not quibble about insignificant matters. Also, he will usually ask you some question about your education, experience or your present job – partly to get you to start talking and to establish the interviewing "rapport." He may start the actual questioning, or turn it over to one of the other members. Frequently, each member undertakes the questioning on a particular area, one in which he is perhaps most competent, so you can expect each member to participate in the examination. Because time is limited, you may also expect some rather abrupt switches in the direction the questioning takes, so do not be upset by it. Normally, a board member will not pursue a single line of questioning unless he discovers a particular strength or weakness.

After each member has participated, the chairman will usually ask whether any member has any further questions, then will ask you if you have anything you wish to add. Unless you are expecting this question, it may floor you. Worse, it may start you off on an extended, extemporaneous speech. The board is not usually seeking more information. The question is principally to offer you a last opportunity to present further qualifications or to indicate that you have nothing to add. So, if you feel that a significant qualification or characteristic has been overlooked, it is proper to point it out in a sentence or so. Do not compliment the board on the thoroughness of their examination – they have been sketchy, and you know it. If you wish, merely say, "No thank you, I have nothing further to add." This is a point where you can "talk yourself out" of a good impression or fail to present an important bit of information. Remember, *you close the interview yourself.*

The chairman will then say, "That is all, Mr. _____, thank you." Do not be startled; the interview is over, and quicker than you think. Thank him, gather your belongings and take your leave. Save your sigh of relief for the other side of the door.

How to put your best foot forward

Throughout this entire process, you may feel that the board individually and collectively is trying to pierce your defenses, seek out your hidden weaknesses and embarrass and confuse you. Actually, this is not true. They are obliged to make an appraisal of your qualifications for the job you are seeking, and they want to see you in your best light. Remember, they must interview all candidates and a non-cooperative candidate may become a failure in spite of their best efforts to bring out his qualifications. Here are 15 suggestions that will help you:

1) Be natural – Keep your attitude confident, not cocky

If you are not confident that you can do the job, do not expect the board to be. Do not apologize for your weaknesses, try to bring out your strong points. The board is interested in a positive, not negative, presentation. Cockiness will antagonize any board member and make him wonder if you are covering up a weakness by a false show of strength.

2) Get comfortable, but don't lounge or sprawl

Sit erectly but not stiffly. A careless posture may lead the board to conclude that you are careless in other things, or at least that you are not impressed by the importance of the occasion. Either conclusion is natural, even if incorrect. Do not fuss with your clothing, a pencil or an ashtray. Your hands may occasionally be useful to emphasize a point; do not let them become a point of distraction.

3) Do not wisecrack or make small talk

This is a serious situation, and your attitude should show that you consider it as such. Further, the time of the board is limited – they do not want to waste it, and neither should you.

4) Do not exaggerate your experience or abilities

In the first place, from information in the application or other interviews and sources, the board may know more about you than you think. Secondly, you probably will not get away with it. An experienced board is rather adept at spotting such a situation, so do not take the chance.

5) If you know a board member, do not make a point of it, yet do not hide it

Certainly you are not fooling him, and probably not the other members of the board. Do not try to take advantage of your acquaintanceship – it will probably do you little good.

6) Do not dominate the interview

Let the board do that. They will give you the clues – do not assume that you have to do all the talking. Realize that the board has a number of questions to ask you, and do not try to take up all the interview time by showing off your extensive knowledge of the answer to the first one.

7) Be attentive

You only have 20 minutes or so, and you should keep your attention at its sharpest throughout. When a member is addressing a problem or question to you, give him your undivided attention. Address your reply principally to him, but do not exclude the other board members.

8) Do not interrupt

A board member may be stating a problem for you to analyze. He will ask you a question when the time comes. Let him state the problem, and wait for the question.

9) Make sure you understand the question

Do not try to answer until you are sure what the question is. If it is not clear, restate it in your own words or ask the board member to clarify it for you. However, do not haggle about minor elements.

10) Reply promptly but not hastily

A common entry on oral board rating sheets is "candidate responded readily," or "candidate hesitated in replies." Respond as promptly and quickly as you can, but do not jump to a hasty, ill-considered answer.

11) Do not be peremptory in your answers

A brief answer is proper – but do not fire your answer back. That is a losing game from your point of view. The board member can probably ask questions much faster than you can answer them.

12) Do not try to create the answer you think the board member wants

He is interested in what kind of mind you have and how it works – not in playing games. Furthermore, he can usually spot this practice and will actually grade you down on it.

13) Do not switch sides in your reply merely to agree with a board member

Frequently, a member will take a contrary position merely to draw you out and to see if you are willing and able to defend your point of view. Do not start a debate, yet do not surrender a good position. If a position is worth taking, it is worth defending.

14) Do not be afraid to admit an error in judgment if you are shown to be wrong

The board knows that you are forced to reply without any opportunity for careful consideration. Your answer may be demonstrably wrong. If so, admit it and get on with the interview.

15) Do not dwell at length on your present job

The opening question may relate to your present assignment. Answer the question but do not go into an extended discussion. You are being examined for a *new* job, not your present one. As a matter of fact, try to phrase ALL your answers in terms of the job for which you are being examined.

Basis of Rating

Probably you will forget most of these "do's" and "don'ts" when you walk into the oral interview room. Even remembering them all will not ensure you a passing grade. Perhaps you did not have the qualifications in the first place. But remembering them will help you to put your best foot forward, without treading on the toes of the board members.

Rumor and popular opinion to the contrary notwithstanding, an oral board wants you to make the best appearance possible. They know you are under pressure – but they also want to see how you respond to it as a guide to what your reaction would be under the pressures of the job you seek. They will be influenced by the degree of poise you display, the personal traits you show and the manner in which you respond.

EXAMINATION SECTION

EXAMINATION SECTION
TEST 1

DIRECTIONS: Each question or incomplete statement is followed by several suggested
answers or completions. Select the one that BEST answers the question or
completes the statement. *PRINT THE LETTER OF THE CORRECT ANSWER
IN THE SPACE AT THE RIGHT.*

Questions 1-3.

DIRECTIONS: Questions 1 through 3 are to be answered on the basis of the following paragraph.

   The Jingle-Dress dance is a popular competitive dance performed at intertribal pow-
wows. The costume of the Jingle-Dress dancer is adorned with small metal cones. The cones
are made from chewing tobacco lids, which are rolled into cylinders and sewn onto the dress.
During the dance, these tin cones strike one another to produce a soft, rhythmic sound. The
dancer blends complicated footwork with a series of gentle hops, causing the cones to jingle
in time to the drumbeat.

1.   The purpose of the cones in the Jingle-Dress dance is to   1._____

     A.   shine and sparkle during the dance
     B.   produce a soft, rhythmic sound
     C.   aid the dancer with the complicated footwork required by the dance
     D.   make use of recycled tobacco can lids

2.   The dancer causes the cones to make sounds by   2._____

     A.   making large cones to sew onto the dress
     B.   sewing the cones as close to another as possible
     C.   jumping up and down as quickly as possible
     D.   combining footwork with gentle hops

3.   The Jingle-Dress dance is performed as a   3._____

     A.   ceremonial dance at semi-annual powwows
     B.   healing dance at intertribal powwows
     C.   competitive dance at intertribal powwows
     D.   costume dance at annual powwows

Questions 4-6.

DIRECTIONS: Questions 4 through 6 are to be answered on the basis of the following paragraph.

   Although volleyball is a unique sport, it shares one important similarity with other well-
known sports. Like most sports, the ability to win doesn't just depend on a team's ability to
score the most points, but on its ability to make the fewest number of errors. In volleyball, a
team cannot score unless it is serving. Serving errors, therefore, are extremely costly since
losing the serve also means granting your opponent a scoring opportunity.

4. To win a volleyball game, it is MOST important to make sure your team
4.__

    A. makes the fewest number of errors
    B. plays good defense
    C. grants scoring opportunities to your opponents
    D. serves first

5. What important similarity does volleyball share with other sports?
5.__

    A. It's exciting to watch.
    B. Winning depends on a powerful serve.
    C. A volleyball team cannot score unless it is serving.
    D. The winning team usually commits the fewest errors.

6. Serving errors are costly in a volleyball game because they
6.__

    A. count as an error against your team
    B. provide your opponent with a scoring opportunity
    C. place your team in a receiving position
    D. can result in a delay-of-game penalty

Questions 7-8.

DIRECTIONS: Questions 7 and 8 are to be answered on the basis of the following paragraph.

Throughout history, solar eclipses have sometimes caused great fear and anxiety. Some cultures believed eclipses predicted the end of the world. Many older cultures believed a dragon was swallowing the sun and, in order to save the sun, people made as much noise as possible to frighten the dragon away. When the sun returned, whole and bright, the noise-makers celebrated their success.

7. Why have eclipses caused such anxiety throughout history?
7.__

    A. People believed they signaled the end of the world
    B. No one knows what causes them
    C. Because people make so much noise when they appear
    D. Because watching one can harm the eyes

8. Why did ancient cultures often make noise during an eclipse?
8.__

    A. People were frightened in the darkness
    B. To celebrate the arrival of the eclipse
    C. To summon the dragon who would swallow the sun
    D. To chase away the dragon they thought had swallowed the sun

Questions 9-11.

DIRECTIONS: Questions 9 through 11 are to be answered on the basis of the following paragraph.

In the films of the 1940s, most American Indians appeared as enemies. They spoke broken English and blocked civilization's progress. During this same time, however, a group of Navajo Indians used their unique language to develop a code for the U.S. military which would become one of the most successful codes in military history. During World War II, this group, known as the Navajo Code Talkers, played a key role in many of the most crucial victories fought by the U.S. military in the Pacific.

9.   What role did the Navajo Code Talkers play in World War II?   9.____
     They

     A.   appeared as enemies in many films
     B.   spoke broken English and blocked civilization's progress
     C.   developed a military code which helped win the war in the Pacific
     D.   used their unique language to block civilization's progress

10.   In films from the 1940s, American Indians were most often depicted as enemies by   10.____

     A.   speaking broken English and blocking civilization's progress
     B.   speaking only in their native Navajo tongue
     C.   using their language to develop secret codes
     D.   trying to block crucial American victories in the Pacific

11.   The Navajo Code Talkers used their language to   11.____

     A.   block civilization's progress
     B.   fight Hollywood stereotypes
     C.   defeat their enemies in other tribes
     D.   develop one of the most effective U.S. military codes in history

Questions 12-13.

DIRECTIONS: Questions 12 and 13 are to be answered on the basis of the following paragraph.

In the last several years, judges throughout the country have attracted controversy by practicing *creative sentencing*. The term refers to the judges' tendency for offering defendants what they consider valid alternatives to jail sentences. For example, to qualify for probation, one defendant had to wear a tee shirt that announced his status as a criminal on probation. An abusive husband had to donate his car to a shelter for battered women. In one case, a judge gave a woman found guilty of child abuse a chance to avoid jail if she would voluntarily allow Norplant, a form of birth control, to be implanted in her arm.

12.   What does the term *creative sentencing* refer to?   12.____

     A.   Various judicial controversies
     B.   Judges who offer defendants alternatives to jail sentences

C. Defendants who are forced to undergo humiliating punishments in addition to jail sentences

D. Judges who have the power to determine how much time a defendant spends in jail

13. Creative sentencing is considered controversial because the

13.__

    A. judges are overstepping the bounds of their power by forcing defendants to submit to these punishments

    B. defendants have no opportunity to defend themselves

    C. alternatives offered to defendants are often surprising and odd

    D. judges have been forced to these extreme measures because of prison overcrowding

Questions 14-16.

DIRECTIONS: Questions 14 through 16 are to be answered on the basis of the following paragraph.

When examined closely, Earth's position in the solar system is something of a miracle. If it were closer to the sun, the heat would be so intense that water would be vaporized. If it were farther away, water would be frozen. Of all the planets in the solar system, only Earth and Mars share the temperature band which allows water to exist in the three states which are necessary to produce and sustain life. But only Earth is surrounded by a protective ozone layer which aids water in making the transition between these three states.

14. Why is Earth's position in the solar system something of a miracle?

14.__

    A. If it were closer to the sun, water would vaporize.

    B. If it were farther from the sun, water would freeze.

    C. It exists in the narrow temperature band which allows water to exist in the three states necessary to sustain life.

    D. It exists in the narrow temperature band which allows a protective ozone layer to form around the planet.

15. What is the difference between Earth and Mars?

15.__

    A. Mars is surrounded by a protective ozone layer.

    B. Earth is surrounded by a protective ozone layer.

    C. Only Earth exists within the narrow temperature band which allows water to exist in the three states necessary to sustain life.

    D. Only Mars exists within the narrow temperature band which allows water to exist in the three states necessary to sustain life.

16. The ozone layer is important to the production and sustenance of life because it

16.__

    A. helps water make the transition between the three forms necessary to sustain life

    B. keeps water from being vaporized by the sun's harmful rays

    C. keeps water from being frozen when the sun sets

    D. keeps water from leaving the atmosphere

Questions 17-19.

DIRECTIONS: Questions 17 through 19 are to be answered on the basis of the following
             paragraph.

During the seventeenth century, sailors at sea often suffered from muscle weakness and
unexplained bleeding. This disease often proved fatal until the discovery that sailors who ate
oranges and lines either didn't get sick, or suffered a much milder form of the illness. As a
result, the British navy required every ship to provide lemons and limes for the entire crew. By
accident, it had discovered that the vitamin C contained in the citrus fruits prevented scurvy.

17. What disease did sailors at sea often suffer from?   17._____

     A. Malnourishment
     B. Overdoses of vitamin C
     C. Muscle weakness and unexplained bleeding
     D. Scurvy

18. How is the disease prevented?   18._____

     A. Consumption of vitamin C   B. Consumption of fresh water
     C. Hard work   D. Bed rest

19. The cure for scurvy was discovered   19._____

     A. as a result of careful testing in laboratories
     B. through the accidental discovery that sailors who consumed vitamin C didn't grow
         ill
     C. through the accidental discovery that sailors who consumed vitamin C often grew
         ill
     D. as a result of years of study and experimentation

Questions 20-22.

DIRECTIONS: Questions 20 through 22 are to be answered on the basis of the following
             paragraph.

     Unlike dogs, cats are typically a solitary animal species who avoid social interaction, but
they do display specific social responses to each other upon meeting. When two cats meet
who are strangers, their first actions and gestures determine who the *dominant* cat will be. If a
cat desires dominance or sees the other cat as a threat to its territory, it will stare directly at
the intruder with a lowered tail. If the other cat responds with a similar gesture, or with the
strong defensive posture of an arched back, laid-back ears, and raised tail, a fight or chase is
likely if neither cat gives in. This is unlikely, however; before such a point of open hostility is
reached, one of the cats will usually take the *submissive* position of crouching down while
looking away from the other cat.

20. A cat signals its dominance over another cat by   20._____

     A. crouching down and looking away from the other cat
     B. arching its back and raising its tail
     C. staring directly at the other cat and lowering its tail
     D. chasing the other cat

21. Cats usually greet each other by

    A. displaying specific social responses
    B. staring directly at one another
    C. raising their tails
    D. arching their backs

21.___

22. Why is it unlikely for cats who are strangers to reach a point of open hostility with one another?

    A. Cats are solitary animals.
    B. One of the cats usually runs away.
    C. One of the cats usually takes a submissive position before they reach the point of open hostility.
    D. The two cats generally stare at each other with lowered tails until the hostility passes.

22.___

Questions 23-25.

DIRECTIONS: Questions 23 through 25 are to be answered on the basis of the following paragraph.

Between the nineteenth and twentieth centuries, the area in America known as the Great Plains underwent startling changes. At the beginning of the nineteenth century, there were few settlements. One could walk for miles without seeing a house. By the end of the century, settlements had sprung up all over. More and more people began to seek their fortunes in this area. In 1800, the Plains were covered by herds of buffalo. These huge animals were the natural cattle of the Plains. By 1900 the buffalo had almost disappeared, however, and the tribes who had roamed the Plains in pursuit of the buffalo had been forced to live on reservations.

23. When did these changes occur on the Great Plains?

    A. Between the 1700s and the 1800s
    B. Between the 1800s and the 1900s
    C. During the 1900s
    D. Between 1850 and 1950

23.___

24. What caused the sudden increase in the number of settlements on the Great Plains?

    A. The disappearance of the buffalo
    B. The disappearance of the Plains tribes
    C. An increased desire to hunt buffalo for sport
    D. An increased number of people seeking their fortunes in the area

24.___

25. What happened to the Plains tribes after the buffalo disappeared?
They

    A. were forced to live on reservations
    B. were all killed
    C. died of starvation
    D. moved farther west, away from the settlers

25.___

Questions 26-28.

DIRECTIONS: Questions 26 through 28 are to be answered on the basis of the following paragraph.

One important line of thinking about stress focuses on the differences between Type A and Type B personalities. Type A individuals are extremely competitive, are very devoted to work, and have a strong sense of time urgency. They are likely to be aggressive, impatient, and very work-oriented. Type B individuals are less competitive, less devoted to work, and have a weaker sense of time urgency. These individuals are less likely to experience conflict with other people and more likely to have a balanced, relaxed approach to life.

26.   Type B individuals are likely to display which of the following characteristics?   26._____

    A.   A strong sense of time urgency
    B.   Devotion to work
    C.   A balanced approach to life
    D.   Aggressiveness

27.   Type A individuals are likely to display which of the following characteristics?   27._____

    A.   A balanced approach to life
    B.   Passivity
    C.   Contentment
    D.   A strong sense of time urgency

28.   These personality types help researchers study which of the following problems?   28._____

    A.   Stress   B.   Apathy
    C.   Criminal behavior   D.   Underachievement

Questions 29-36.

The paragraphs which follow contain blank spaces with numbers corresponding to the questions. Each of the corresponding questions contains one lettered choice whose meaning fits in the space. Place the letter of the correct choice in the answer space to the right of the question.

Most successful job interviews _(29)_ three basic steps. Step 1 lasts about three minutes and _(30)_ when you first introduce yourself. Those people who have a firm handshake, who maintain eye contact, smile, and seem friendly, are the _(31)_ successful during this phase. Step 2 is the _(32)_ phase. This is the point at which interviewees _(33)_ their skills and work to *sell* themselves. Step 3 comes at the _(34)_ of the interview and, like Step 1, lasts only a few minutes. After the employer says, *We'll call you,* successful interviewees are quick _(35)_ respond, *I'll get in touch with you if I don't hear from you in a few days.* This final gesture conveys _(36)_.

29. A. lack   B. mimic   29.___
     C. follow   D. end with

30. A. begins   B. ends   C. stalls   D. fails   30.___

31. A. least   B. mostly   C. more   D. most   31.___

32. A. least challenging   B. most boring   32.___
     C. longest   D. shortest

33. A. brag about   B. explain   C. enunciate   D. lie about   33.___

34. A. middle   B. outset   C. beginning   D. end   34.___

35. A. to   B. at   C. with   D. for   35.___

36. A. insistence   B. impatience   36.___
     C. enthusiasm   D. hope

Questions 37-40.

The idea of duty is important to the followers of Hinduism, the major (37) in India. In fact, the many duties prescribed by Hinduism make it a way of life that (38) each day. From an early age, children learn that nothing is more important (39) doing one's duty. In fact doing (40) duty is, in itself, a form of worship.

37. A. belief   B. religion   37.___
     C. system   D. political institution

38. A. organizes   B. disrupts   38.___
     C. produces   D. destabilizes

39. A. if   B. with   C. of   D. than   39.___

40. A. your   B. his   C. one's   D. its   40.___

Questions 41-46.

Strong emotions are accompanied (41) physiological changes. When we are extremely fearful or angry, for example, (42) heartbeat speeds up, our pulse races, and our breathing rate tends to increase. The body's metabolism (43), burning up sugar in the bloodstream and fats in the tissues at a faster rate. The salivary glands become less active, making the mouth feel (44). The sweat glands may overreact, (45) a dripping forehead, clammy hands, and cold sweat. Finally, the pupils may (46), producing the wide-eyed look that is characteristic of both terror and rage.

41. A. with   B. to   C. beside   D. by   41.___

42. A. your   B. our   C. the   D. a   42.___

43.	A. accelerates			B. slows down			43.____
	C. works			D. stays the same			
44.	A. hot	B. cold		C. wet		D. dry	44.____
45.	A. with	B. showing		C. producing		D. fearing	45.____
46.	A. dilate	B. enlarge		C. blacken		D. disappear	46.____

Questions 47-52.

Increased numbers of women are (47) going to college and graduating with degrees in law and medicine. More women than ever before are (48) careers and earning as much as men. Many career women who are married have also achieved economic equality (49) their husbands. The number of women in elected office has also increased, and a large majority of Americans are now willing to vote for a qualified (50) for president. A growing number of women are entering the military, with the U.S. now having more female soldiers than any other (51). These are all signs that women have made significant headway toward (52) equality.

47.	A. now	B. then	C. yet	D. not	47.____
48.	A. leaving	B. changing	C. avoiding	D. pursuing	48.____
49.	A. to	B. with	C. at	D. for	49.____
50.	A. Republican	B. candidate	C. woman	D. man	50.____
51.	A. woman	B. country	C. man	D. branch	51.____
52.	A. racial	B. economic	C. religious	D. gender	52.____

Questions 53-56.

Understanding does not mean manipulating someone to agree (53) your point of view. Although a manipulative person views understanding as having someone else come around to his or her opinion, an understanding person conveys a sense of open-mindedness and (54). A communicator who is understanding does (55) insist upon agreement. He or she understands that, in order to be understood, you must also (56) others.

53.	A. to	B. at	C. with	D. for	53.____
54.	A. acceptance	B. exclusion	C. anger	D. elation	54.____
55.	A. always	B. not	C. sometimes	D. generally	55.____
56.	A. disagree with		B. judge		56.____
	C. love		D. understand		

Questions 57-62.

DIRECTIONS: Questions 57 through 62 are to be answered on the basis of the following facts.

Apollo Elementary School serves students in grades kindergarten through fifth. The school library is located in the center of the school. Classrooms surround the library, forming a large circle. Throughout the school day, teachers bring their classes into the library to conduct research and reading activities. There are usually several classes using the library at any one time.

The school librarian is Mrs. Samuels. She is a tall, middle-aged woman with brown hair and green eyes. Her part-time assistant is Velma Thomas. Velma is a student at the local community college, where she studies library science.

On the afternoon of Wednesday, April 11, Mrs. Simon brought her fourth-grade class to the library at approximately 1:50 P.M. Mrs. Samuels was already working with a third-grade class, so Velma began assisting the fourth grade students. A young girl from Mrs. Simon's class asked Velma how to find her book in the card catalog. As Velma guided the girl through the procedure, she noticed that one of the third graders had drifted away from his class and was attempting to reach a book by standing on one of the bookshelves.

Just as Velma called to the boy, he lost his footing and fell. Mrs. Samuels rushed to his side and checked him for injuries. The boy had a slight bruise on his wrist, but was otherwise uninjured.

57.   Who checked the boy for injuries after his fall?   57.__

    A.   Mrs. Samuels   B.   Velma Thomas
    C.   Mrs. Simon   D.   The third grade teacher

58.   Who is the school librarian?   58.__

    A.   Mrs. Samuels
    B.   Velma Thomas
    C.   Mrs. Simon
    D.   She is not named in this passage

59.   On what day of the week did the incident occur?   59.__

    A.   Monday   B.   Tuesday   C.   Wednesday   D.   Friday

60.   In what grade was the boy who fell from the shelf?   60.__

    A.   Fifth   B.   Fourth   C.   Third   D.   Second

61.   What grade does Mrs. Simon teach?   61.__

    A.   Fifth   B.   Fourth   C.   Third   D.   Second

62. What grades does Apollo Elementary serve?

    A. First through fifth
    B. First through sixth
    C. Kindergarten through fourth
    D. Kindergarten through fifth

62.____

Questions 63-68.

DIRECTIONS: Questions 63 through 68 are to be answered on the basis of the following facts.

There is a small hot dog cart located in the outdoor plaza of the Smith County Courthouse. The cart sells Polish hot dogs, sausages, bratwurst, soft pretzels, and soda. In the mornings between 7:00 and 9:30, fresh coffee and danishes are also sold. Employees of the court and other nearby businesses often purchase their lunch there, and eat on the plaza benches and tables.

The cart opens at 7:00 A.M. and closes at 3:00 P.M. during weekdays. It does not operate on weekends. It is owned and operated by Luisa Gonzalez, who is a 21-year-old college student with brown hair and brown eyes. Her father is Martin Gonzalez, a retired police officer, and he often works with her. At approximately 12:00 P.M. on October 3, Court Officer Laura Innes stopped at the cart to buy her lunch. After paying Luisa, Laura moved to the condiment table, located just to the right of the cart. She noticed Martin Gonzalez struggling to pour a large tub of boiling water into the hot dog steamer. Before she could move to help him, however, Martin lost his grip and dropped the tub of water, splashing himself.

The Court Officer administered first aid, and Martin was taken to St. Luke's hospital. He had received second degree burns on his arms and feet and was not able to return to the hot dog cart for three weeks.

63. What hospital was Martin taken to?

    A. St. Mark's   B. St. Peter's
    C. St. Mary's   D. St. Luke's

63.____

64. What part of his body did Martin burn?
His

    A. arms and feet   B. arms
    C. feet and ankles   D. arms and face

64.____

65. Who owns the hot dog cart?

    A. Martin Gonzalez   B. Luisa Gonzalez
    C. Laura Innes   D. Luke Martin

65.____

66. During what hours does the cart operate on weekends?

    A. 7:00 A.M. to 3:00 P.M.
    B. 9:30 A.M. to 3:00 P.M.
    C. 7:00 A.M. to 9:30 A.M.
    D. The cart does not operate on weekends

66.____

67. Where is the hot dog cart located?
On the _____ of the courthouse.

    A. first floor   B. roof
    C. outdoor plaza   D. third floor

  67.__

68. Who was first to administer first aid to Martin?

    A. Laura Innes   B. Luisa Gonzalez
    C. Luke Martin   D. Paramedics

  68.__

Questions 69-74.

DIRECTIONS: Questions 69 through 74 are to be answered on the basis of the following facts.

The offices of Judge Anjelica Chen are located on the third floor of the Peak County Courthouse. The offices of Judge Benjamin Laurence are also located on the third floor of the courthouse, across a courtyard. The windows of these offices face one another.

Judge Chen keeps her pet parrot, Mabel, in her offices. Although Mabel has a cage, Judge Chen keeps the door open, allowing Mabel to perch on bookshelves and lamps while the Judge finishes paperwork late in the evenings. Judge Laurence has no pets, but he often feeds pigeons from his window, sprinkling breadcrumbs along his sill.

On the evening of Tuesday, May 2, Court Officer Roger Crawford heard a scream from Judge Chen's office. He arrived to find the judge searching frantically through her office for Mabel, who had apparently disappeared. The window to the judge's office was open. The court officer assisted the judge in her search. At approximately 7:30, nearly 45 minutes after he had arrived in Judge Chen's office, the court officer heard someone hollering from the other side of the building.

Officer Crawford rushed toward the noise and found Judge Laurence in his office, trying to fend off the bright parrot flying back and forth across his office. The court officer summoned Judge Chen, who calmed Mabel and led her back to her cage.

69. Where was Mabel found?

    A. In Judge Chen's office   B. In Judge Laurence's office
    C. In the courtyard   D. In her cage

  69.__

70. What kind of bird is Mabel?

    A. Pigeon   B. Canary   C. Chickadee   D. Parrot

  70.__

71. Where is Judge Chen's office located?
_____ Judge Laurence's office.

    A. Below   B. Next to   C. Across from   D. Above

  71.__

72. Why does Judge Laurence leave breadcrumbs on his window-sill?   72.____

    A. To feed pigeons
    B. To feed Mabel
    C. To feed squirrels
    D. To keep food litter out of his office

73. How long did Judge Chen and Officer Crawford look for Mabel before they heard Judge   73.____
Laurence yelling in his office?
_____ minutes.

    A. 30   B. 45   C. 60   D. 15

74. Why does Judge Chen leave Mabel's cage door open?   74.____

    A. To allow Mabel to escape
    B. To allow Mabel a clearer view of Judge Laurence's windowsill
    C. Judge Chen does not leave Mabel's cage door open
    D. To allow Mabel to perch on bookshelves and lamps while the Judge finishes her paperwork

Questions 75-80.

DIRECTIONS: Questions 75 through 80 are to be answered on the basis of the following facts.

The Hickory Ridge Courthouse is located just across the street from the Hickory Ridge Public Library. Employees begin arriving at the courthouse at approximately 7:00 A.M. each weekday morning. The library opens at 9:00 A.M. and closes at 5:00 P.M. each weekday. Both the courthouse and the library have bicycle stands in front of them. Bicyclists lock their bikes to the stands while they run their errands and conduct their business.

Court Officer Melinda Thompson eats her lunch each day at a small cafe next to the library. The cafe caters mainly to employees of the library and courthouse. It operates from 11:00 A.M. to 3:00 P.M. each day.

On the afternoon of August 11, the court officer observed a young man with a backpack lock his bike to a stand in front of the library. The young man had blond hair, green eyes, and long sideburns. Approximately 30 minutes after the young man entered the library, a dark-haired man emerged from the cafe where the court officer was eating her lunch. The man had a beard, and was of medium build. He walked to the bicycle stand and began jiggling a lock on one of the bikes.

The court officer recognized the bicycle as the same one the blond-haired young man had locked to the stand. By the time the court officer reached the bicycle stand, the second man had already broken the lock. Although she called for him to stop, he rode away on the young man's bicycle. Her excellent description, however, helped police locate the bicycle thief and the bicycle a short time later.

75. What time does the library open?   75.____

    A. 7:00 A.M.   B. 9:00 A.M.   C. 11:00 A.M.   D. 3:00 P.M.

76. Where is the cafe located?   76.___

    A. Next to the courthouse
    B. Across from the library
    C. Next to the library
    D. Between the library and the courthouse

77. Who stole the bicycle?   77.___

    A. The blond-haired man
    B. The dark-haired man
    C. The man with the backpack
    D. The man with the long sideburns

78. What hours is the cafe open?   78.___

    A. 11:00 A.M. to 3:00 P.M.   B. 9:00 A.M. to 5:00 P.M.
    C. 7:00 A.M. to 5:00 P.M.   D. 7:00 A.M. to 3:00 P.M.

79. When do employees begin arriving at the courthouse each day?   79.___

    A. 7:00 A.M.   B. 9:00 A.M.   C. 10:00 A.M.   D. 11:00 A.M.

80. What did the bicycle thief do when the court officer ordered him to stop? 80.___

    A. He stopped.
    B. He rode away.
    C. He threw down the bicycle and ran.
    D. He insisted the bicycle was his.

Questions 81-87.

DIRECTIONS: Questions 81 through 87 are to be answered on the basis of the following
              facts.

The Jade Market is located on the first floor of the Angel County Courthouse. The court-house is located across the street from San Gabriel High School. Jade Market sells newspa-pers, magazines, sandwiches, beverages, and sodas. In the mornings, between 7:00 A.M. and 9:00 A.M., the market is frequented mostly by employees of the courthouse. In the after-noons, between 1:45 and 2:45, the small market is crowded with teenagers wearing cumber-some backpacks. Classes at San Gabriel High School end at 1:30 P.M.

Jade Market is operated by James Chang, who is 55 years old, with graying black hair and brown eyes. His wife, Lola, also helps at the market during the afternoon and evening hours.

On the afternoon of Thursday, September 1, Court Officer Mason Stewart stopped at Jade Market to buy a newspaper and some coffee. While he was talking with Lola Chang, twelve to fifteen high school students walked into the market. They moved noisily up and down the narrow aisles. They each carried a heavy backpack. As they walked through the store, their packs often knocked items from the shelves.

As the court officer watched the students, he noticed one young woman knock several magazines from the magazine stand located at the back of the store. Several other students walked past the magazine stand before the young woman was able to turn around and pick the magazines up. The young woman had blond hair and brown eyes, and she carried a red backpack. When she returned to the stand, Officer Stewart saw that she only replaced one magazine.

When the court officer approached the girl about the missing magazines, she insisted that she had not seen them. He asked her to wait at the front counter, which she did. Officer Stewart studied the magazine stand for a brief moment, and then bent down to peer beneath it. He saw the magazines lying there, where they had been accidentally kicked by the other passing students. The young woman helped gather the magazines, and then left the store after apologizing to Mr. and Mrs. Chang.

81. What hours is the market open?   81.____

    A. 7:00 A.M. to 2:45 P.M.
    B. 7:00 A.M. to 9:00 A.M.
    C. 7:00 A.M. to 1:30 P.M.
    D. The passage doesn't contain this information

82. Where were the missing magazines found?   82.____

    A. Inside the girl's backpack
    B. On the magazine stand
    C. Beneath the magazine stand
    D. They were never found

83. What did the girl do when Officer Stewart asked her about the missing magazines?   83.____
She

    A. ran from the store
    B. denied stealing them
    C. confessed
    D. ran to the front counter

84. Where is the Jade Market located?   84.____

    A. On the first floor of the courthouse
    B. On the third floor of the courthouse
    C. Next to Angel High School
    D. In the plaza of Angel High School

85. When does Lola Chang work in the market?   85.____

    A. All day
    B. Afternoons
    C. Afternoons and evenings
    D. The passage doesn't contain this information

86. On what day of the week did the incident occur?   86.____

    A. Monday   B. Tuesday   C. Wednesday   D. Thursday

87. What time are students at San Gabriel High School dismissed from class?   87._____
    A. 1:30 P.M.
    B. 1:45 P.M.
    C. 2:45 P.M.
    D. The passage does not contain this information

Questions 88-89.

DIRECTIONS: Questions 88 and 89 are to be answered on the basis of the following facts.

Procedure: The Service Station at the Friendly Car Dealership has a policy which allows customers to drop off their cars the night before they are to be worked on. This allows customers the convenience of not having to take time off from work to have their cars serviced. Cars must be dropped off between 9 P.M. and 11 P.M. the night before. Keys must be labeled with the make and license plate number of the car to which they belong. They are then placed into envelopes and dropped into a locked drop box outside the service station office. Cars must be picked up by 9:00 P.M. on the day repairs are completed. If the car cannot be picked up on that day, other arrangements must be made with the service department by 3:00 P.M. of that day.

Situation: Sarah Stone drops her car off at 10:45 P.M. the night before it is to be serviced. She labels her key, places it in the envelope and leaves it in the drop box. Her car is repaired by 11:00 A.M. the next morning. Because Sarah has to catch up on a backlog of work, she is unable to pick her car up before 6:00 P.M. on the day after the repairs have been completed.

88. Based on the above procedure, which one of the following statements regarding Stone's   88.___
    actions is correct?
    Stone

    A. should have dropped her car off before 10:45 P.M. the night before it was to be serviced
    B. should have given her keys to someone in the service department instead of dropping them in a box
    C. should have notified the service department of her plans by 3:00 P.M. on the day the car was repaired
    D. did everything according to proper procedure

89. If Stone wishes to pick her car up at 8:00 P.M. the day the repairs are completed, which   89.___
    of the following things must she do?
    She

    A. must make special arrangements with the service department
    B. must wait until the following morning to pick up her car
    C. must make a special appointment to pick up her car after hours
    D. does not need to do anything

Questions 90-91.

DIRECTIONS: Questions 90 and 91 are to be answered on the basis of the following facts.

Procedure: Notification of absence due to illness must be made between 9:00 A.M. and 10:00 A.M. on the first day of illness. Illness which results in more than four days of consecutive absence must be confirmed by a doctor's note stating the nature of the illness and the approximate date of return to work.

Situation: Officer Janus Lee becomes sick on the night of June 25 while at home. At 10:15 on the morning of June 26, Lee notifies his office that he will not be in. On July 4, Lee submits a doctor's note confirming and identifying his illness and stating that Lee will return to work on July 5.

90.   Based on the above procedure, which one of the following statements regarding Lee's actions is correct?
Officer Lee

    A.   should have notified his office of his absence by 10:00 A.M. on the morning of June 26
    B.   should have notified his office of his absence by 10:00 A.M. on the morning of June 25
    C.   should have submitted the doctor's note on June 26
    D.   followed the procedure correctly

90._____

91.   Officer Lee's note from the doctor states that he will be absent from the office from June 26 through July 4. Which of the following notification procedures should he follow on those days?

    A.   Officer Lee must notify his office of his absence on each morning between June 26 and July 4 by 10:00 A.M.
    B.   Officer Lee's doctor must notify his office of Officer Lee's absence on each morning between June 26 and July 4 by 10:00 A.M.
    C.   Officer Lee must contact his office periodically between June 26 and July 4 to notify them of his progress.
    D.   Once he has submitted his doctor's note, Officer Lee does not need to notify his office any further so long as he returns to work on July 5.

91._____

Questions 92-93.

DIRECTIONS: Questions 92 and 93 are to be answered on the basis of the following facts.

Procedure: Court officers in Montgomery County who work overtime are awarded compensation time instead of overtime pay. Each hour of over-time is equal to one hour of compensation time. In order to use compensation time, court officers must submit a written vacation request two weeks in advance of the desired time off. The request must contain the beginning and ending dates of the requested vacation. It must be signed by the officer's supervisor before the officer may utilize the compensation time.

Situation: Officer Sabrina Hellman wishes to use compensation time for a vacation beginning October 1 and ending October 10. The vacation will require 7 days of compensation time. Officer Hellman submits her vacation request on September 24. The request contains the beginning and ending dates of her desired vacation.

92. Based on the above procedure, which of the following statements regarding Officer Hell-   92.___
man's actions is correct?
Officer Hellman

    A.   should have submitted her vacation request by September 17
    B.   should have submitted her vacation request by September 1
    C.   should have submitted the beginning and ending dates of her vacation
    D.   followed the procedures correctly

93. How many hours of overtime must Officer Hellman have in order to accumulate 100   93.___
hours of compensation time?

    A. 50   B. 75   C. 150   D. 100

Questions 94-95.

DIRECTIONS: Questions 94 and 95 are to be answered on the basis of the following facts.

Procedure: Court officers in Salinas County who work overtime are awarded compensation time instead of overtime pay. Each hour of overtime is equal to one hour of compensation time. At the end of each calendar year, compensation time which has not been used is automatically erased unless employees submit a written request to have their compensation time rolled over to the next year. Rollover requests must be submitted no later than November 1. They must contain the employee's name, social security, and the total number of compensation hours s/he wishes to rollover.

Situation: Officer Larry Bernstein accumulated 20 hours of compensation time during calendar year 2008. In addition to that, he has 40 hours of compensation time which was rolled over from 2007. On October 30, Officer Bernstein submits a written request asking that his remaining compensation time be rolled over to calendar year 2009.

94. Based on the above procedure, which of the following statements regarding Officer Bern-   94.___
stein's actions is correct? Officer Bernstein

    A.   should have submitted his rollover request by November 1, 2008
    B.   should have submitted his vacation request by October 1, 2008
    C.   should have submitted the total number of hours he wanted to be rolled over
    D.   followed the procedures correctly

95. Based on the above procedure and situation, how many hours of compensation time can   95.___
Officer Bernstein expect to be rolled over to calendar year 2009?

    A. 20   B. 40   C. 60   D. 80

Questions 96-97.

DIRECTIONS: Questions 96 and 97 are to be answered on the basis of the following facts.

Procedure: Court officers in Salinas County who work overtime are awarded compensation time instead of overtime pay. Each hour of overtime is equal to one hour of compensation time. If a court officer is laid off or chooses to leave his or her employment as a court officer with the county, and he or she has compensation time remaining, then he or she can choose one of two options. The first option is for the employee to use the remaining compensation time as paid vacation time. This would allow the officer to cease his or her duties early, but still be paid until the end of his or her regular employment. In order to utilize this option, employees must submit a written request 30 days before the start of the paid vacation. The second option is for the employee to remain through the end of his or her regular employment, and receive a check for any remaining compensation time. In order to utilize this option, employees must submit a written request 90 days before the scheduled departure date.

Situation: Officer Glen Regan is due to retire at the end of calendar year 2008. Through the course of his career as a court officer, Glen has accumulated 200 hours of compensation time. This equals approximately 25 standard working days.

96. If Officer Regan decides that he would like to retire early, he should submit a written request by _____ 1, 2008.

    A. December   B. November   C. October   D. September

97. If Officer Regan decides to receive a check for his unused compensation time, he should submit a written request by _____ 1, 2008.

    A. December   B. November   C. October   D. September

Questions 98-100.

DIRECTIONS: Questions 98 through 100 are to be answered on the basis of the following facts.
Procedure: Court officers in James County are granted 10 paid sick days each year. Sick days are to be used only in the case of unforeseen illness. Employees are also granted 5 paid personal days. Officers who work overtime are also granted compensation time instead of overtime pay. Each hour of overtime is equal to one hour of compensation time. In order to use a sick day, employees must notify a supervisor by 10:00 A.M. on the day of their absence. In order to use a personal day, employees must notify a supervisor two working days in advance. In order to use a compensation-time day, employees must notify a supervisor two weeks in advance.

Situation: Court Officer Carla Lewis has a doctor and a dentist appointment on Monday, October 5.

98. In order to use a compensation day for these appointments, by what date must Carla notify her supervisor?

    A. Friday, September 4   B. Monday, September 14
    C. 10:00 A.M. October 5   D. Thursday, September 1

99. If Officer Carla Lewis wants to use a personal day for these appointments, by what date must she notify her supervisor?

    A. Friday, September 4   B. Monday, September 14
    C. 10:00 A.M. October 5   D. Thursday, October 1

100. If Officer Carla Lewis wants to use a sick day for these appointments, by what date must   100.___
she notify her supervisor?

    A.   10:00 A.M. on October 5
    B.   Monday, September 14
    C.   She cannot use a sick day for these appointments
    D.   She does not have to notify her supervisor until after she returns to work

---

KEY (CORRECT ANSWERS)

1. B	21. A	41. D	61. B	81. D
2. D	22. C	42. B	62. D	82. C
3. C	23. B	43. A	63. D	83. B
4. A	24. D	44. D	64. A	84. A
5. D	25. A	45. C	65. B	85. C
6. B	26. C	46. B	66. D	86. D
7. A	27. D	47. A	67. C	87. A
8. D	28. A	48. D	68. A	88. C
9. C	29. C	49. B	69. B	89. D
10. A	30. A	50. C	70. D	90. A
11. D	31. D	51. B	71. C	91. D
12. B	32. C	52. D	72. A	92. A
13. C	33. B	53. C	73. B	93. D
14. C	34. D	54. A	74. D	94. D
15. B	35. A	55. B	75. B	95. C
16. A	36. C	56. D	76. C	96. B
17. D	37. B	57. A	77. B	97. C
18. A	38. A	58. A	78. A	98. B
19. B	39. D	59. C	79. A	99. D
20. C	40. C	60. C	80. B	100. C

READING COMPREHENSION
UNDERSTANDING AND INTERPRETING WRITTEN MATERIAL
EXAMINATION SECTION
TEST 1

DIRECTIONS: Each question or incomplete statement is followed by several suggested
answers or completions. Select the one that BEST answers the question or
completes the statement. *PRINT THE LETTER OF THE CORRECT ANSWER
IN THE SPACE AT THE RIGHT.*

Questions 1-4.

DIRECTIONS: Questions 1 through 4 are to be answered SOLELY on the basis of the following passage.

Those engaged in the exercise of First Amendment rights by pickets, marches, parades,
and open-air assemblies are not exempted from obeying valid local traffic ordinances. In a
recent pronouncement, Mr. Justice Baxter, speaking for the Supreme Court, wrote:

The rights of free speech and assembly, while fundamental to our democratic society, still
do not mean that everyone with opinions or beliefs to express may address a group at any
public place and at any time. The constitutional guarantee of liberty implies the existence of
an organized society maintaining public order, without which liberty itself would be lost in the
excesses of anarchy. The control of travel on the streets is a clear example of governmental
responsibility to insure this necessary order. A restriction in that relation, designed to promote
the public convenience in the interest of all, and not susceptible to abuses of discriminatory
application, cannot be disregarded by the attempted exercise of some civil rights which, in
other circumstances, would be entitled to protection. One would not be justified in ignoring
the familiar red light because this was thought to be a means of social protest. Governmental
authorities have the duty and responsibility to keep their streets open and available for movement. A group of demonstrators could not insist upon the right to cordon off a street, or
entrance to a public or private building, and allow no one to pass who did not agree to listen
to their exhortations.

1. Which of the following statements BEST reflects Mr. Justice Baxter's view of the relationship between liberty and public order?   1.____

    A. Public order cannot exist without liberty.
    B. Liberty cannot exist without public order.
    C. The existence of liberty undermines the existence of public order.
    D. The maintenance of public order insures the existence of liberty.

2. According to the above passage, local traffic ordinances result from   2.____

    A. governmental limitations on individual liberty
    B. governmental responsibility to insure public order
    C. majority rule as determined by democratic procedures
    D. restrictions on expression of dissent

3. The above passage suggests that government would be acting improperly if a local traffic ordinance

    A. was enforced in a discriminatory manner
    B. resulted in public inconvenience
    C. violated the right of free speech and assembly
    D. was not essential to public order

4. Of the following, the MOST appropriate title for the above passage is

    A. THE RIGHTS OF FREE SPEECH AND ASSEMBLY
    B. ENFORCEMENT OF LOCAL TRAFFIC ORDINANCES
    C. FIRST AMENDMENT RIGHTS AND LOCAL TRAFFIC ORDINANCES
    D. LIBERTY AND ANARCHY

Questions 5-8

DIRECTIONS: Questions 5 through 8 are to be answered SOLELY on the basis of the following passage

On November 8, 1976, the Supreme Court refused to block the payment of Medicaid funds for elective abortions. The Court's action means that a new Federal statute that bars the use of Federal funds for abortions unless abortion is necessary to save the life of the mother will not go into effect for many months, if at all.

A Federal District Court in Brooklyn ruled the following month that the statute was unconstitutional and ordered that Federal reimbursement for the costs of abortions continue on the same basis as reimbursements for the costs of pregnancy and childbirth-related services.

Technically, what the Court did today was to deny a request by Senator Howard Ramsdell and others for a stay blocking enforcement of the District Court order pending appeal. The Court's action was a victory for New York City. The City's Health and Hospitals Corporation initiated one of the two lawsuits challenging the new statute that led to the District Court's decision. The Corporation also opposed the request for a Supreme Court stay of that decision, telling the Court in a memorandum that a stay would subject the Corporation to a *grave and irreparable injury.*

5. According to the above passage, it would be CORRECT to state that the Health and Hospitals Corporation

    A. joined Senator Ramsdell in his request for a stay
    B. opposed the statute which limited reimbursement for the cost of abortions
    C. claimed that it would experience a loss if the District Court order was enforced
    D. appealed the District Court decision

6. The above passage indicates that the Supreme Court acted in DIRECT response to

    A. a lawsuit initiated by the Health and Hospitals Corporation
    B. a ruling by a Federal District Court
    C. a request for a stay
    D. the passage of a new Federal statute

7. According to the above passage, it would be CORRECT to state that the Supreme Court   7._____

   A. blocked enforcement of the District Court order
   B. refused a request for a stay to block enforcement of the Federal statute
   C. ruled that the new Federal statute was unconstitutional
   D. permitted payment of Federal funds for abortion to continue

8. Following are three statements concerning abortion that might be correct: 8._____
   I. Abortion costs are no longer to be Federally reimbursed on the same basis as those for pregnancy and childbirth
   II. Federal funds have not been available for abortions except to save the life of the mother
   III. Medicaid has paid for elective abortions in the past
   According to the passage above, which of the following CORRECTLY classifies the above statements into those that are true and those that are not true?

   A. I is true, but II and III are not.
   B. I and III are true, but II is not.
   C. I and II are true, but III is not.
   D. III is true, but I and II are not.

Questions 9-12.

DIRECTIONS: Questions 9 through 12 are to be answered SOLELY on the basis of the following passage.

   A person may use physical force upon another person when and to the extent he reasonably believes such to be necessary to defend himself or a third person from what he reasonably believes to be the use or imminent use of unlawful physical force by such other person, unless (a) the latter's conduct was provoked by the actor himself with intent to cause physical injury to another person; or (b) the actor was the initial aggressor; or (c) the physical force involved is the product of a combat by agreement not specifically authorized by law.

   A person may not use deadly physical force upon another person under the circumstances specified above unless (a) he reasonably believes that such other person is using or is about to use deadly physical force. Even in such case, however, the actor may not use deadly physical force if he knows he can, with complete safety, as to himself and others avoid the necessity of doing so by retreating; except that he is under no duty to retreat if he is in his dwelling and is not the initial aggressor; or (b) he reasonably believes that such other person is committing or attempting to commit a kidnapping, forcible rape, or forcible sodomy.

9. Jones and Smith, who have not met before, get into an argument in a tavern. Smith takes   9._____
   a punch at Jones, but misses. Jones then hits Smith on the chin with his fist. Smith falls to the floor and suffers minor injuries.
   According to the above passage, it would be CORRECT to state that _____ justified in using physical force.

   A. only Smith was   B. only Jones was
   C. both Smith and Jones were   D. neither Smith nor Jones was

10. While walking down the street, Brady observes Miller striking Mrs. Adams on the head   1(
    with his fist in an attempt to steal her purse.
    According to the above passage, it would be CORRECT to state that Brady would

    A. not be justified in using deadly physical force against Miller since Brady can safely
       retreat
    B. be justified in using physical force against Miller but not deadly physical force
    C. not be justified in using physical force against Miller since Brady himself is not
       being attacked
    D. be justified in using deadly physical force

11. Winters is attacked from behind by Sharp, who attempts to beat up Winters with a black-   11.__
    jack. Winters disarms Sharp and succeeds in subduing him with a series of blows to the
    head. Sharp stops fighting and explains that he thought Winters was the person who had
    robbed his apartment a few minutes before, but now realizes his mistake.
    According to the above passage, it would be CORRECT to state that

    A. Winters was justified in using physical force on Sharp only to the extent necessary
       to defend himself
    B. Winters was not justified in using physical force on Sharp since Sharp's attack was
       provoked by what he believed to be Winters' behavior
    C. Sharp was justified in using physical force on Winters since he reasonably believed
       that Winters had unlawfully robbed him
    D. Winters was justified in using physical force on Sharp only because Sharp was act-
       ing mistakenly in attacking him

12. Roberts hears a noise in the cellar of his home, and, upon investigation, discovers an   12.__
    intruder, Welch. Welch moves towards Roberts in a threatening manner, thrusts his hand
    into a bulging pocket, and withdraws what appears to be a gun. Roberts thereupon
    strikes Welch over the head with a golf club. He then sees that the *gun* is a toy. Welch
    later dies of head injuries. According to the above passage, it would be CORRECT to
    state that Roberts was

    A. justified in using deadly physical force because he reasonably believed Welch was
       about to use deadly physical force
    B. not justified in using deadly physical force
    C. justified in using deadly physical force only because he did not provoke Welch's
       conduct
    D. justified in using deadly physical force only because he was not the initial aggres-
       sor

Questions 13-16.

DIRECTIONS: Questions 13 through 16 are to be answered SOLELY on the basis of the fol-
              lowing passage.

From the beginning, the Supreme Court has supervised the fairness of trials conducted
by the Federal government. But the Constitution, as originally drafted, gave the court no such
general authority in state cases. The court's power to deal with state cases comes from the
Fourteenth Amendment, which became part of the Constitution in 1868. The crucial provision
forbids any state to *deprive any person of life, liberty, or property without due process of law.*

The guarantee of *due process* would seem, at the least, to require fair procedure in criminal trials. But curiously the Supreme Court did not speak on the question for many decades. During that time, however, the due process clause was interpreted to bar *unreasonable* state economic regulations, such as minimum wage laws.

In 1915, there came the case of Leo M. Frank, a Georgian convicted of murder in a trial that he contended was dominated by mob hysteria. Historians now agree that there was such hysteria, with overtones of anti-semitism.

The Supreme Court held that it could not look past the findings of the Georgia courts that there had been no mob atmosphere at the trial. Justices Oliver Wendell Holmes and Charles Evans Hughes dissented, arguing that the constitutional guarantee would be *a barren one* if the Federal courts could not make their own inferences from the facts.

In 1923, the case of Moore v. Dempsey involved five Arkansas Blacks convicted of murder and sentenced to death in a community so aroused against them that at one point they were saved from lynching only by Federal troops. Witnesses against them were said to have been beaten into testifying.

The court, though not actually setting aside the convictions, directed a lower Federal court to hold a habeas corpus hearing to find out whether the trial had been fair, or whether the whole proceeding had been *a mask—that counsel, jury, and judge were swept to the fatal end by an irresistible wave of public passion.*

13. According to the above passage, the Supreme Court's INITIAL interpretation of the Fourteenth Amendment   13.____

    A. protected state supremacy in economic matters
    B. increased the scope of Federal jurisdiction
    C. required fair procedures in criminal trials
    D. prohibited the enactment of minimum wage laws

14. According to the above passage, the Supreme Court in the Frank case   14.____

    A. denied that there had been mob hysteria at the trial
    B. decided that the guilty verdict was supported by the evidence
    C. declined to question the state court's determination of the facts
    D. found that Leo Frank had not received *due process*

15. According to the above passage, the dissenting judges in the Frank case maintained that   15.____

    A. due process was an empty promise in the circumstances of that case
    B. the Federal courts could not guarantee certain provisions of the Constitution
    C. the Federal courts should not make their own inferences from the facts in state cases
    D. the Supreme Court had rendered the Constitution *barren*

16. Of the following, the MOST appropriate title for the above passage is
    A. THE CONDUCT OF FEDERAL TRIALS
    B. THE DEVELOPMENT OF STATES' RIGHTS: 1868-1923
    C. MOORE V. DEMPSEY: A CASE STUDY IN CRIMINAL JUSTICE
    D. DUE PROCESS-THE EVOLUTION OF A CONSTITUTIONAL CORNERSTONE

Questions 17-20.

DIRECTIONS: Questions 17 through 20 are to be answered SOLELY on the basis of the following passage.

The difficulty experienced in determining which party has the burden of proving payment or non-payment is due largely to a lack of consistency between the rules of pleading and the rules of proof. In some cases, a plaintiff is obligated by a rule of pleading to allege non-payment on his complaint, yet is not obligated to prove non-payment on the trial. An action upon a contract for the payment of money will serve as an illustration. In such a case, the plaintiff must allege non-payment in his complaint, but the burden of proving payment on the trial is upon the defendant. An important and frequently cited case on this problem is Conkling v. Weatherwax. In that case, the action was brought to establish and enforce a legacy as a lien upon real property. The defendant alleged in her answer that the legacy had been paid. There was no witness competent to testify for the plaintiff to show that the legacy had not been paid. Therefore, the question of the burden of proof became of primary importance since, if the plaintiff had the burden of proving non-payment, she must fail in her action; whereas if the burden of proof was on the defendant to prove payment, the plaintiff might win. The Court of Appeals held that the burden of proof was on the plaintiff. In the course of his opinion, Judge Vann attempted to harmonize the conflicting cases on this subject, and for that purpose formulated three rules. These rules have been construed and applied to numerous subsequent cases. As so construed and applied, these may be summarized as follows:

Rule 1. In an action upon a contract for the payment of money only, where the complaint does not allege a balance due over and above all payments made, the plaintiff must allege nonpayment in his complaint, but the burden of proving payment is upon the defendant. In such a case, payment is an affirmative defense which the defendant must plead in his answer. If the defendant fails to plead payment, but pleads a general denial instead, he will not be permitted to introduce evidence of payment.

Rule 2. Where the complaint sets forth a balance in excess of all payments, owing to the structure of the pleading, burden is upon the plaintiff to prove his allegation. In this case, the defendant is not required to plead payment as a defense in his answer but may introduce evidence of payment under a general denial.

Rule 3. When the action is not upon contract for the payment of money, but is upon an obligation created by operation of law, or is for the enforcement of a lien where non-payment of the amount secured is part of the cause of action, it is necessary both to allege and prove the fact of nonpayment.

17. In the above passage, the case of Conkling v. Weatherwax was cited PRIMARILY to illus-   17.____
trate

    A. a case where the burden of proof was on the defendant to prove payment
    B. how the question of the burden of proof can affect the outcome of a case
    C. the effect of a legacy as a lien upon real property
    D. how conflicting cases concerning the burden of proof were harmonized

18. According to the above passage, the pleading of payment is a defense in Rule(s)   18.____

    A. 1, but not Rules 2 and 3
    B. 2, but not Rules 1 and 3
    C. 1 and 3, but not Rule 2
    D. 2 and 3, but not Rule 1

19. The facts in Conkling v. Weatherwax CLOSELY resemble the conditions described in   19.____

    A. Rule #1
    B. Rule #2
    C. Rule #3
    D. none of the rules

20. The MAJOR topic of the above passage may BEST be described as   20.____

    A. determining the ownership of property
    B. providing a legal definition
    C. placing the burden of proof
    D. formulating rules for deciding cases

Questions 21-25.

DIRECTIONS: Questions 21 through 25 are to be answered SOLELY on the basis of the following passage.

The law is quite clear that evidence obtained in violation of Section 605 of the Federal Communications Act is not admissible in Federal court. However, the law as to the admissibility of evidence in state court is far from clear. Had the Supreme Court of the United States made the wiretap exclusionary rule applicable to the states, such confusion would not exist.

In the case of Alton v. Texas, the Supreme Court was called upon to determine whether wiretapping by state and local officers came within the proscription of the Federal statute and, if so, whether Section 605 required the same remedies for its vindication in state courts. In answer to the first question, Mr. Justice Minton, speaking for the court, flatly stated that Section 605 made it a federal crime for anyone to intercept telephone messages and divulge what he learned. The court went on to say that a state officer who testified in state court concerning the existence, contents, substance, purport, effect, or meaning of an intercepted conversation violated the Federal law and committed a criminal act. In regard to the second question, how-ever, the Supreme Court felt constrained by due regard for federal-state relations to answer in the negative. Mr. Justice Minton stated that the court would not presume, in the absence of a clear manifestation of congressional intent, that Congress intended to supersede state rules of evidence.

Because the Supreme Court refused to apply the exclusionary rule to wiretap evidence that was being used in state courts, the states respectively made this decision for themselves. According to hearings held before a congressional committee in 1975, six states authorize wiretapping by statute, 33 states impose total bans on wiretapping, and 11 states have no definite statute on the subject. For examples of extremes, a statute in Pennsylvania will be compared with a statute in New York.

The Pennsylvania statute provides that no communications by telephone or telegraph can be intercepted without permission of both parties. It also specifically prohibits such interception by public officials and provides that evidence obtained cannot be used in court.

The lawmakers in New York, recognizing the need for legal wire-tapping, authorized wire-tapping by statute. A New York law authorizes the issuance of an ex parte order upon oath or affirmation for limited wiretapping. The aim of the New York law is to allow court-ordered wire-tapping and to encourage the testimony of state officers concerning such wiretapping in court. The New York law was found to be constitutional by the New York State Supreme Court in 1975. Other states, including Oregon, Maryland, Nevada, and Massachusetts, enacted similar laws which authorize court-ordered wiretapping.

To add to this legal disarray, the vast majority of the states, including New Jersey and New York, permit wiretapping evidence to be received in court even though obtained in violation of the state laws and of Section 605 of the Federal act. However, some states, such as Rhode Island, have enacted statutory exclusionary rules which provide that illegally procured wiretap evidence is incompetent in civil as well as criminal actions.

21. According to the above passage, a state officer who testifies in New York State court concerning the contents of a conversation he overheard through a court-ordered wire-tap is in violation of _____ law.

    A. state law but not federal
    B. federal law but not state
    C. federal law and state
    D. neither federal nor state

22. According to the above passage, which of the following statements concerning states statutes on wiretapping is CORRECT?

    A. The number of states that impose total bans on wiretapping is three times as great as the number of states with no definite statute on wiretapping.
    B. The number of states having no definite statute on wiretapping is more than twice the number of states authorizing wiretapping.
    C. The number of states which authorize wiretapping by statute and the number of states having no definite statute on wiretapping exceed the number of states imposing total bans on wiretapping.
    D. More states authorize wiretapping by statute than impose total bans on wiretapping.

23. Following are three statements concerning wiretapping that might be valid: 23._____
     I.   In Pennsylvania, only public officials may legally intercept telephone commu-
          nications.
     II. In Rhode Island, evidence obtained through an illegal wiretap is incompetent
          in criminal, but not civil, actions.
     III. Neither Massachusetts nor Pennsylvania authorizes wiretapping by public
          officials.
     According to the above passage, which of the following CORRECTLY classifies these
     statements into those that are valid and those that are not?

     A.   I is valid, but II and III are not.
     B.   II is valid, but I and III are not.
     C.   II and III are valid, but I is not.
     D.   None of the statements is valid.

24. According to the above passage, evidence obtained in violation of Section 605 of the   24._____
     Federal Communications Act is inadmissible in

     A.   federal court but not in any state courts
     B.   federal court and all state courts
     C.   all state courts but not in federal court
     D.   federal court and some state courts

25. In regard to state rules of evidence, Mr. Justice Minton expressed the Court's opinion   25._____
     that Congress

     A.   intended to supersede state rules of evidence, as manifested by Section 605 of the
          Federal Communications Act
     B.   assumed that federal statutes would govern state rules of evidence in all wiretap
          cases
     C.   left unclear whether it intended to supersede state rules of evidence
     D.   precluded itself from superseding state rules of evidence through its regard for fed-
          eral-state relations

KEY (CORRECT ANSWERS)

1.	B		11.	A
2.	B		12.	A
3.	A		13.	D
4.	C		14.	C
5.	B		15.	A
6.	C		16.	D
7.	D		17.	B
8.	D		18.	A
9.	B		19.	C
10.	B		20.	C

21.	B
22.	A
23.	D
24.	D
25.	C

TEST 2

Questions 1-3.

DIRECTIONS: Questions 1 through 3 are to be answered SOLELY on the basis of the following passage.

The State Assembly has passed a bill that would require all state agencies, public authorities, and local governments to refuse bids in excess of $2,000 from any foreign firm or corporation. The only exceptions to this outright prohibition against public buying of foreign goods or services would be for products not available in this country, goods of a quality unobtainable from an American supplier, and products using foreign materials that are *substantially* manufactured in the United States.

This bill is a flagrant violation of the United States' officially espoused trade principles. It would add to the costs of state and local governments. It could provoke retaliatory action from many foreign governments against the state and other American producers, and foreign governments would be fully entitled to take such retaliatory action under the General Agreement on Tariffs and Trade, which the United States has signed.

The State Senate, which now has the Assembly bill before it, should reject this protectionist legislation out of enlightened regard for the interests of the taxpayers and producers of the State—as well as for those of the nation and its trading partners generally. In this time of unemployment and international monetary disorder, the State—with its reputation for intelligent and progressive law-making—should avoid contributing to what could become a tidal wave of protectionism here and overseas.

1. Under the requirements of the bill passed by the State Assembly, a bid from a foreign manufacturer in excess of $2,000 can be accepted by a state agency or local government only if it meets which one of the following requirements?
The

    A. bid is approved individually by the State Legislature
    B. bidder is willing to accept payment in United States currency
    C. bid is for an item of a quality unobtainable from an American supplier
    D. bid is for an item which would be more expensive if it were purchased from an American supplier

1.____

2. The author of the above passage feels that the bill passed by the State Assembly should be

    A. passed by the State Senate and put into effect
    B. passed by the State Senate but vetoed by the Governor
    C. reintroduced into the State Assembly and rejected
    D. rejected by the State Senate

2.____

3. The author of the above passage calls the practice of prohibiting purchase of products manufactured by foreign countries

   A. prohibition
   C. retaliatory action
   B. protectionism
   D. isolationism

Questions 4-7.

DIRECTIONS: Questions 4 through 7 are to be answered SOLELY on the basis of the following passage.

Data processing is by no means a new invention. In one form or another, it has been carried on throughout the entire history of civilization. In its most general sense, data processing means organizing data so that it can be used for a specific purpose-a procedure commonly known simply as *record-keeping* or *paperwork*. With the development of modern office equipment, and particularly with the recent introduction of computers, the techniques of data processing have become highly elaborate and sophisticated, but the basic purpose remains the same: Turning raw data into useful information.

The key concept here is usefulness. The data, or input, that is to be processed can be compared to the raw material that is to go into a manufacturing process. The information, or output, that results from data processing—like the finished product of a manufacturer—should be clearly usable. A collection of data has little value unless it is converted into information that serves a specific function.

4. The expression *paperwork,* as it is used in this passage,

   A. shows that the author regards such operations as a waste of time
   B. has the same general meaning as *data processing*
   C. refers to methods of record-keeping that are no longer in use
   D. indicates that the public does not understand the purpose of data processing

5. The above passage indicates that the use of computers has

   A. greatly simplified the clerical work in an office
   B. led to more complicated systems for the handling of data
   C. had no effect whatsoever on data processing
   D. made other modern office machines obsolete

6. Which of the following BEST expresses the basic principle of data processing as it is described in the above passage?

   A. Input-processing-output
   B. Historical record-keeping-modern techniques -specific functions
   C. Office equipment-computer-accurate data
   D. Raw material-manufacturer-retailer

7. According to the above passage, data processing may be described as

   A. a new management technique
   B. computer technology
   C. information output
   D. record-keeping

Questions 8-10.

DIRECTIONS: Questions 8 through 10 are to be answered SOLELY on the basis of the following passage.

A loan receipt is an instrument devised to permit the insurance company to bring an
action against the wrongdoer in the name of the insured despite the fact that the insured no
longer has any financial interest in the outcome. It provides, in effect, that the amount of the
loss is advanced to the insured as a loan which is repayable only up to the extent of any
recovery made from the wrongdoer. The insured further agrees to enter and prosecute suit
against the wrongdoer in his own name. Such a receipt substitutes a loan for a payment for
the purpose of permitting the insurance company to press its action against the wrongdoer in
the name of the insured.

8. According to the above passage, the purpose behind the use of a loan receipt is to   8.____

    A. guarantee that the insurance company gets repayment from the person insured
    B. insure repayment of all expenditures to the named insured
    C. make it possible for the insurance company to sue in the name of the policyowner
    D. prevent the wrongdoer from escaping the natural consequences of his act

9. According to the above passage, the amount of the loan which must be paid back to the   9.____
    insurance company equals but does NOT exceed the amount

    A. of the loss
    B. on the face of the policy
    C. paid to the insured
    D. recovered from the wrongdoer

10. According to the above passage, by giving a loan receipt, the person insured agrees to   10.____

    A. a suit against the wrongdoer in his own name
    B. forego any financial gain from the outcome of the suit
    C. institute an action on behalf of the insurance company
    D. repay the insurance company for the loan received

Questions 11-12.

DIRECTIONS: Questions 11 and 12 are to be answered SOLELY on the basis of the following
passage.

Open air markets originally came into existence spontaneously when groups of pushcart
peddlers congregated in spots where business was good. Good business induced them to
return to these spots daily and, thus, unofficial open air markets arose. These peddlers paid
no fees, and the city received no revenue from them. Confusion and disorder reigned in these
unsupervised markets; the earliest arrivals secured the best locations, unless or until forcibly
ejected by stronger or tougher peddlers. Although the open air markets supplied a definite
need in the community, there were many detrimental factors involved in their operation. They
were unsightly, created unsanitary conditions in market streets by the deposit of garbage and
waste and were a definite obstruction to traffic, as well as a fire hazard.

11. On the basis of the above passage, the MOST accurate of the following statements is: 1

   A. Each peddler in the original open air markets had his own fixed location.
   B. Open air markets were originally organized by means of agreements between groups of pushcart peddlers.
   C. The locations of these markets depended upon the amount of business the vendors were able to do.
   D. There was confusion and disorder in these open air markets because the peddlers were not required to pay any fees to the city.

12. Of the following, the MOST valid implication which can be made on the basis of the above passage is that the   12.__

   A. detrimental aspect of the operations of open air markets was the probable reason for the creation of enclosed markets under the supervision of the Department of Markets
   B. open air markets could not supply any community need without proper supervision
   C. original open air markets were good examples of the operation of fair competition in business
   D. possibility of obtaining a source of revenue was probably the most important reason for the city's ultimate undertaking of the supervision of open air markets

Questions 13-14.

DIRECTIONS: Questions 13 and 14 are to be answered SOLELY on the basis of the following passage.

   A person who displays on his window, door, or in his place of business words or letters in Hebraic characters other than the word *kosher,* or any sign, emblem, insignia, six-pointed star, symbol or mark in simulation of same, without displaying in conjunction there-with in English letters of at least the same size as such characters, signs, emblems, insignia or marks, the words *we sell kosher meat and food only* or *we sell non-kosher meat and food only* or *we sell both kosher and non-kosher meat and food,* as the case may be, is guilty of a misdemeanor. Possession of non-kosher meat and food in any place of business advertising the sale of kosher meat and food only is presumptive evidence that the person in possession exposes the same for sale with intent to defraud, in violation of the provisions of this section.

13. Of the following, the MOST valid implication that can be made on the basis of the above passage is that a person who   13.__

   A. displays on his window a six-pointed star in addition to the word *kosher* in Hebraic letters is guilty of intent to defraud
   B. displays on his window the word *kosher* in Hebraic characters intends to indicate that he has only kosher food for sale
   C. sells both kosher and non-kosher food in the same place of business is guilty of a misdemeanor
   D. sells only that type of food which can be characterized as neither kosher nor non-kosher, such as fruit and vegetables, without an explanatory sign in English is guilty of intent to defraud

14. Of the following, the one which would constitute a violation of the rules of the above passage is a case in which a person   14._____

    A. displays the word *kosher* on his window in Hebraic letters has only kosher meat and food in the store but has some non-kosher meat in the rear of the establishment

    B. selling both kosher and non-kosher meat and food uses words in Hebraic letters, other than the word *kosher,* on his window and a sign of the same size letters in English stating *we sell both kosher and non-kosher meat and food*

    C. selling only kosher meat and food uses words in Hebraic letters, other than the word *kosher,* on his window and a sign of the same size letters in English stating *we sell kosher meat and food only*

    D. selling only non-kosher meat and food displays a six-pointed star on his window and a sign of the same size letters in English stating *we sell only non-kosher meat and food*

Questions 15-16.

DIRECTIONS: Questions 15 and 16 are to be answered SOLELY on the basis of the following passage.

COMMODITIES IN GLASS BOTTLES OR JARS

    The contents of the bottle may be stated in terms of weight or of fluid measure, the weight being indicated in terms of pounds and ounces and the fluid measure being indicated in terms of gallons, quarts, pints, half-pints, gills, or fluid ounces. When contents are liquid, the amount should not be stated in terms of weight. The marking indicating content is to be on a tag attached to the bottle or upon a label. The letters shall be in bold-faced type at least one-ninth of an inch (1/9") in height for bottles or jars having a capacity of a gill, half-pint, pint, or multiples of a pint, and letters at least three-sixteenths of an inch (3/16") in height for bottles of other capacities, on a part of the tag or label free from other printing or ornamentation, leaving a clear space around the marking which indicates the contents.

15. Of the following, the one which does NOT meet the requirements of the above passage is a   15._____

    A. bottle of cooking oil with a label stating *contents—16 fluid ounces* in appropriate sized letters

    B. bottle of vinegar with a label stating *contents—8 ounces avoir.* in appropriate sized letters

    C. glass jar filled with instant coffee with a label stating *contents—1 lb. 3 ozs. avoir.* in appropriate sized letters

    D. glass jar filled with liquid bleach with a label stating *contents—1 quart* in appropriate sized letters

16. Of the following, the one which does meet the requirements of the above passage is a   16._____

    A. bottle filled with a low-calorie liquid sweetener with a label stating *contents—3 fluid ounces* in letters 1/12" high

    B. bottle filled with ammonia solution for cleaning with a label stating *contents—1 pint* in letters 1/10" high

C.   jar filled with baking powder with a label stating *contents—$\frac{1}{2}$ pint* in letters $\frac{1}{4}$" high

D.   jar filled with hard candy with a label stating *contents—1 lb. avoir.* in letters $\frac{1}{2}$" high

Question 17.

DIRECTIONS: Question 17 is to be answered SOLELY on the basis of the information contained in the following passage.

DEALERS IN SECOND HAND DEVICES

1.   It shall be unlawful for any person to engage in or conduct the business of dealing in, trading in, selling, receiving, or repairing condemned, rebuilt, or used weighing or measuring devices without a permit therefor.

2.   Such permit shall expire on the twenty-eighth day of February next succeeding the date of issuance thereof.

3.   Every person engaged in the above business, within five days after the making of a repair, or the sale and delivery of a repaired, rebuilt, or used weighing or measuring device, shall serve notice in writing on the commissioner giving the name and address of the person for whom the repair has been made or to whom a repaired, rebuilt, or used weighing or measuring device has been sold or delivered, and shall include a statement that such device has been so altered, repaired, or rebuilt as to conform to the regulations of the department.

17.   According to the above passage, the MOST accurate of the following statements is: 17.__

A.   A permit issued to engage in the business mentioned above, first issued on April 23, 1968, expired on February 28, 1969.
B.   A rebuilt or repaired weighing or measuring device should not operate with less error than the tolerances permitted by the regulations of the department.
C.   If a used scale in good condition is sold, it is not necessary for the seller to notify the commissioner of the name and address of the buyer.
D.   There is a difference in the time required to notify the commissioner of a repair or of a sale of a repaired device.

Questions 18-19.

DIRECTIONS: Questions 18 and 19 are to be answered SOLELY on the basis of the following passage.

A.   It shall be unlawful for any person, firm, or corporation to sell or offer for sale at retail for use in internal combustion engines in motor vehicles any gasoline unless such seller shall post and keep continuously posted on the individual pump or other dispensing device from which such gasoline is sold or offered for sale a sign or placard not less than seven inches in height and eight inches in width nor larger than twelve inches in height and twelve inches in width and stating clearly in numbers of uniform size the selling price or prices per gallon of such gasoline so sold or offered for sale from such pump or other dispensing device.

B. The amount of governmental tax to be collected in connection with the sale of such gasoline shall be stated on such sign or placard and separately and apart from such selling price or prices.

18. The one of the following price signs posted on a gasoline pump which would be in violation of the above passage is a sign _____ square inches in size and _____ inches high.   18._____

   A. 144; 12   B. 84; 7   C. 72; 12   D. 60; 8

19. According to the above passage, the LEAST accurate of the following statements is: 19._____

   A. Gasoline may be sold from a dispensing device other than a pump.
   B. If two different pumps are used to sell the same grade of gasoline, a price sign must appear on each pump.
   C. The amount of governmental tax and the price of the gasoline must not be stated on the same sign.
   D. The sizes of the numbers used on a sign to indicate the price of gasoline must be the same.

Questions 20-21.

DIRECTIONS: Questions 20 and 21 are to be answered SOLELY on the basis of the following passage.

In all systems of weights and measures based on one or more arbitrary fundamental units, the concrete representation of the unit in the form of a standard is necessary, and the construction and preservation of such a standard is a matter of primary importance. Therefore, it is essential that the standard should be so constructed as to be as nearly permanent and invariable as human ingenuity can contrive. The reference of all measures to an original standard is essential for their correctness, and such a standard must be maintained and preserved in its integrity by some responsible authority which is thus able to provide against the use of false weights and measures. Accordingly, from earliest times, standards were constructed and preserved under the direction of kings and priests, and the temples were a favorite place for their deposit. Later, this duty was assumed by the government, and today we find the integrity of standards of weights and measures safeguarded by international agreement.

20. Of the following, the MOST valid implication which can be made on the basis of the above passage is that   20._____

   A. fundamental units of systems of weights and measures should be represented by quantities so constructed that they are specific and constant
   B. in the earliest times, standards were so constructed that they were as permanent and invariable as modern ones
   C. international agreement has practically relieved the U.S. government of the necessity of preserving standards of weights and measures
   D. the preservation of standards is of less importance than the ingenuity used in their construction

21. Of the following, the MOST appropriate title for the above passage is

    A. THE CONSTRUCTION AND PRESERVATION OF STANDARDS OF WEIGHTS
       AND MEASURES
    B. THE FIXING OF RESPONSIBILITY FOR THE ESTABLISHMENT OF STAN-
       DARDS OF WEIGHTS AND MEASURES
    C. THE HISTORY OF SYSTEMS OF WEIGHTS AND MEASURES
    D. THE VALUE OF PROPER STANDARDS IN PROVIDING CORRECT WEIGHTS
       AND MEASURES

Questions 22-23.

DIRECTIONS: Questions 22 and 23 are to be answered SOLELY on the basis of the following
           passage.

Accurate weighing and good scales insure that excess is not given just for the sake of
good measure. No more striking example of the fundamental importance of correct weighing
to the business man is found than in the simple and usual relation where a charge or value is
obtained by multiplying a weight by a unit price. For example, a scale may weigh *light,* that is,
the actual quantity delivered is in excess by 1 percent. The actual result is that the seller
taxes himself. If his profit is supposed to be 10 percent of total sales, an overweight of 1 percent represents 10 percent of that profit. Under these conditions, the situation is as though
the seller were required to pay a sales tax equivalent to what he is taxing himself.

22. Of the following, the MOST valid implication which can be made on the basis of the
    above passage is that

    A. consistent use of scales that weigh *light* will reduce sellers' profits
    B. no good businessman would give any buyer more than the weight required even if
       his scale is accurate
    C. the kind of situation described in the above passage could not arise if sales were
       being made of merchandise sold by the yard
    D. the use of incorrect scales is one of the reasons causing governments to impose
       sales taxes

23. According to the above passage, the MOST accurate of the following statements is:

    A. If his scale weighs *light* by an amount of 2 percent, the seller would deliver only 98
       pounds when 100 pounds was the amount agreed upon.
    B. If the seller's scale weighs *heavy,* the buyer will receive an amount in excess of
       what he intended to purchase.
    C. If the seller's scale weighs *light* by an amount of 1 percent, a buyer who agreed to
       purchase 50 pounds of merchandise would actually receive $50 \frac{1}{2}$ pounds.
    D. The use of a scale which delivers an amount which is in excess of that required is
       an example of deliberate fraud.

Questions 24-25.

DIRECTIONS: Questions 24 and 25 are to be answered SOLELY on the basis of the following passage.

Food shall be deemed to be misbranded:
1. If its labeling is false or misleading in any particular.

2. If any word, statement, or other information required by or under authority of this article to appear on the label or labeling is not prominently placed thereon with such conspicuousness (as compared with other words, statements, designs, or devices in the labeling) and in such terms as to render it likely to be read and understood by the ordinary individual under customary conditions of purchase and use.

3. If it purports to be or is represented as a food for which a standard of quality has been prescribed and its quality falls below such standard, unless its label bears a statement that it falls below such standard.

24. According to the above passage, the MOST accurate of the following statements is: 24._____

A. A food may be considered misbranded if the label contains a considerable amount of information which is not required.
B. If a consumer purchased one type of canned food, although he intended to buy another, the food is probably misbranded.
C. If a food is used in large amounts by a group of people of certain foreign origin, it can be considered misbranded unless the label is in the foreign language with which they are familiar.
D. The required information on a label is likely to be in larger print than other information which may appear on it.

25. According to the above passage, the one of the following foods which may be considered   25._____
to be misbranded is a

A. can of peaches with a label which carries the brand name of the packer but states *Below Standard in Quality*
B. can of vegetables with a label on which is printed a shield which states *U.S. Grade B*
C. package of frozen food which has some pertinent information printed on it in very small type which a customer cannot read and which the store manager cannot read when asked to do so by the customer
D. package of margarine of the same size as the usual package of butter, kept near the butter, but clearly labeled as margarine

_____

KEY (CORRECT ANSWERS)

1.	C		11.	C
2.	D		12.	A
3.	B		13.	B
4.	B		14.	A
5.	B		15.	B
6.	A		16.	D
7.	D		17.	A
8.	C		18.	C
9.	D		19.	C
10.	A		20.	A

21.	D
22.	A
23.	C
24.	D
25.	C

EXAMINATION SECTION
TEST 1

DIRECTIONS: Each question or incomplete statement is followed by several suggested answers or completions. Select the one that BEST answers the question or completes the statement. *PRINT THE LETTER OF THE CORRECT ANSWER IN THE SPACE AT THE RIGHT.*

Questions 1-6.

DIRECTIONS: Questions 1 through 6 consist of descriptions of material to which a filing designation must be assigned.

Assume that the matters and oases described in the questions were referred for handling to a government legal office which has its files set up according to these file designations. The file designation consists of a number of characters and punctuation marks as described below.

The first character refers to agencies whose legal work is handled by this office. These agencies are numbered consecutively in the order in which they first submit a matter for attention, and are identified in an alphabetical card index. To date numbers have been assigned to agencies as follows:

Department of Correction	1
Police Department	2
Department of Traffic	3
Department of Consumer Affairs	4
Commission on Human Rights	5
Board of Elections	6
Department of Personnel	7
Board of Estimate	8

The second character is separated from the first character by a dash. The second character is the last digit of the year in which a particular lawsuit or matter is referred to the legal office.

The third character is separated from the second character by a colon and may consist of either of the following:

I.   *A sub-number assigned to each lawsuit to which the agency is a party. Lawsuits are numbered consecutively regardless of year. (Lawsuits are brought by or against agency heads rather than agencies themselves, but references are made to agencies for the purpose of simplification.)*

or II.   *A capital letter assigned to each matter other than a lawsuit according to subject, the subject being identified in an alphabetical index. To date, letters have been assigned to subjects as follows:*

Citizenship	A	Housing	E
Discrimination	B	Gambling	F
Residence Requirements	C	Freedom of Religion	G
Civil Service Examinations	D		

These referrals are numbered consecutively regardless of year. The first referral by a particular agency on citizenship, for example, would be designated A1, followed by A2, A3, etc.

If no reference is made in a question as to how many letters involving a certain subject or how much lawsuits have been referred by an agency, assume that it is the first.

For each question, choose the file designation which is MOST appropriate for filing the material described in the question.

1. In January, 2000, two candidates in a 1999 civil service examination for positions with the Department of Correction filed a suit against the Department of Personnel seeking to set aside an educational requirement for the title.
   The Department of Personnel immediately referred the law-suit to the legal office for handling.

   A. 1-9:1   B. 1-0:D1   C. 7-9:D1   D. 7-0:1

2. In 2004, the Police Department made its sixth request for an opinion on whether an employee assignment proposed for 2005 could be considered discriminatory.

   A. 2-5:1-B6   B. 2-4:6   C. 2-4:1-B6   D. 2-4:B6

3. In 2005, a lawsuit was brought by the Bay Island Action Committee against the Board of Estimate in which the plaintiff sought withdrawal of approval of housing for the elderly in the Bay Island area given by the Board in 2005.

   A. 8-3:1   B. 8-5:1   C. 8-3:B1   D. 8-5:E1

4. In December 2004, community leaders asked the Police Department to ban outdoor meetings of a religious group on the grounds that the meetings were disrupting the area. Such meetings had been held from time to time during 2004. On January 31, 2005, the Police Department asked the government legal office for an opinion on whether granting this request would violate the worshippers' right to freedom of religion.

   A. 2-4:G-1   B. 2-5:G1   C. 2-5:B-1   D. 2-4:B1

5. In 2004, a woman filed suit against the Board of Elections. She alleged that she had not been permitted to vote at her usual polling place in the 2003 election and had been told she was not registered there. She claimed that she had always voted there and that her record card had been lost. This was the fourth case of its type for this agency.

   A. 6-4:4   B. 6-3:C4   C. 3-4:6   D. 6-3:4

6. A lawsuit was brought in 2001 by the Ace Pinball Machine Company against the Commissioner of Consumer Affairs. The lawsuit contested an ordinance which banned the use of pinball machines on the ground that they are gambling devices.
   This was the third lawsuit to which the Department of Consumer Affairs was a party.

   A. 4-1:1   B. 4-3:F1   C. 4-1:3   D. 3F-4:1

7. You are instructed by your supervisor to type a statement that must be signed by the per-   7.____
son making the statement and by three witnesses to the signature. The typed statement
will take two pages and will leave no room for signatures if the normal margin is maintained at the bottom of the second page.
In this situation, the PREFERRED method is to type

    A.   the signature lines below the normal margin on the second page
    B.   nothing further and have the witnesses sign without a typed signature line
    C.   the signature lines on a third page
    D.   some of the text and the signature lines on a third page

8. Certain legal documents always begin with a statement of venue - that is, the county and   8.____
state in which the document is executed. This is usually boxed with a parentheses or
colons.
The one of the following documents that ALWAYS bears a statement of venue in a
prominent position at its head is a(n)

    A.   affidavit   B.   memorandum of law
    C.   contract of sale   D.   will

9. You are requested to take stenographic notes and to transcribe the statements of a per-   9.____
son under oath. The person has a heavy accent and speaks in ungrammatical and broken English.
When you are transcribing the testimony, of the following, the BEST thing for you to do
is to

    A.   transcribe the testimony exactly as spoken, making no grammatical changes
    B.   make only the grammatical changes which would clarify the client's statements
    C.   make all grammatical changes so that the testimony is in standard English form
    D.   ask the client's permission before making any grammatical changes

10. When the material typed on a printed form does not fill the space provided, a Z-ruling is   10.____
frequently drawn to fill up the unused space.
The MAIN purpose of this practice is to

    A.   make the document more pleasing to the eye
    B.   indicate that the preceding material is correct
    C.   insure that the document is not altered
    D.   show that the lawyer has read it

11. After you had typed an original and five copies of a certain document, some changes   11.____
were made in ink on the original and were initialed by all the parties. The original was
signed by all the parties, and the signatures were notarized.
Which of the following should *generally* be typed on the copies BEFORE filing the original and the copies? The inked changes

    A.   but not the signatures, initials, or notarial data
    B.   the signatures and the initials but not the notarial data
    C.   and the notarial data but not the signatures or initials
    D.   the signatures, the initials, and the notarial data

12. The first paragraph of a noncourt agreement *generally* contains all of the following EXCEPT the

    A. specific terms of the agreement
    B. date of the agreement
    C. purpose of the agreement
    D. names of the parties involved

12.____

13. When typing an answer in a court proceeding, the place where the word ANSWER should be typed on the first page of the document is

    A. at the upper left-hand corner
    B. below the index number and to the right of the box containing the names of the parties to the action
    C. above the index number and to the right of the box containing the names of the parties to the action
    D. to the left of the names of the attorneys for the defendant

13.____

14. Which one of the following statements BEST describes the legal document called an acknowledgment?
It is

    A. an answer to an affidavit
    B. a receipt issued by the court when a document is filed
    C. proof of service of a summons
    D. a declaration that a signature is valid

14.____

15. Suppose you typed the original and three carbon copies of a legal document which was dictated by an attorney in your office. He has already signed the original copy, and corrections have been made on all copies.
Regarding the carbon copies, which one of the following procedures is the PROPER one to follow?

    A. Leave the signature line blank on the carbon copies
    B. Ask the attorney to sign the carbon copies
    C. Print or type the attorney's name on the signature line on the carbon copies
    D. Sign your name to the carbon copies followed by the attorney's initials

15.____

16. Suppose your office is defending a particular person in a court action. This person comes to the office and asks to see some of the lawyer's working papers in his file. The lawyer assigned to the case is out of the office at the time.
You SHOULD

    A. permit him to examine his entire file as long as he does not remove any materials from it
    B. make an appointment for the caller to come back later when the lawyer will be there
    C. ask him what working papers he wants to see and show him only those papers
    D. tell him that he needs written permission from the lawyer in order to see any records

16.____

17. Suppose that you receive a phone call from an official who is annoyed about a letter from   17._____
your office which she just received. The lawyer who dictated the letter is not in the office
at the moment.
Of the following, the BEST action for you to take is to

    A. explain that the lawyer is out but that you will ask the lawyer to return her call when
he returns
    B. take down all of the details of her complaint and tell her that you will get back to her
with an explanation
    C. refer to the proper file so that you can give her an explanation of the reasons for the
letter over the phone
    D. make an appointment for her to stop by the office to speak with the lawyer

18. Suppose that you have taken dictation for an interoffice memorandum. You are asked to   18._____
prepare it for distribution to four lawyers in your department whose names are given to
you. You will type an original and four carbon copies. Which one of the following is COR-
RECT with regard to the typing of the lawyers' names?
The names of all of the lawyers should appear

    A. *only* on the original
    B. on the original and each copy should have the name of one lawyer
    C. on each of the copies but not on the original
    D. on the original and on all of the copies

19. Regarding the correct typing of punctuation, the GENERALLY accepted practice is that   19._____
there should be

    A. two spaces after a semi-colon
    B. one space before an apostrophe used in the body of a word
    C. no space between parentheses and the matter enclosed
    D. one space before and after a hyphen

20. Suppose you have just completed typing an original and two copies of a letter   20._____
requesting information. The original is to be signed by a lawyer in your office. The first
copy is for the files, and the second is to be used as a reminder to follow up.
The PROPER time to file the file copy of the letter is

    A. after the letter has been signed and corrections have been made on the copies
    B. before you take the letter to the lawyer for his signature
    C. after a follow-up letter has been sent
    D. after a response to the letter has been received

21. A secretary in a legal office has just typed a letter. She has typed the copy distribution   21._____
notation on the copies to indicate *blind copy distribution*. This *blind copy* notation shows
that

    A. copies of the letter are being sent to persons that the addressee does not know
    B. copies of the letter are being sent to other persons without the addressee's knowledge
    C. a copy of the letter will be enlarged for a legally blind person
    D. a copy of the letter is being given as an extra copy to the addressee

22. Suppose that one of the attorneys in your office dictates material to you without indicat-   22.___
ing punctuation. He has asked that you give him, as soon as possible, a single copy of a
rough draft to be triple-spaced so that he can make corrections.
Of the following, what is the BEST thing for you to do in this situation?

    A. Assume that no punctuation is desired in the material
    B. Insert the punctuation as you type the rough draft
    C. Transcribe the material exactly as dictated, but attach a note to the attorney stating
       your suggested changes
    D. Before you start to type the draft, tell the attorney you want to read back your notes
       so that he can indicate punctuation

23. When it is necessary to type a mailing notation such as CERTIFIED, REGISTERED, or   23.___
FEDEX on an envelope, the GENERALLY accepted place to type it is

    A. directly above the address
    B. in the area below where the stamp will be affixed
    C. in the lower left-hand corner
    D. in the upper left-hand corner

24. When taking a citation of a case in shorthand, which of the following should you write   24.___
FIRST if you are having difficulty keeping up with the dictation?

    A. Volume and page number   B. Title of volume
    C. Name of plaintiff   D. Name of defendant

25. All of the following abbreviations and their meanings are correctly paired EXCEPT   25.___

    A. viz. - namely   B. ibid. - refer
    C. n.b. - note well   D. q.v. - which see

KEY (CORRECT ANSWERS)

1.	D		11.	D
2.	D		12.	A
3.	B		13.	B
4.	B		14.	D
5.	A		15.	C
6.	C		16.	B
7.	D		17.	A
8.	A		18.	D
9.	A		19.	C
10.	C		20.	A

21.	B
22.	B
23.	B
24.	A
25.	B

EXAMINATION SECTION
TEST 1

DIRECTIONS: Each question or incomplete statement is followed by several suggested answers or completions. Select the one that BEST answers the question or completes the statement. *PRINT THE LETTER OF THE CORRECT ANSWER IN THE SPACE AT THE RIGHT.*

Questions 1-9.

DIRECTIONS: Questions 1 through 9 consist of sentences which may or may not be examples of good English usage. Consider grammar, punctuation, spelling, capitalization, awkwardness, etc. Examine each sentence, and then choose the correct statement about it from the four choices below it. If the English usage in the sentence given is better than it would be with any of the changes suggested in options B, C, and D, choose option A. Do not choose an option that will change the meaning of the sentence.

1. According to Judge Frank, the grocer's sons found guilty of assault and sentenced last Thursday. 1.____

    A. This is an example of acceptable writing.
    B. A comma should be placed after the word *sentenced.*
    C. The word *were* should be placed after *sons*
    D. The apostrophe in *grocer's* should be placed after the *s.*

2. The department heads assistant said that the stenographers should type duplicate copies of all contracts, leases, and bills. 2.____

    A. This is an example of acceptable writing.
    B. A comma should be placed before the word *contracts.*
    C. An apostrophe should be placed before the *s* in *heads.*
    D. Quotation marks should be placed before *the stenographers* and after *bills.*

3. The lawyers questioned the men to determine who was the true property owner? 3.____

    A. This is an example of acceptable writing.
    B. The phrase *questioned the men* should be changed to *asked the men questions.*
    C. The word *was* should be changed to *were.*
    D. The question mark should be changed to a period.

4. The terms stated in the present contract are more specific than those stated in the previous contract. 4.____

    A. This is an example of acceptable writing.
    B. The word *are* should be changed to *is.*
    C. The word *than* should be changed to *then.*
    D. The word *specific* should be changed to *specified.*

5. Of the lawyers considered, the one who argued more skillful was chosen for the job. 5.____

    A. This is an example of acceptable writing.
    B. The word *more* should be replaced by the word *most.*
    C. The word *skillful* should be replaced by the word *skillfully,*
    D. The word *chosen* should be replaced by the word *selected.*

6. Each of the states has a court of appeals; some states have circuit courts.　　6.___

    A. This is an example of acceptable writing.
    B. The semi-colon should be changed to a comma.
    C. The word *has* should be changed to *have*.
    D. The word *some* should be capitalized.

7. The court trial has greatly effected the child's mental condition.　　7.___

    A. This is an example of acceptable writing.
    B. The word *effected* should be changed to *affected*.
    C. The word *greatly* should be placed after *effected*.
    D. The apostrophe in *child's* should be placed after the *s*.

8. Last week, the petition signed by all the officers was sent to the Better Business Bureau.　　8.___

    A. This is an example of acceptable writing.
    B. The phrase *last week* should be placed after *officers*.
    C. A comma should be placed after *petition*.
    D. The word *was* should be changed to *were*.

9. Mr. Farrell claims that he requested form A-12, and three booklets describing court procedures.　　9.___

    A. This is an example of acceptable writing.
    B. The word *that* should be eliminated.
    C. A colon should be placed after *requested*.
    D. The comma after *A-12* should be eliminated.

Questions 10-21.

DIRECTIONS:　Questions 10 through 21 contain a word in capital letters followed by four suggested meanings of the word. For each question, choose the BEST meaning for the word in capital letters.

10. SIGNATORY - A　　10.___

    A. lawyer who draws up a legal document
    B. document that must be signed by a judge
    C. person who signs a document
    D. true copy of a signature

11. RETAINER - A　　11.___

    A. fee paid to a lawyer for his services
    B. document held by a third party
    C. court decision to send a prisoner back to custody pending trial
    D. legal requirement to keep certain types of files

12. BEQUEATH - To　　12.___

    A. receive assistance from a charitable organization
    B. give personal property by will to another
    C. transfer real property from one person to another
    D. receive an inheritance upon the death of a relative

13. RATIFY - To   13._____

    A. approve and sanction   B. forego
    C. produce evidence   D. summarize

14. CODICIL - A   14._____

    A. document introduced in evidence in a civil action
    B. subsection of a law
    C. type of legal action that can be brought by a plaintiff
    D. supplement or an addition to a will

15. ALIAS   15._____

    A. Assumed name   B. In favor of
    C. Against   D. A writ

16. PROXY - A(n)   16._____

    A. phony document in a real estate transaction
    B. opinion by a judge of a civil court
    C. document containing appointment of an agent
    D. summons in a lawsuit

17. ALLEGED   17._____

    A. Innocent   B. Asserted
    C. Guilty   D. Called upon

18. EXECUTE - To   18._____

    A. complete a legal document by signing it
    B. set requirements
    C. render services to a duly elected executive of a municipality
    D. initiate legal action such as a lawsuit

19. NOTARY PUBLIC - A   19._____

    A. lawyer who is running for public office
    B. judge who hears minor cases
    C. public officer, one of whose functions is to administer oaths
    D. lawyer who gives free legal services to persons unable to pay

20. WAIVE - To   20._____

    A. disturb a calm state of affairs
    B. knowingly renounce a right or claim
    C. pardon someone for a minor fault
    D. purposely mislead a person during an investigation

21. ARRAIGN - To   21._____

    A. prevent an escape   B. defend a prisoner
    C. verify a document   D. accuse in a court of law

Questions 22-40.

DIRECTIONS: Questions 22 through 40 each consist of four words which may or may not be
spelled correctly. If you find an error in
only one word, mark your answer A;
any two words, mark your answer B;
any three words, mark your answer C;
none of these words, mark your answer D.

22.	occurrence	Febuary	privilege	similiar	22.__
23.	separate	transferring	analyze	column	23.__
24.	develop	license	bankrupcy	abreviate	24.__
25.	subpoena	arguement	dissolution	foreclosure	25.__
26.	exaggerate	fundamental	significance	warrant	26.__
27.	citizen	endorsed	marraige	appraissal	27.__
28.	precedant	univercity	observence	preliminary	28.__
29.	stipulate	negligence	judgment	prominent	29.
30.	judisial	whereas	release	guardian	30.
31.	appeal	larcenny	transcrip	jurist	31.__
32.	petition	tenancy	agenda	insurance	32.__
33.	superfical	premise	morgaged	maintainance	33.__
34.	testamony	publically	installment	possessed	34.__
35.	escrow	decree	eviction	miscelaneous	35.__
36.	securitys	abeyance	adhere	corporate	36.__
37.	kaleidoscope	anesthesia	vermilion	tafetta	37.__
38.	congruant	barrenness	plebescite	vigilance	38.__
39.	picnicing	promisory	resevoir	omission	39.__
40.	supersede	banister	wholly	seize	40.__

KEY (CORRECT ANSWERS)

1.	C	11.	A	21.	D	31.	B
2.	C	12.	B	22.	B	32.	D
3.	D	13.	A	23.	D	33.	C
4.	A	14.	D	24.	B	34.	B
5.	C	15.	A	25.	A	35.	A
6.	A	16.	C	26.	D	36.	A
7.	B	17.	B	27.	B	37.	A
8.	A	18.	A	28.	C	38.	B
9.	D	19.	C	29.	D	39.	C
10.	C	20.	B	30.	A	40.	D

EXAMINATION SECTION
TEST 1

DIRECTIONS: Each question or incomplete statement is followed by several suggested answers or completions. Select the one that BEST answers the question or completes the statement. *PRINT THE LETTER OF THE CORRECT ANSWER IN THE SPACE AT THE RIGHT.*

Questions 1-25.

DIRECTIONS: In each of Questions 1 through 25, select the lettered word or phrase which means MOST NEARLY the same as the capitalized word.

1. INTERROGATE   1.____
   A. question   B. arrest   C. search   D. rebuff

2. PERVERSE   2.____
   A. manageable   B. poetic
   C. contrary   D. patient

3. ADVOCATE   3.____
   A. champion   B. employ
   C. select   D. advise

4. APPARENT   4.____
   A. desirable   B. clear
   C. partial   D. possible

5. INSINUATE   5.____
   A. survey   B. strengthen
   C. suggest   D. insist

6. MOMENTOUS   6.____
   A. important   B. immediate   C. delayed   D. short

7. AUXILIARY   7.____
   A. exciting   B. assisting   C. upsetting   D. available

8. ADMONISH   8.____
   A. praise   B. increase   C. warn   D. polish

9. ANTICIPATE   9.____
   A. agree   B. expect   C. conceal   D. approve

10. APPREHEND   10.____
    A. confuse   B. sentence   C. release   D. seize

11. CLEMENCY   11.____
    A. silence   B. freedom   C. mercy   D. severity

12. THWART   12.____
    A. enrage   B. strike   C. choke   D. block

13. RELINQUISH   13.___

    A. stretch   B. give up   C. weaken   D. flee from

14. CURTAIL   14.___

    A. stop   B. reduce   C. repair   D. insult

15. INACCESSIBLE   15.___

    A. obstinate   B. unreachable

    C. unreasonable   D. puzzling

16. PERTINENT   16.___

    A. related   B. saucy   C. durable   D. impatient

17. INTIMIDATE   17.___

    A. encourage   B. hunt   C. beat   D. frighten

18. INTEGRITY   18.___

    A. honesty   B. wisdom

    C. understanding   D. persistence

19. UTILIZE   19.___

    A. use   B. manufacture

    C. help   D. include

20. SUPPLEMENT   20.___

    A. regulate   B. demand   C. add   D. answer

21. INDISPENSABLE   21.___

    A. essential   B. neglected

    C. truthful   D. unnecessary

22. ATTAIN   22.___

    A. introduce   B. spoil   C. achieve   D. study

23. PRECEDE   23.___

    A. break away   B. go ahead

    C. begin   D. come before

24. HAZARD   24.___

    A. penalty   B. adventure   C. handicap   D. danger

25. DETRIMENTAL   25.___

    A. uncertain   B. harmful   C. fierce   D. horrible

KEY (CORRECT ANSWERS)

1. A	6. A	11. C	16. A	21. A
2. C	7. B	12. D	17. D	22. C
3. A	8. C	13. B	18. A	23. D
4. B	9. B	14. B	19. A	24. D
5. C	10. D	15. B	20. C	25. B

TEST 2

DIRECTIONS: Each question or incomplete statement is followed by several suggested answers or completions. Select the one that BEST answers the question or completes the statement. *PRINT THE LETTER OF THE CORRECT ANSWER IN THE SPACE AT THE RIGHT.*

Questions 1-20.

DIRECTIONS: In each of Questions 1 through 20, select the lettered word or phrase which means MOST NEARLY the same as the capitalized word.

1. IMPLY   1.____
   A. agree to   B. hint at   C. laugh at
   D. mimic   E. reduce

2. APPRAISAL   2.____
   A. allowance   B. composition   C. prohibition
   D. quantity   E. valuation

3. DISBURSE   3.____
   A. approve   B. expend   C. prevent
   D. relay   E. restrict

4. POSTERITY   4.____
   A. back payment   B. current procedure   C. final effort
   D. future generations E. rare specimen

5. PUNCTUAL   5.____
   A. clear   B. honest   C. polite
   D. prompt   E. prudent

6. PRECARIOUS   6.____
   A. abundant   B. alarmed   C. cautious
   D. insecure   E. placid

7. FOSTER   7.____
   A. delegate   B. demote   C. encourage
   D. plead   E. surround

8. PINNACLE   8.____
   A. center   B. crisis   C. outcome
   D. peak   E. personification

9. COMPONENT   9.____
   A. flattery   B. opposite   C. part
   D. revision   E. trend

10. SOLICIT   10.____
    A. ask   B. prohibit   C. promise
    D. revoke   E. surprise

11. LIAISON   11.___
    A. asset   B. coordination   C. difference
    D. policy   E. procedure

12. ALLEGE   12.___
    A. assert   B. break   C. irritate
    D. reduce   E. wait

13. INFILTRATION   13.___
    A. consumption   B. disposal   C. enforcement
    D. penetration   E. seizure

14. SALVAGE   14.___
    A. announce   B. combine   C. prolong
    D. save   E. try

15. MOTIVE   15.___
    A. attack   B. favor   C. incentive
    D. patience   E. tribute

16. PROVOKE   16.___
    A. adjust   B. incite   C. leave
    D. obtain   E. practice

17. SURGE   17.___
    A. branch   B. contract   C. revenge
    D. rush   E. want

18. MAGNIFY   18.___
    A. attract   B. demand   C. generate
    D. increase   E. puzzle

19. PREPONDERANCE   19.___
    A. decision   B. judgment   C. outweighing
    D. submission   E. warning

20. ABATE   20.___
    A. assist   B. coerce   C. diminish
    D. indulge   E. trade

Questions 21-30.

DIRECTIONS: In each of Questions 21 through 30, select the lettered word or phrase which
              means MOST NEARLY, the same as, or the opposite of, the capitalized word.

21. VINDICTIVE   21.___
    A. centrifugal   B. forgiving   C. molten
    D. tedious   E. vivacious

22. SCOPE   22.___
    A. compact   B. detriment   C. facsimile
    D. potable   E. range

23. HINDER   23.___
    A. amplify   B. aver   C. method
    D. observe   E. retard

24. IRATE   24.___
    A. adhere   B. angry   C. authentic
    D. peremptory   E. vacillate

25. APATHY   25.___
    A. accessory   B. availability   C. fervor
    D. pacify   E. stride

26. LUCRATIVE   26.___
    A. effective   B. imperfect   C. injurious
    D. timely   E. worthless

27. DIVERSITY   27.___
    A. convection   B. slip   C. temerity
    D. uniformity   E. viscosity

28. OVERT   28.___
    A. laugh   B. lighter   C. orifice
    D. quay   E. sly

29. SPORADIC   29.___
    A. divide   B. incumbrance   C. livid
    D. occasional   E. original

30. PREVARICATE   30.___
    A. hesitate   B. increase   C. lie
    D. procrastinate   E. reject

_____

KEY (CORRECT ANSWERS)

1.	B	11.	B	21.	B
2.	E	12.	A	22.	E
3.	B	13.	D	23.	E
4.	D	14.	D	24.	B
5.	D	15.	C	25.	C
6.	D	16.	B	26.	E
7.	C	17.	D	27.	D
8.	D	18.	D	28.	E
9.	C	19.	C	29.	D
10.	A	20.	C	30.	C

_____

TEST 3

DIRECTIONS: Each question or incomplete statement is followed by several suggested answers or completions. Select the one that BEST answers the question or completes the statement. *PRINT THE LETTER OF THE CORRECT ANSWER IN THE SPACE AT THE RIGHT.*

Questions 1-30.

DIRECTIONS: In each of Questions 1 through 30, select the lettered word which means MOST NEARLY the same as the capitalized word.

1. AVARICE   1.___
   A. flight   B. greed   C. pride   D. thrift

2. PREDATORY   2.___
   A. offensive   B. plundering
   C. previous   D. timeless

3. VINDICATE   3.___
   A. clear   B. conquer   C. correct   D. illustrate

4. INVETERATE   4.___
   A. backward   B. erect   C. habitual   D. lucky

5. DISCERN   5.___
   A. describe   B. fabricate   C. recognize   D. seek

6. COMPLACENT   6.___
   A. indulgent   B. listless   C. overjoyed   D. satisfied

7. ILLICIT   7.___
   A. insecure   B. unclear   C. unlawful   D. unlimited

8. PROCRASTINATE   8.___
   A. declare   B. multiply   C. postpone   D. steal

9. IMPASSIVE   9.___
   A. calm   B. frustrated
   C. thoughtful   D. unhappy

10. AMICABLE   10.___
    A. cheerful   B. flexible
    C. friendly   D. poised

11. FEASIBLE   11.___
    A. breakable   B. easy
    C. likeable   D. practicable

12. INNOCUOUS   12.___
    A. harmless   B. insecure
    C. insincere   D. unfavorable

13. OSTENSIBLE   13.___
 A. apparent B. hesitant C. reluctant D. showy

14. INDOMITABLE   14.___
 A. excessive   B. unconquerable
 C. unreasonable   D. unthinkable

15. CRAVEN   15.___
 A. cowardly B. hidden C. miserly D. needed

16. ALLAY   16.___
 A. discuss B. quiet C. refine D. remove

17. ALLUDE   17.___
 A. denounce B. refer C. state D. support

18. NEGLIGENCE   18.___
 A. carelessness   B. denial
 C. objection   D. refusal

19. AMEND   19.___
 A. correct B. destroy C. end D. list

20. RELEVANT   20.___
 A. conclusive   B. careful
 C. obvious   D. related

21. VERIFY   21.___
 A. challenge B. change C. confirm D. reveal

22. INSIGNIFICANT   22.___
 A. incorrect   B. limited
 C. unimportant   D. undesirable

23. RESCIND   23.___
 A. annul B. deride C. extol D. indulge

24. AUGMENT   24.___
 A. alter B. increase C. obey D. perceive

25. AUTONOMOUS   25.___
 A. conceptual   B. constant
 C. defamatory   D. independent

26. TRANSCRIPT   26.___
 A. copy B. report C. sentence D. termination

27. DISCORDANT   27.___
 A. quarrelsome   B. comprised
 C. effusive   D. harmonious

28. DISTEND   28.___
 A. constrict B. dilate C. redeem D. silence

29. EMANATE

    A. bridge   B. coherency   C. conquer   D. flow

29.___

30. EXULTANT

    A. easily upset   B. in high spirits
    C. subject to moods   D. very much over-priced

30.___

KEY (CORRECT ANSWERS)

1.	B	11.	D	21.	C
2.	B	12.	A	22.	C
3.	A	13.	A	23.	A
4.	C	14.	B	24.	B
5.	C	15.	A	25.	D
6.	D	16.	B	26.	A
7.	C	17.	B	27.	A
8.	C	18.	A	28.	B
9.	A	19.	A	29.	D
10.	C	20.	D	30.	B

RECORD KEEPING
EXAMINATION SECTION
TEST 1

DIRECTIONS: Each question or incomplete statement is followed by several suggested answers or completions. Select the one that BEST answers the question or completes the statement. *PRINT THE LETTER OF THE CORRECT ANSWER IN THE SPACE AT THE RIGHT.*

Questions 1-15.

DIRECTIONS: Questions 1 through 15 are to be answered on the basis of the following list of company names below. Arrange a file alphabetically, word-by-word, disregarding punctuation, conjunctions, and apostrophes. Then answer the questions.
A Bee C Reading Materials
ABCO Parts
A Better Course for Test Preparation
AAA Auto Parts Co.
A-Z Auto Parts, Inc.
Aabar Books
Abbey, Joanne
Boman-Sylvan Law Firm
BMW Autowerks
C Q Service Company
Chappell-Murray, Inc.
E&E Life Insurance
Emcrisco
Gigi Arts
Gordon, Jon & Associates
SOS Plumbing
Schmidt, J.B. Co.

1.   Which of these files should appear FIRST?   1._____

    A.   ABCO Parts
    B.   A Bee C Reading Materials
    C.   A Better Course for Test Preparation
    D.   AAA Auto Parts Co.

2.   Which of these files should appear SECOND?   2._____

    A.   A-Z Auto Parts, Inc.
    B.   A Bee C Reading Materials
    C.   A Better Course for Test Preparation
    D.   AAA Auto Parts Co.

3.   Which of these files should appear THIRD?   3._____

    A.   ABCO Parts
    B.   A Bee C Reading Materials
    C.   Aabar Books
    D.   AAA Auto Parts Co.

4. Which of these files should appear FOURTH?   4.___

    A. ABCO Parts
    B. A Bee C Reading Materials
    C. Abbey, Joanne
    D. AAA Auto Parts Co.

5. Which of these files should appear LAST?   5.___

    A. Gordon, Jon & Associates
    B. Gigi Arts
    C. Schmidt, J.B. Co.
    D. SOS Plumbing

6. Which of these files should appear between A-Z Auto Parts, Inc. and Abbey, Joanne?   6.___

    A. A Bee C Reading Materials
    B. AAA Auto Parts Co.
    C. Aabar Books
    D. A Better Course for Test Preparation

7. Which of these files should appear between ABCO Parts and Aabar Books?   7.___

    A. A Bee C Reading Materials
    B. Abbey, Joanne
    C. Aabar Books
    D. A-Z Auto Parts

8. Which of these files should appear between Abbey, Joanne and Boman-Sylvan Law   8.___
    Firm?

    A. A Better Course for Test Preparation
    B. BMW Autowerks
    C. A-Z Auto Parts,Inc.
    D. Aabar Books

9. Which of these files should appear between Abbey, Joanne and C Q Service?   9.___

    A. A-Z Auto Parts,Inc.   B. BMW Autowerks
    C. Choices A and B   D. Chappell-Murray, Inc.

10. Which of these files should appear between C Q Service Company and Emcrisco?   10.___

    A. Chappell-Murray,Inc.   B. E&E Life Insurance
    C. C. Gigi Arts   D. Choices A and B

11. Which of these files should NOT appear between C Q Service Company and E&E Life   11.___
    Insurance?

    A. Gordon, Jon & Associates
    B. Emcrisco
    C. Gigi Arts
    D. All of the above

12. Which of these files should appear between Chappell-Murray Inc., and Gigi Arts?　　12.____

    A.　CQ Service Inc. E&E Life Insurance, and Emcrisco
    B.　Emcrisco, E&E Life Insurance, and Gordon, Jon & Associates
    C.　E&E Life Insurance and Emcrisco
    D.　Emcrisco and Gordon, Jon & Associates

13. Which of these files should appear between Gordon, Jon & Associates and SOS Plumb-　13.____
ing?

    A.　Gigi Arts
    B.　Schmidt, J.B. Co.
    C.　Choices A and B
    D.　None of the above

14. Ea ch of the choices lists the four files in their proper alphabetical order except　　14.____

    A.　E&E Life Insurance; Gigi Arts; Gordon, Jon & Associates; SOS Plumbing
    B.　E&E Life Insurance; Emcrisco; Gigi Arts; SOS Plumbing
    C.　Emcrisco; Gordon, Jon & Associates; Schmidt, J.B. Co.; SOS Plumbing
    D.　Emcrisco; Gigi Arts; Gordon, Jon & Associates; SOS Plumbing

15. Which of the choices lists the four files in their proper alphabetical order?　　15.____

    A.　Gigi Arts; Gordon, Jon & Associates; SOS Plumbing; Schmidt, J.B. Co.
    B.　Gordon, Jon & Associates; Gigi Arts; Schmidt, J.B. Co.; SOS Plumbing
    C.　Gordon, Jon & Associates; Gigi Arts; SOS Plumbing; Schmidt, J.B. Co.
    D.　Gigi Arts; Gordon, Jon & Associates; Schmidt, J.B. Co.; SOS Plumbing

16. The alphabetical filing order of two businesses with identical names is determined by the　16.____

    A.　length of time each business has been operating
    B.　addresses of the businesses
    C.　last name of the company president
    D.　none of the above

17. In an alphabetical filing system, if a business name includes a number, it should be　　17.____

    A.　disregarded
    B.　considered a number and placed at the end of an alphabetical section
    C.　treated as though it were written in words and alphabetized accordingly
    D.　considered a number and placed at the beginning of an alphabetical section

18. If a business name includes a contraction (such as *don't* or *it's*), how should that word be　18.____
treated in an alphabetical filing system?

    A.　Divide the word into its separate parts and treat it as two words.
    B.　Ignore the letters that come after the apostrophe.
    C.　Ignore the word that contains the contraction.
    D.　Ignore the apostrophe and consider all letters in the contraction.

19. In what order should the parts of an address be considered when using an alphabetical　19.____
filing system?

    A.　City or town; state; street name; house or building number
    B.　State; city or town; street name; house or building number
    C.　House or building number; street name; city or town; state
    D.　Street name; city or town; state

20. A business record should be cross-referenced when a(n)   20._

    A. organization is known by an abbreviated name
    B. business has a name change because of a sale, incorporation, or other reason
    C. business is known by a *coined* or common name which differs from a dictionary spelling
    D. all of the above

21. A geographical filing system is MOST effective when   21._

    A. location is more important than name
    B. many names or titles sound alike
    C. dealing with companies who have offices all over the world
    D. filing personal and business files

Questions 22-25.

DIRECTIONS: Questions 22 through 25 are to be answered on the basis of the list of items below, which are to be filed geographically. Organize the items geographically and then answer the questions.
    1. University Press at Berkeley, U.S.
    2. Maria Sanchez, Mexico City, Mexico
    3. Great Expectations Ltd. in London, England
    4. Justice League, Cape Town, South Africa, Africa
    5. Crown Pearls Ltd. in London, England
    6. Joseph Prasad in London, England

22. Which of the following arrangements of the items is composed according to the policy of: 22._
    Continent, Country, City, Firm or Individual Name?

    A. 5, 3, 4, 6, 2, 1   B. 4, 5, 3, 6, 2, 1
    C. 1, 4, 5, 3, 6, 2   D. 4, 5, 3, 6, 1, 2

23. Which of the following files is arranged according to the policy of: *Continent, Country,*   23._
    City, Firm or Individual Name?

    A. South Africa. Africa. Cape Town. Justice League
    B. Mexico. Mexico City, Maria Sanchez
    C. North America. United States. Berkeley. University Press
    D. England. Europe. London. Prasad, Joseph

24. Which of the following arrangements of the items is composed according to the policy of: 24._
    Country, City, Firm or Individual Name?

    A. 5, 6, 3, 2, 4, 1   B. 1, 5, 6, 3, 2, 4
    C. 6, 5, 3, 2, 4, 1   D. 5, 3, 6, 2, 4, 1

25. Which of the following files is arranged according to a policy of: *Country, City, Firm or*   25._
    Individual Name?

    A. England. London. Crown Pearls Ltd.
    B. North America. United States. Berkeley. University Press
    C. Africa. Cape Town. Justice League
    D. Mexico City. Mexico. Maria Sanchez

26. Under which of the following circumstances would a phonetic filing system be MOST effective?

    26._____

    A. When the person in charge of filing can't spell very well
    B. With large files with names that sound alike
    C. With large files with names that are spelled alike
    D. All of the above

Questions 27-29.

DIRECTIONS: Questions 27 through 29 are to be answered on the basis of the following list of numerical files.

    1. 391-023-100
    2. 361-132-170
    3. 385-732-200
    4. 381-432-150
    5. 391-632-387
    6. 361-423-303
    7. 391-123-271

27. Which of the following arrangements of the files follows a consecutive-digit system?

    27._____

    A. 2, 3, 4, 1   B. 1, 5, 7, 3
    C. 2, 4, 3, 1   D. 3, 1, 5, 7

28. Which of the following arrangements follows a terminal-digit system?

    28._____

    A. 1, 7, 2, 4, 3   B. 2, 1, 4, 5, 7
    C. 7, 6, 5, 4, 3   D. 1, 4, 2, 3, 7

29. Which of the following lists follows a middle-digit system?

    29._____

    A. 1, 7, 2, 6, 4, 5, 3   B. 1, 2, 7, 4, 6, 5, 3
    C. 7, 2, 1, 3, 5, 6, 4   D. 7, 1, 2, 4, 6, 5, 3

Questions 30-31.

DIRECTIONS: Questions 30 and 31 are to be answered on the basis of the following information.

    1. Reconfirm Laura Bates appointment with James Caldecort on December 12 at 9:30 A.M.
    2. Laurence Kinder contact Julia Lucas on August 3 and set up a meeting for week of September 23 at 4 P.M.
    3. John Lutz contact Larry Waverly on August 3 and set up appointment for September 23 at 9:30 A.M.
    4. Call for tickets for Gerry Stanton August 21 for New Jersey on September 23, flight 143 at 4:43 P.M.

30. A chronological file for the above information would be 30.____

    A. 4, 3, 2, 1   B. 3, 2, 4, 1
    C. 4, 2, 3, 1   D. 3, 1, 2, 4

31. Using the above information, a chronological file for the date of September 23 would be   31.____

    A. 2, 3, 4   B. 3, 1, 4   C. 3, 2, 4   D. 4, 3, 2

Questions 32-34.

DIRECTIONS: Questions 32 through 34 are to be answered on the basis of the following information.
1. Call Roger Epstein, Ashoke Naipaul, Jon Anderson, and Sarah Washington on April 19 at 1:00 P.M. to set up meeting with Alika D'Ornay for June 6 in New York.
2. Call Martin Ames before noon on April 19 to confirm afternoon meeting with Bob Greenwood on April 20th
3. Set up meeting room at noon for 2:30 P.M. meeting on April 19th;
4. Ashley Stanton contact Bob Greenwood at 9:00 A.M. on April 20 and set up meeting for June 6 at 8:30 A.M.
5. Carol Guiland contact Shelby Van Ness during afternoon of April 20 and set up meeting for June 6 at 10:00 A.M.
6. Call airline and reserve tickets on June 6 for Roger Epstein trip *to* Denver on July 8
7. Meeting at 2:30 P.M. on April 19th

32. A chronological file for all of the above information would be 32.____

    A. 2, 1, 3, 7, 5, 4, 6   B. 3, 7, 2, 1, 4, 5, 6
    C. 3, 7, 1, 2, 5, 4, 6   D. 2, 3, 1, 7, 4, 5, 6

33. A chronological file for the date of April 19th would be 33.____

    A. 2, 3, 7, 1   B. 2, 3, 1, 7
    C. 7, 1, 3, 2   D. 3, 7, 1, 2

34. Add the following information to the file, and then create a chronological file for April 20th: 34.____
    8. April 20: 3:00 P.M. meeting between Bob Greenwood and Martin Ames.

    A. 4, 5, 8   B. 4, 8, 5   C. 8, 5, 4   D. 5, 4, 8

35. The PRIMARY advantage of computer records filing over a manual system is 35.____

    A. speed of retrieval   B. accuracy
    C. cost   D. potential file loss

KEY (CORRECT ANSWERS)

1.	B		16.	B
2.	C		17.	C
3.	D		18.	D
4.	A		19.	A
5.	C		20.	D
6.	C		21.	A
7.	D		22.	B
8.	B		23.	C
9.	B		24.	D
10.	D		25.	A
11.	D		26.	B
12.	C		27.	C
13.	D		28.	D
14.	C		29.	A
15.	A		30.	B

31.	C
32.	D
33.	B
34.	A
35.	A

―――――――

PREPARING WRITTEN MATERIAL

EXAMINATION SECTION
TEST 1

Questions 1-15.

DIRECTIONS: For each of Questions 1 through 15, select from the options given below the MOST applicable choice, and mark your answer accordingly.

A. The sentence is correct.
B. The sentence contains a spelling error *only*.
C. The sentence contains an English grammar error *only*.
D. The sentence contains both a spelling error and an English grammar error.

1. He is a very dependible person whom we expect will be an asset to this division.   1.____

2. An investigator often finds it necessary to be very diplomatic when conducting an interview.   2.____

3. Accurate detail is especially important if court action results from an investigation.   3.____

4. The report was signed by him and I since we conducted the investigation jointly.   4.____

5. Upon receipt of the complaint, an inquiry was begun.   5.____

6. An employee has to organize his time so that he can handle his workload efficiantly.   6.____

7. It was not apparant that anyone was living at the address given by the client.   7.____

8. According to regulations, there is to be at least three attempts made to locate the client.   8.____

9. Neither the inmate nor the correction officer was willing to sign a formal statement.   9.____

10. It is our opinion that one of the persons interviewed were lying.   10.____

11. We interviewed both clients and departmental personel in the course of this investigation.   11.____

12. It is concievable that further research might produce additional evidence.   12.____

13. It is concievable that further research might produce additional evidence.   13.____

14. We cannot accede to the candidate's request.   14.____

15. The submission of overdue reports is the reason that there was a delay in completion of this investigation.   15.____

Questions 16-25.

DIRECTIONS: Each of Questions 16 through 25 may be classified under one of the following four categories:

    A.   Faulty because of incorrect grammar or sentence structure
    B.   Faulty because of incorrect punctuation
    C.   Faulty because of incorrect spelling
    D.   Correct

Examine each sentence carefully to determine under which of the above four options it is best classified. Then, in the space at the right, write the letter preceding the option which is the BEST of the four suggested above. Each incorrect sentence contains but one type of error. Consider a sentence to be correct if it contains none of the types of errors mentioned, even though there may be other correct ways of expressing the same thought.

16.   Although the department's supply of scratch pads and stationary have diminished considerably, the allotment for our division has not been reduced.   16.___

17.   You have not told us whom you wish to designate as your secretary.   17.___

18.   Upon reading the minutes of the last meeting, the new proposal was taken up for consideration.   18.___

19.   Before beginning the discussion, we locked the door as a precautionery measure.   19._

20.   The supervisor remarked, "Only those clerks, who perform routine work, are permitted to take a rest period."   20.___

21.   Not only will this duplicating machine make accurate copies, but it will also produce a quantity of work equal to fifteen transcribing typists.   21.___

22.   "Mr. Jones," said the supervisor, "we regret our inability to grant you an extention of your leave of absence."   22.___

23.   Although the employees find the work monotonous and fatigueing, they rarely complain.   23.___

24.   We completed the tabulation of the receipts on time despite the fact that Miss Smith our fastest operator was absent for over a week.   24.___

25.   The reaction of the employees who attended the meeting, as well as the reaction of those who did not attend, indicates clearly that the schedule is satisfactory to everyone concerned.   25.___

KEY (CORRECT ANSWERS)

1.	D		11.	B
2.	A		12.	B
3.	A		13.	B
4.	C		14.	A
5.	A		15.	C
6.	B		16.	A
7.	B		17.	D
8.	C		18.	A
9.	A		19.	C
10.	C		20.	B

21.	A
22.	C
23.	C
24.	B
25.	D

———

TEST 2

Questions 1-15.

DIRECTIONS: Questions 1 through 15 consist of two sentences. Some are correct according to ordinary formal English usage. Others are incorrect because they contain errors in English usage, spelling, or punctuation. Consider a sentence correct if it contains no errors in English usage, spelling, or punctuation, even if there may be other ways of writing the sentence correctly. Mark your answer:

    A. If only sentence I is correct
    B. If only sentence II is correct
    C. If sentences I and II are correct
    D. If neither sentence I nor II is correct

1.   I. The influence of recruitment efficiency upon administrative standards is readily apparant.   1.____
    II. Rapid and accurate thinking are an essential quality of the police officer.

2.   I. The administrator of a police department is constantly confronted by the demands of subordinates for increased personnel in their respective units.   2.____
    II. Since a chief executive must work within well-defined fiscal limits, he must weigh the relative importance of various requests.

3.   I. The two men whom the police arrested for a parking violation were wanted for robbery in three states.   3.____
    II. Strong executive control from the top to the bottom of the enterprise is one of the basic principals of police administration.

4.   I. When he gave testimony unfavorable to the defendant loyalty seemed to mean very little.   4.____
    II. Having run off the road while passing a car, the patrolman gave the driver a traffic ticket.

5.   I. The judge ruled that the defendant's conversation with his doctor was a priviliged communication.   5.____
    II. The importance of our training program is widely recognized; however, fiscal difficulties limit the program's effectiveness.

6.   I. Despite an increase in patrol coverage, there were less arrests for crimes against property this year.   6.____
    II. The investigators could hardly have expected greater cooperation from the public.

7.   I. Neither the patrolman nor the witness could identify the defendant as the driver of the car.   7.____
    II. Each of the officers in the class received their certificates at the completion of the course.

8.
   I. The new commander made it clear that those kind of procedures would no longer be permitted.
   II. Giving some weight to performance records is more advisable then making promotions solely on the basis of test scores.
         8.____

9.
   I. A deputy sheriff must ascertain whether the debtor, has any property.
   II. A good deputy sheriff does not cause histerical excitement when he executes a process.
         9.____

10.
   I. Having learned that he has been assigned a judgment debtor, the deputy sheriff should call upon him.
   II. The deputy sheriff may seize and remove property without requiring a bond.
         10.____

11.
   I. If legal procedures are not observed, the resulting contract is not enforseable.
   II. If the directions from the creditor's attorney are not in writing, the deputy sheriff should request a letter of instructions from the attorney.
         11.____

12.
   I. The deputy sheriff may confer with the defendant and may enter this defendants' place of business.
   II. A deputy sheriff must ascertain from the creditor's attorney whether the debtor has any property against which he may proceede.
         12.____

13.
   I. The sheriff has a right to do whatever is reasonably necessary for the purpose of executing the order of the court.
   II. The written order of the court gives the sheriff general authority and he is governed in his acts by a very simple principal.
         13.____

14.
   I. Either the patrolman or his sergeant are always ready to help the public.
   II. The sergeant asked the patrolman when he would finish the report.
         14.____

15.
   I. The injured man could not hardly talk.
   II. Every officer had ought to hand in their reports on time.
         15.____

Questions 16-25.

DIRECTIONS: For each of the sentences given below, numbered 16 through 25, select from the following choices the MOST correct choice and print your choice in the space at the right. Select as your answer:

    A. If the statement contains an unnecessary word or expression
    B. If the statement contains a slang term or expression ordinarily not acceptable in government report writing
    C. If the statement contains an old-fashioned word or expression, where a concrete, plain term would be more useful
    D. If the statement contains no major faults

16. Every one of us should try harder
         16.____

17. Yours of the first instant has been received.
         17.____

18. We will have to do a real snow job on him.
         18.____

19. I shall contact him next Thursday.
         19.____

20. None of us were invited to the meeting with the community.   20.__

21. We got this here job to do.   21.____

22. She could not help but see the mistake in the checkbook.   22.____

23. Don't bug the Director about the report.   23.____

24. I beg to inform you that your letter has been received.   24.____

25. This project is all screwed up.   25.____

KEY (CORRECT ANSWERS)

1.	D	11.	B
2.	C	12.	D
3.	A	13.	A
4.	D	14.	D
5.	B	15.	D
6.	B	16.	D
7.	A	17.	C
8.	D	18.	B
9.	D	19.	D
10.	C	20.	D

21.	B
22.	D
23.	B
24.	C
25.	B

TEST 3

DIRECTIONS: Questions 1 through 25 are sentences taken from reports. Some are correct according to ordinary formal English usage. Others are incorrect because they contain errors in English usage, spelling, or punctuation. Consider a sentence correct if it contains no errors in English usage, spelling, or punctuation, even if there may be other ways of writing the sentence correctly. Mark your answer:

A. If only sentence I is correct
B. If only sentence II is correct
C. If sentences I and II are correct
D. If neither sentence I nor II is correct.

1. I. The Neighborhood Police Team Commander and Team Patrol- men are encouraged to give to the public the widest possible verbal and written disemination of information regarding the existence and purposes of the program.
   II. The police must be vitally interelated with every segment of the public they serve.

1.____

2. I. If social gambling, prostitution, and other vices are to be prohibited, the law makers should provide the manpower and method for enforcement.
   II. In addition to checking on possible crime locations such as hallways, roofs yards and other similar locations, Team Patrolmen are encouraged to make known their presence to members of the community.

2.____

3. I. The Neighborhood Police Team Commander is authorized to secure, the cooperation of local publications, as well as public and private agencies, to further the goals of the program.
   II. Recruitment from social minorities is essential to effective police work among minorities and meaningful relations with them.

3.____

4. I. The Neighborhood Police Team Commander and his men have the responsibility for providing patrol service within the sector territory on a twenty-four hour basis.
   II. While the patrolman was walking his beat at midnight he noticed that the clothing stores' door was partly open.

4.____

5. I. Authority is granted to the Neighborhood Police Team to device tactics for coping with the crime in the sector.
   II. Before leaving the scene of the accident, the patrolman drew a map showing the positions of the automobiles and indicated the time of the accident as 10 M. in the morning.

5.____

6. I. The Neighborhood Police Team Commander and his men must be kept apprised of conditions effecting their sector.
   II. Clear, continuous communication with every segment of the public served based on the realization of mutual need and founded on trust and confidence is the basis for effective law enforcement.

6.____

7.   I.   The irony is that the police are blamed for the laws they enforce when they are doing their duty.   7.___

       II.   The Neighborhood Police Team Commander is authorized to prepare and distribute literature with pertinent information telling the public whom to contact for assistance.

8.   I.   The day is not far distant when major parts of the entire police compliment will need extensive college training or degrees.   8.____

       II.   Although driving under the influence of alcohol is a specific charge in making arrests, drunkeness is basically a health and social problem.

9.   I.   If a deputy sheriff finds that property he has to attach is located on a ship, he should notify his supervisor.   9.____

       II.   Any contract that tends to interfere with the administration of justice is illegal.

10.   I.   A mandate or official order of the court to the sheriff or other officer directs it to take into possession property of the judgment debtor.   10.____

       II.   Tenancies from month-to-month, week-to-week, and sometimes year-to-year are termenable.

11.   I.   A civil arrest is an arrest pursuant to an order issued by a court in civil litigation.   11.____

       II.   In a criminal arrest, a defendant is arrested for a crime he is alleged to have committed.

12.   I.   Having taken a defendant into custody, there is a complete restraint of personal liberty.   12.____

       II.   Actual force is unnecessary when a deputy sheriff makes an arrest.

13.   I.   When a husband breaches a separation agreement by failing to supply to the wife the amount of money to be paid to her periodically under the agreement, the same legal steps may be taken to enforce his compliance as in any other breach of contract.   13.____

       II.   Having obtained the writ of attachment, the plaintiff is then in the advantageous position of selling the very property that has been held for him by the sheriff while he was obtaining a judgment.

14.   I.   Being locked in his desk, the investigator felt sure that the records would be safe.   14.____

       II.   The reason why the witness changed his statement was because he had been threatened.

15.   I.   The investigation had just began then an important witness disappeared.   15.____

       II.   The check that had been missing was located and returned to its owner, Harry Morgan, a resident of Suffolk County, New York.

16.   I.   A supervisor will find that the establishment of standard procedures enables his staff to work more efficiently.   16.____

       II.   An investigator hadn't ought to give any recommendations in his report if he is in doubt.

17.   I.   Neither the investigator nor his supervisor is ready to interview the witnesses.   17.____

       II.   Interviewing has been and always will be an important asset in investigation.

18.   I.   One of the investigator's reports has been forwarded to the wrong person.   18.____
      II.   The investigator stated that he was not familiar with those kind of cases.

19.   I.   Approaching the victim of the assault, two large bruises were noticed by me.   19.____
      II.   The prisoner was arrested for assault, resisting arrest, and use of a deadly weapon.

20.   I.   A copy of the orders, which had been prepared by the captain, was given to each   20.____
        patrolman.
      II.   It's always necessary to inform an arrested person of his constitutional rights before asking him any questions.

21.   I.   To prevent further bleeding, I applied a tourniquet to the wound.   21.____
      II.   John Rano a senior officer was on duty at the time of the accident.

22.   I.   Limiting the term "property" to tangible property, in the criminal mischief setting,   22.____
        accords with prior case law holding that only tangible property came within the purview of the offense of malicious mischief.
      II.   Thus, a person who intentionally destroys the property of another, but under an honest belief that he has title to such property, cannot be convicted of criminal mischief under the Revised Penal Law.

23.   I.   Very early in it's history, New York enacted statutes from time to time punishing,   23.____
        either as a felony or as a misdemeanor, malicious injuries to various kinds of property: piers, booms, dams, bridges, etc.
      II.   The application of the statute is necessarily restricted to trespassory takings with larcenous intent: namely with intent permanently or virtually permanently to "appropriate" property or "deprive" the owner of its use.

24.   I.   Since the former Penal Law did not define the instruments of forgery in a general   24.____
        fashion, its crime of forgery was held to be narrower than the common law offense in this respect and to embrace only those instruments explicitly specified in the substantive provisions.
      II.   After entering the barn through an open door for the purpose of stealing, it was closed by the defendants.

25.   I.   The use of fire or explosives to destroy tangible property is proscribed by the crim-   25.____
        inal mischief provisions of the Revised Penal Law.
      II.   The defendant's taking of a taxicab for the immediate purpose of affecting his escape did not constitute grand larceny.

KEY (CORRECT ANSWERS)

1.	D	11.	C
2.	D	12.	B
3.	B	13.	C
4.	A	14.	D
5.	D	15.	B
6.	D	16.	A
7.	C	17.	C
8.	D	18.	A
9.	C	19.	B
10.	D	20.	C

21.	A
22.	C
23.	B
24.	A
25.	A

TEST 4

Questions 1-4.

DIRECTIONS: Each of the two sentences in Questions 1 through 4 may be correct or may contain errors in punctuation, capitalization, or grammar. Mark your answer:

     A. If there is an error only in sentence I
     B. If there is an error only in sentence II
     C. If there is an error in both sentences I and II
     D. If both sentences are correct.

1.   I. It is very annoying to have a pencil sharpener, which is not in working order.   1.____
     II. Patrolman Blake checked the door of Joe's Restaurant and found that the lock has been jammed.

2.   I. When you are studying a good textbook is important.   2.____
     II. He said he would divide the money equally between you and me.

3.   I. Since he went on the city council a year ago, one of his primary concerns has been safety in the streets.   3.____
     II. After waiting in the doorway for about 15 minutes, a black sedan appeared.

Questions 5-9.

DIRECTIONS: Each of the sentences in Questions 5 through 9 may be classified under one of the following four categories:
     A. Faulty because of incorrect grammar
     B. Faulty because of incorrect punctuation
     C. Faulty because of incorrect capitalization or incorrect spelling
     D. Correct

Examine each sentence carefully to determine under which of the above four options it is BEST classified. Then, in the space at the right, print the capitalized letter preceding the option which is the BEST of the four suggested above. Each faulty sentence contains but one type of error. Consider a sentence to be correct if it contains none of the types of errors mentioned, even though there may be other correct ways of expressing the same thought.

5. They told both he and I that the prisoner had escaped.   5.____

6. Any superior officer, who, disregards the just complaints of his subordinates, is remiss in the performance of his duty.   6.____

7. Only those members of the national organization who resided in the Middle west attended the conference in Chicago.   7.____

8. We told him to give the investigation assignment to whoever was available.   8.____

9. Please do not disappoint and embarass us by not appearing in court.   9.____

Questions 10-14.

DIRECTIONS: Each of Questions 10 through 14 consists of three sentences lettered A, B, and C. In each of these questions, one of the sentences may contain an error in grammar, sentence structure, or punctuation, or all three sentences may be correct. If one of the sentences in a question contains an error in grammar, sentence structure, or punctuation, print in the space at the right the capital letter preceding the sentence which contains the error. If all three sentences are correct, print the letter D.

10.   A.   Mr. Smith appears to be less competent than I in performing these duties.   10.____
        B.   The supervisor spoke to the employee, who had made the error, but did not reprimand him.
        C.   When he found the book lying on the table, he immediately notified the owner.

11.   A.   Being locked in the desk, we were certain that the papers would not be taken.   11.____
        B.   It wasn't I who dictated the telegram; I believe it was Eleanor.
        C.   You should interview whoever comes to the office today.

12.   A.   The clerk was instructed to set the machine on the table before summoning the manager.   12.____
        B.   He said that he was not familiar with those kind of activities.
        C.   A box of pencils, in addition to erasers and blotters, was included in the shipment of supplies.

13.   A.   The supervisor remarked, "Assigning an employee to the proper type of work is not always easy."   13.____
        B.   The employer found that each of the applicants were qualified to perform the duties of the position.
        C.   Any competent student is permitted to take this course if he obtains the consent of the instructor.

14.   A.   The prize was awarded to the employee whom the judges believed to be most deserving.   14.____
        B.   Since the instructor believes this book is the better of the two, he is recommending it for use in the school.
        C.   It was obvious to the employees that the completion of the task by the scheduled date would require their working overtime.

Questions 15-21.

DIRECTIONS: In answering Questions 15 through 21, choose the sentence which is BEST from the point of view of English usage suitable for a business report.

15.   A.   The client's receiving of public assistance checks at two different addresses were   15.____
             disclosed by the investigation.
       B.   The investigation disclosed that the client was receiving public assistance
             checks at two different addresses.
       C.   The client was found out by the investigation to be receiving public assistance
             checks at two different addresses.
       D.   The client has been receiving public assistance checks at two different
             addresses, disclosed the investigation.

16.   A.   The investigation of complaints are usually handled by this unit, which deals with   16.____
             internal security problems in the department.
       B.   This unit deals with internal security problems in the department usually investi-
             gating complaints.
       C.   Investigating complaints is this unit's job, being that it handles internal security
             problems in the department.
       D.   This unit deals with internal security problems in the department and usually
             investigates complaints.

17.   A.   The delay in completing this investigation was caused by difficulty in obtaining the   17.____
             required documents from the candidate.
       B.   Because of difficulty in obtaining the required documents from the candidate is
             the reason that there was a delay in completing this investigation.
       C.   Having had difficulty in obtaining the required documents from the candidate,
             there was a delay in completing this investigation.
       D.   Difficulty in obtaining the required documents from the candidate had the affect
             of delaying the completion of this investigation.

18.   A.   This report, together with documents supporting our recommendation, are being   18.____
             submitted for your approval.
       B.   Documents supporting our recommendation is being submitted with the report
             for your approval.
       C.   This report, together with documents supporting our recommendation, is being
             submitted for your approval.
       D.   The report and documents supporting our recommendation is being submitted
             for your approval.

19.   A.   The chairman himself, rather than his aides, has reviewed the report.   19.____
       B.   The chairman himself, rather than his aides, have reviewed the report.
       C.   The chairmen, not the aide, has reviewed the report.
       D.   The aide, not the chairmen, have reviewed the report.

20.   A.   Various proposals were submitted but the decision is not been made.   20.____
       B.   Various proposals has been submitted but the decision has not been made.
       C.   Various proposals were submitted but the decision is not been made.
       D.   Various proposals have been submitted but the decision has not been made.

21.   A.   Everyone were rewarded for his successful attempt.   21.____
       B.   They were successful in their attempts and each of them was rewarded.
       C.   Each of them are rewarded for their successful attempts.
       D.   The reward for their successful attempts were made to each of them.

22. The following is a paragraph from a request for departmental recognition consisting of five numbered sentences submitted to a Captain for review. These sentences may or may not have errors in spelling, grammar, and punctuation:

22.

1. The officers observed the subject Mills surreptitiously remove a wallet from the woman's handbag and entered his automobile. 2. As they approached Mills, he looked in their direction and drove away. 3. The officers pursued in their car. 4. Mills executed a series of complicated manuvers to evade the pursuing officers. 5. At the corner of Broome and Elizabeth Streets, Mills stopped the car, got out, raised his hands and sur-rendered to the officers.

Which one of the following BEST classifies the above with regard to spelling, grammar and punctuation?

    A. 1, 2, and 3 are correct, but 4 and 5 have errors.
    B. 2, 3, and 5 are correct, but 1 and 4 have errors.
    C. 3, 4, and 5 are correct, but 1 and 2 have errors.
    D. 1, 2, 3, and 5 are correct, but 4 has errors.

23. The one of the following sentences which is grammatically PREFERABLE to the others is:

23._____

    A. Our engineers will go over your blueprints so that you may have no problems in construction.
    B. For a long time he had been arguing that we, not he, are to blame for the confu-sion.
    C. I worked on this automobile for two hours and still cannot find out what is wrong with it.
    D. Accustomed to all kinds of hardships, fatigue seldom bothers veteran policemen.

24. The MOST accurate of the following sentences is:

24._____

    A. The commissioner, as well as his deputy and various bureau heads, were present.
    B. A new organization of employers and employees have been formed.
    C. One or the other of these men have been selected.
    D. The number of pages in the book is enough to discourage a reader.

25. The MOST accurate of the following sentences is:

25._____

    A. Between you and me, I think he is the better man.
    B. He was believed to be me.
    C. Is it us that you wish to see?
    D. The winners are him and her.

KEY (CORRECT ANSWERS)

1.	C		11.	A
2.	A		12.	B
3.	C		13.	B
4.	B		14.	D
5.	A		15.	B
6.	B		16.	D
7.	C		17.	A
8.	D		18.	C
9.	C		19.	A
10.	B		20.	D

21.	B
22.	B
23.	A
24.	D
25.	A

———

PREPARING WRITTEN MATERIALS

EXAMINATION SECTION
TEST 1

DIRECTIONS: Each of the following questions consists of a sentence which may be classified appropriately under one of the following four categories:
  A. Incorrect because of faulty grammar or sentence structure
  B. Incorrect because of faulty punctuation
  C. Incorrect because of faulty spelling or capitalization
  D. Correct

Examine each sentence carefully. Then, in the space at the right, print the letter preceding the best of the four alternatives suggested above. All incorrect sentences contain but one type of error. Consider a sentence correct if it contains none of the types of errors mentioned, even though there may be other correct ways of expressing the same thought.

1.   The fire apparently started in the storeroom, which is usually locked.   1._____

2.   On approaching the victim two bruises were noticed by this officer.   2._____

3.   The officer, who was there examined the report with great care.   3._____

4.   Each employee in the office had a separate desk.   4._____

5.   Each employee in the office had a separate desk.   5._____

6.   The suggested procedure is similar to the one now in use.   6._____

7.   No one was more pleased with the new procedure than the chauffeur.   7._____

8.   He tried to pursuade her to change the procedure.   8._____

9.   The total of the expenses charged to petty cash were high.   9._____

10. An understanding between him and I was finally reached.   10._____

11. It was at the supervisor's request that the clerk agreed to postpone his vacation.   11._____

12. We do not believe that it is necessary for both he and the clerk to attend the conference.   12._____

13. All employees, who display perseverance, will be given adequate recognition.   13._____

14. He regrets that some of us employees are dissatisfied with our new assignments.   14._____

15. "Do you think that the raise was merited," asked the supervisor?   15._____

16. The new manual of procedure is a valuable supplament to our rules and regulation.   16._____

17. The typist admitted that she had attempted to pursuade the other employees to assist her in her work.   17._____

18. The supervisor asked that all amendments to the regulations be handled by you and I.   18.___

19. They told both he and I that the prisoner had escaped.   19.___

20. Any superior officer, who, disregards the just complaints of his subordinates, is remiss in   20.___
the performance of his duty.

21. Only those members of the national organization who resided in the Middle west   21.___
attended the conference in Chicago.

22. We told him to give the investigation assignment to whoever was available.   22.___

23. Please do not disappoint and embarass us by not appearing in court.   23.___

24. Despite the efforts of the Supervising mechanic, the elevator could not be started.   24.___

25. The U.S. Weather Bureau, weather record for the accident date was checked.   25.___

———

KEY (CORRECT ANSWERS)

1.	D	11.	D
2.	A	12.	A
3.	B	13.	B
4.	D	14.	D
5.	B	15.	B
6.	C	16.	C
7.	D	17.	C
8.	C	18.	A
9.	A	19.	A
10.	A	20.	B

21. C
22. D
23. C
24. C
25. B

———

TEST 2

DIRECTIONS: Each question consists of a sentence. Some of the sentences contain errors in English grammar or usage, punctuation, spelling, or capitalization. A sentence does not contain an error simply because it could be written in a different manner. Choose answer
    A. If the sentence contains an error in English grammar or usage
    B. If the sentence contains an error in punctuation
    C. If the sentence contains an error in spelling or capitalization
    D. If the sentence does not contain any errors.

1. The severity of the sentence prescribed by contemporary statutes - including both the former and the revised New York Penal Laws - do not depend on what crime was intended by the offender.　1.____

2. It is generally recognized that two defects in the early law of attempt played a part in the birth of burglary: (1) immunity from prosecution for conduct short of the last act before completion of the crime, and (2) the relatively minor penalty imposed for an attempt (it being a common law misdemeanor) vis-a-vis the completed offense.　2.____

3. The first sentence of the statute is applicable to employees who enter their place of employment, invited guests, and all other persons who have an express or implied license or privilege to enter the premises.　3.____

4. Contemporary criminal codes in the United States generally divide burglary into various degrees, differentiating the categories according to place, time and other attendent circumstances.　4.____

5. The assignment was completed in record time but the payroll for it has not yet been preparid.　5.____

6. The operator, on the other hand, is willing to learn me how to use the mimeograph.　6.____

7. She is the prettiest of the three sisters.　7.____

8. She doesn't know; if the mail has arrived.　8.____

9. The doorknob of the office door is broke.　9.____

10. Although the department's supply of scratch pads and stationery have diminished considerably, the allotment for our division has not been reduced.　10.____

11. You have not told us whom you wish to designate as your secretary.　11.____

12. Upon reading the minutes of the last meeting, the new proposal was taken up for consideration.　12.____

13. Before beginning the discussion, we locked the door as a precautionery measure.　13.____

14. The supervisor remarked, "Only those clerks, who perform routine work, are permitted to take a rest period."　14.____

15. Not only will this duplicating machine make accurate copies, but it will also produce a quantity of work equal to fifteen transcribing typists.　15.____

16. "Mr. Jones," said the supervisor, "we regret our inability to grant you an extent ion of your leave of absence." 16.___

17. Although the employees find the work monotonous and fatigueing, they rarely complain. 17.___

18. We completed the tabulation of the receipts on time despite the fact that Miss Smith our fastest operator was absent for over a week. 18.___

19. The reaction of the employees who attended the meeting, as well as the reaction of those who did not attend, indicates clearly that the schedule is satisfactory to everyone concerned. 19.___

20. Of the two employees, the one in our office is the most efficient. 20.___

21. No one can apply or even understand, the new rules and regulations. 21.___

22. A large amount of supplies were stored in the empty office. 22.___

23. If an employee is occassionally asked to work overtime, he should do so willingly. 23.___

24. It is true that the new procedures are difficult to use but, we are certain that you will learn them quickly. 24.___

25. The office manager said that he did not know who would be given a large allotment under the new plan. 25.___

———————

KEY (CORRECT ANSWERS)

1.	A		11.	D
2.	D		12.	A
3.	D		13.	C
4.	C		14.	B
5.	C		15.	A
6.	A		16.	C
7.	D		17.	C
8.	B		18.	B
9.	A		19.	D
10.	A		20.	A

21.	B
22.	A
23.	C
24.	B
25.	D

———————

TEST 3

DIRECTIONS: Each of the following sentences may be classified MOST appropriately under one of the following our categories:
- A. faulty because of incorrect grammar;
- B. faulty because of incorrect punctuation;
- C. faulty because of incorrect capitalization;
- D. correct

Examine each sentence carefully. Then, in the space at the right, print the capital letter preceding the option which is the BEST of the four suggested above. All incorrect sentences contain but one type of error. Consider a sentence correct if it contains none of the types of errors mentioned, even though there may be other correct ways of expressing the same thought.

1. The desk, as well as the chairs, were moved out of the office.   1.____

2. The clerk whose production was greatest for the month won a day's vacation as first prize.   2.____

3. Upon entering the room, the employees were found hard at work at their desks.   3.____

4. John Smith our new employee always arrives at work on time.   4.____

5. Punish whoever is guilty of stealing the money.   5.____

6. Intelligent and persistent effort lead to success no matter what the job may be.   6.____

7. The secretary asked, "can you call again at three o'clock?"   7.____

8. He told us, that if the report was not accepted at the next meeting, it would have to be rewritten.   8.____

9. He would not have sent the letter if he had known that it would cause so much excitement.   9.____

10. We all looked forward to him coming to visit us.   10.____

11. If you find that you are unable to complete the assignment please notify me as soon as possible.   11.____

12. Every girl in the office went home on time but me; there was still some work for me to finish.   12.____

13. He wanted to know who the letter was addressed to, Mr. Brown or Mr. Smith.   13.____

14. "Mr. Jones, he said, please answer this letter as soon as possible."   14.____

15. The new clerk had an unusual accent inasmuch as he was born and educated in the south.   15.____

16. Although he is younger than her, he earns a higher salary.   16.____

17. Neither of the two administrators are going to attend the conference being held in Washington, D.C.   17.___

18. Since Miss Smith and Miss Jones have more experience than us, they have been given more responsible duties.   18.___

19. Mr. Shaw the supervisor of the stock room maintains an inventory of stationery and office supplies.   19.___

20. Inasmuch as this matter affects both you and I, we should take joint action.   20.___

21. Who do you think will be able to perform this highly technical work?   21.___

22. Of the two employees, John is considered the most competent.   22.___

23. He is not coming home on tuesday; we expect him next week.   23.___

24. Stenographers, as well as typists must be able to type rapidly and accurately.   24.___

25. Having been placed in the safe we were sure that the money would not be stolen.   25.___

KEY (CORRECT ANSWERS)

1.	A		11.	B
2.	D		12.	D
3.	A		13.	A
4.	B		14.	B
5.	D		15.	C
6.	A		16.	A
7.	C		17.	A
8.	A		18.	A
9.	D		19.	B
10.	A		20.	A

21.	D
22.	A
23.	C
24.	B
25.	A

TEST 4

DIRECTIONS: Each of the following sentences consist of four sentences lettered A, B, C, and D. One of the sentences in each group contains an error in grammar or punctuation. Indicate the INCORRECT sentence in each group. *PRINT THE LETTER OF THE CORRECT ANSWER IN THE SPACE AT THE RIGHT.*

1. A. Give the message to whoever is on duty.
   B. The teacher who's pupil won first prize presented the award.
   C. Between you and me, I don't expect the program to succeed.
   D. His running to catch the bus caused the accident.

   1.____

2. A. The process, which was patented only last year is already obsolete.
   B. His interest in science (which continues to the present) led him to convert his basement into a laboratory.
   C. He described the book as "verbose, repetitious, and bombastic".
   D. Our new director will need to possess three qualities: vision, patience, and fortitude.

   2.____

3. A. The length of ladder trucks varies considerably.
   B. The probationary fireman reported to the officer to whom he was assigned.
   C. The lecturer emphasized the need for we firemen to be punctual.
   D. Neither the officers nor the members of the company knew about the new procedure.

   3.____

4. A. Ham and eggs is the specialty of the house.
   B. He is one of the students who are on probation.
   C. Do you think that either one of us have a chance to be nominated for president of the class?
   D. I assume that either he was to be in charge or you were.

   4.____

5. A. Its a long road that has no turn.
   B. To run is more tiring than to walk.
   C. We have been assigned three new reports: namely, the statistical summary, the narrative summary, and the budgetary summary.
   D. Had the first payment been made in January, the second would be due in April.

   5.____

6. A. Each employer has his own responsibilities.
   B. If a person speaks correctly, they make a good impression.
   C. Every one of the operators has had her vacation.
   D. Has anybody filed his report?

   6.____

7. A. The manager, with all his salesmen, was obliged to go.
   B. Who besides them is to sign the agreement?
   C. One report without the others is incomplete.
   D. Several clerks, as well as the proprietor, was injured.

   7.____

8. A. A suspension of these activities is expected.
   B. The machine is economical because first cost and upkeep are low.
   C. A knowledge of stenography and filing are required for this position.
   D. The condition in which the goods were received shows that the packing was not done properly.

   8.____

9. A. There seems to be a great many reasons for disagreement.
    B. It does not seem possible that they could have failed.
    C. Have there always been too few applicants for these positions?
    D. There is no excuse for these errors.

9.___

10. A. We shall be pleased to answer your question.
    B. Shall we plan the meeting for Saturday?
    C. I will call you promptly at seven.
    D. Can I borrow your book after you have read it?

10.___

11. A. You are as capable as I.
    B. Everyone is willing to sign but him and me.
    C. As for he and his assistant, I cannot praise them too highly.
    D. Between you and me, I think he will be dismissed.

11.___

12. A. Our competitors bid above us last week.
    B. The survey which was began last year has not yet been completed.
    C. The operators had shown that they understood their instructions.
    D. We have never ridden over worse roads.

12.___

13. A. Who did they say was responsible?
    B. Whom did you suspect?
    C. Who do you suppose it was?
    D. Whom do you mean?

13.___

14. A. Of the two propositions, this is the worse.
    B. Which report do you consider the best -- the one in January or the one in July?
    C. I believe this is the most practicable of the many plans submitted.
    D. He is the youngest employee in the organization.

14.___

15. A. The firm had but three orders last week.
    B. That doesn't really seem possible.
    C. After twenty years scarcely none of the old business remains.
    D. Has he done nothing about it?

15.___

_____

KEY (CORRECT ANSWERS)

1.	B		6.	B
2.	A		7.	D
3.	C		8.	C
4.	C		9.	A
5.	A		10.	D

11.	C
12.	B
13.	A
14.	B
15.	C

_____

PREPARING WRITTEN MATERIAL

PARAGRAPH REARRANGEMENT
COMMENTARY

The sentences which follow are in scrambled order. You are to rearrange them in proper order and indicate the letter choice containing the correct answer at the space at the right.

Each group of sentences in this section is actually a paragraph presented in scrambled order. Each sentence in the group has a place in that paragraph; no sentence is to be left out. You are to read each group of sentences and decide upon the best order in which to put the sentences so as to form as well-organized paragraph.

The questions in this section measure the ability to solve a problem when all the facts relevant to its solution are not given.

More specifically, certain positions of responsibility and authority require the employee to discover connections between events sometimes, apparently, unrelated. In order to do this, the employee will find it necessary to correctly infer that unspecified events have probably occurred or are likely to occur. This ability becomes especially important when action must be taken on incomplete information.

Accordingly, these questions require competitors to choose among several suggested alternatives, each of which presents a different sequential arrangement of the events. Competitors must choose the MOST logical of the suggested sequences.

In order to do so, they may be required to draw on general knowledge to infer missing concepts or events that are essential to sequencing the given events. Competitors should be careful to infer only what is essential to the sequence. The plausibility of the wrong alternatives will always require the inclusion of unlikely events or of additional chains of events which are NOT essential to sequencing the given events.

It's very important to remember that you are looking for the best of the four possible choices, and that the best choice of all may not even be one of the answers you're given to choose from.

There is no one right way to these problems. Many people have found it helpful to first write out the order of the sentences, as they would have arranged them, on their scrap paper before looking at the possible answers. If their optimum answer is there, this can save them some time. If it isn't, this method can still give insight into solving the problem. Others find it most helpful to just go through each of the possible choices, contrasting each as they go along. You should use whatever method feels comfortable, and works, for you.

While most of these types of questions are not that difficult, we've added a higher percentage of the difficult type, just to give you more practice. Usually there are only one or two questions on this section that contain such subtle distinctions that you're unable to answer confidently, and you then may find yourself stuck deciding between two possible choices, neither of which you're sure about.

———

EXAMINATION SECTION
TEST 1

DIRECTIONS: The sentences that follow are in scrambled order. You are to rearrange them in proper order and indicate the letter choice containing the correct answer. *PRINT THE LETTER OF THE CORRECT ANSWER IN THE SPACE AT THE RIGHT.*

1. Below are four statements labeled W., X., Y., and Z.   1.____
    W.   He was a strict and fanatic drillmaster.
    X.   The word is always used in a derogatory sense and generally shows resent-
          ment and anger on the part of the user.
    Y.   It is from the name of this Frenchman that we derive our English word, martinet.
    Z.   Jean Martinet was the Inspector-General of Infantry during the reign of King
          Louis XIV.
    The *PROPER* order in which these sentences should be placed in a paragraph is:

    A. X, Z, W, Y   B. X, Z, Y, W   C. Z, W, Y, X   D. Z, Y, W, X

2. In the following paragraph, the sentences which are numbered, have been jumbled.   2.____
    1.   Since then it has undergone changes.
    2.   It was incorporated in 1955 under the laws of the State of New York.
    3.   Its primary purpose, a cleaner city, has, however, remained the same.
    4.   The Citizens Committee works in cooperation with the Mayor's Inter-departmen-
          tal Committee for a Clean City.
    The order in which these sentences should be arranged to form a well-organized para-
    graph is:

    A. 2, 4, 1, 3   B. 3, 4, 1, 2   C. 4, 2, 1, 3   D. 4, 3, 2, 1

Questions 3-5.

DIRECTIONS: The sentences listed below are part of a meaningful paragraph but they are not given in their proper order. You are to decide what would be the *best order* in which to put the sentences so as to form a well-organized paragraph. Each sentence has a place in the paragraph; there are no extra sentences. You are then to answer questions 3 to 5 inclusive on the basis of your rearrangements of these secrambled sentences into a properly organized paragraph.

In 1887 some insurance companies organized an Inspection Department to advise their clients on all phases of fire prevention and protection. Probably this has been due to the smaller annual fire losses in Great Britain than in the United States. It tests various fire prevention devices and appliances and determines manufacturing hazards and their safeguards. Fire research began earlier in the United States and is more advanced than in Great Britain. Later they established a laboratory specializing in electrical, mechanical, hydraulic, and chemical fields.

3. When the five sentences are arranged in proper order, the paragraph starts with the sentence which begins   3.___

    A. "In 1887 ..."   B. "Probably this ..."   C. "It tests ..."
    D. "Fire research ..."   E. "Later they ..."

4. In the last sentence listed above, "they" refers to   4.___

    A. insurance companies
    B. the United States and Great Britain
    C. the Inspection Department
    D. clients
    E. technicians

5. When the above paragraph is properly arranged, it ends with the words   5.___

    A. "... and protection."   B. "... the United States."
    C. "... their safeguards."   D. "... in Great Britain."
    E. "... chemical fields."

KEY (CORRECT ANSWERS)

    1. C
    2. C
    3. D
    4. A
    5. C

TEST 2

DIRECTIONS: In each of the questions numbered 1 through 5, several sentences are given. For each question, choose as your answer the group of numbers that represents the *most logical* order of these sentences if they were arranged in paragraph form. *PRINT THE LETTER OF THE CORRECT ANSWER IN THE SPACE AT THE RIGHT.*

1.
   1. It is established when one shows that the landlord has prevented the tenant's enjoyment of his interest in the property leased.
   2. Constructive eviction is the result of a breach of the covenant of quiet enjoyment implied in all leases.
   3. In some parts of the United States, it is not complete until the tenant vacates within a reasonable time.
   4. Generally, the acts must be of such serious and permanent character as to deny the tenant the enjoyment of his possessing rights.
   5. In this event, upon abandonment of the premises, the tenant's liability for that ceases.

   The CORRECT answer is:

   A. 2, 1, 4, 3, 5 B. 5, 2, 3, 1, 4 C. 4, 3, 1, 2, 5
   D. 1, 3, 5, 4, 2

   1.____

2.
   1. The powerlessness before private and public authorities that is the typical experience of the slum tenant is reminiscent of the situation of blue-collar workers all through the nineteenth century.
   2. Similarly, in recent years, this chapter of history has been reopened by anti-poverty groups which have attempted to organize slum tenants to enable them to bargain collectively with their landlords about the conditions of their tenancies.
   3. It is familiar history that many of the workers remedied their condition by joining together and presenting their demands collectively.
   4. Like the workers, tenants are forced by the conditions of modern life into substantial dependence on these who possess great political arid economic power.
   5. What's more, the very fact of dependence coupled with an absence of education and self-confidence makes them hesitant and unable to stand up for what they need from those in power.

   The CORRECT answer is:

   A. 5, 4, 1, 2, 3 B. 2, 3, 1, 5, 4 C. 3, 1, 5, 4, 2
   D. 1, 4, 5, 3, 2

   2.____

3.
   1. A railroad, for example, when not acting as a common carrier may contract; away responsibility for its own negligence.
   2. As to a landlord, however, no decision has been found relating to the legal effect of a clause shifting the statutory duty of repair to the tenant.
   3. The courts have not passed on the validity of clauses relieving the landlord of this duty and liability.
   4. They have, however, upheld the validity of exculpatory clauses in other types of contracts.
   5. Housing regulations impose a duty upon the landlord to maintain leased premises in safe condition.

   3.____

6. As another example, a bailee may limit his liability except for gross negligence, willful acts, or fraud.

The CORRECT answer is:

A. 2, 1, 6, 4, 3, 5   B. 1, 3, 4, 5, 6, 2   C. 3, 5, 1, 4, 2, 6
D. 5, 3, 4, 1, 6, 2

4.   1. Since there are only samples in the building, retail or consumer sales are generally eschewed by mart occupants, and,in some instances, rigid controls are maintained to limit entrance to the mart only to those persons engaged in retailing.
    2. Since World War I, in many larger cities, there has developed a new type of property, called the mart building.
    3. It can, therefore, be used by wholesalers and jobbers for the display of sample merchandise.
    4. This type of building is most frequently a multi-storied, finished interior property which is a cross between a retail arcade and a loft building.
    5. This limitation enables the mart occupants to ship the orders from another location after the retailer or dealer makes his selection from the samples.

4.____

The CORRECT answer is:

A. 2, 4, 3, 1, 5   B. 4, 3, 5, 1, 2   C. 1, 3, 2, 4, 5
D. 1, 4, 2, 3, 5

5.   1. In general, staff-line friction reduces the distinctive contribution of staff personnel.
    2. The conflicts, however, introduce an uncontrolled element into the managerial system.
    3. On the other hand, the natural resistance of the line to staff innovations probably usefully restrains over-eager efforts to apply untested procedures on a large scale.
    4. Under such conditions, it is difficult to know when valuable ideas are being sacrificed.
    5. The relatively weak position of staff, requiring accommodation to the line, tends to restrict their ability to engage .in free, experimental innovation.

5.____

The CORRECT answer is:

A. 4, 2, 3, 1, 3   B. 1, 5, 3, 2, 4   C. 5, 3, 1, 2, 4
D. 2, 1, 4, 5, 3

_____

KEY (CORRECT ANSWERS)

1. A
2. D
3. D
4. A
5. B

_____

TEST 3

DIRECTIONS: Questions 1 through 4 consist of six sentences which can be arranged in a logical sequence. For each question, select the choice which places the numbered sentences in the *most logical* sequence. *PRINT THE LETTER OF THE CORRECT ANSWER IN THE SPACE AT THE RIGHT.*

1.
1. The burden of proof as to each issue is determined before trial and remains upon the same party throughout the trial.
2. The jury is at liberty to believe one witness' testimony as against a number of contradictory witnesses.
3. In a civil case, the party bearing the burden of proof is required to prove his contention by a fair preponderance of the evidence.
4. However, it must be noted that a fair preponderance of evidence does not necessarily mean a greater number of witnesses.
5. The burden of proof is the burden which rests upon one of the parties to an action to persuade the trier of the facts, generally the jury, that a proposition he asserts is true.
6. If the evidence is equally balanced, or if it leaves the jury in such doubt as to be unable to decide the controversy either way, judgment must be given against the party upon whom the burden of proof rests.

The CORRECT answer is:

A. 3, 2, 5, 4, 1, 6   B. 1, 2, 6, 5, 3, 4   C. 3, 4, 5, 1, 2, 6
D. 5, 1, 3, 6, 4, 2

1.＿＿＿

2.
1. If a parent is without assets and is unemployed, he cannot be convicted of the crime of non-support of a child.
2. The term "sufficient ability" has been held to mean sufficient financial ability.
3. It does not matter if his unemployment is by choice or unavoidable circumstances.
4. If he fails to take any steps at all, he may be liable to prosecution for endangering the welfare of a child.
5. Under the penal law, a parent is responsible for the support of his minor child only if the parent is "of sufficient ability."
6. An indigent parent may meet his obligation by borrowing money or by seeking aid under the provisions of the Social Welfare Law.

The CORRECT answer is:

A. 6, 1, 5, 3, 2, 4   B. 1, 3, 5, 2, 4, 6   C. 5, 2, 1, 3, 6, 4
D. 1, 6, 4, 5, 2, 3

2.＿＿＿

3. 1. Consider, for example, the case of a rabble rouser who urges a group of twenty people to go out and break the windows of a nearby factory.
    2. Therefore, the law fills the indicated gap with the crime of inciting to riot."
    3. A person is considered guilty of inciting to riot when he urges ten or more persons to engage in tumultuous and violent conduct of a kind likely to create public alarm.
    4. However, if he has not obtained the cooperation of at least four people, he cannot be charged with unlawful assembly.
    5. The charge of inciting to riot was added to the law to cover types of conduct which cannot be classified as either the crime of "riot" or the crime of "unlawful assembly."
    6. If he acquires the acquiescence of at least four of them, he is guilty of unlawful assembly even if the project does not materialize.

    The CORRECT answer is:

    A. 3, 5, 1, 6, 4, 2   B. 5, 1, 4, 6, 2, 3   C. 3, 4, 1, 5, 2, 6
    D. 5, 1, 4, 6, 3, 2

4. 1. If, however, the rebuttal evidence presents an issue of credibility, it is for the jury to determine whether the presumption has, in fact, been destroyed.
    2. Once sufficient evidence to the contrary is introduced, the presumption disappears from the trial.
    3. The effect of a presumption is to place the burden upon the adversary to come forward with evidence to rebut the presumption.
    4. When a presumption is overcome and ceases to exist in the case, the fact or facts which gave rise to the presumption still remain.
    5. Whether a presumption has been overcome is ordinarily a question for the court.
    6. Such information may furnish a basis for a logical inference.

    The CORRECT answer is:

    A. 4, 6, 2, 5, 1, 3   B. 3, 2, 5, 1, 4, 6   C. 5, 3, 6, 4, 2, 1
    D. 5, 4, 1, 2, 6, 3

KEY (CORRECT ANSWERS)

1. D
2. C
3. A
4. B

EXAMINATION SECTION
Preparing Written Material

Directions: The following groups of sentences need to be arranged in an order that makes sense. Select the letter preceding the sequence that represents the best sentence order. *PRINT THE LETTER OF THE CORRECT ANSWER IN THE SPACE AT THE RIGHT.*

Group 1

1. _____

1) The ostrich egg shell's legendary toughness makes it an excellent substitute for certain types of dishes or dinnerware, and in parts of Africa ostrich shells are cut and decorated for use as containers for water.

2) Since prehistoric times, people have used the enormous egg of the ostrich as a part of their diet, a practice which has required much patience and hard work—to hard-boil an ostrich egg takes about four hours.

3) Opening the egg's shell, which is rock hard and nearly an inch thick, requires heavy tools, such as a saw or chisel; from inside, a baby ostrich must use a hornlike projection on its beak as a miniature pick-axe to escape from the egg.

4) The offspring of all higher-order animals originate from single egg cells that are carried by mothers, and most of these eggs are relatively small, often microscopic.

5) The egg of the African ostrich, however, weighs a massive thirty pounds, making it the largest single cell on earth, and a common object of human curiosity and wonder.

The best order is

A.   5 4 1 2 3
B.   1 4 5 3 2
C.   4 2 3 5 1
D.   4 5 2 3 1

Group 2

1)   Typically only a few feet high on the open sea, individual tsunami have been known to circle the entire globe two or three times if their progress is not interrupted, but are not usually dangerous until they approach the shallow water that surrounds land masses.

2)   Some of the most terrifying and damaging hazards caused by earthquakes are tsunami, which were once called "tidal waves"—a poorly chosen name, since these waves have nothing to do with tides.

3)   Then a wave, slowed by the sudden drag on the lower part of its moving water column, will pile upon itself, sometimes reaching a height of over 100 feet.

4)   Tsunami (Japanese for "great harbor wave") are seismic waves that are caused by earthquakes near oceanic trenches, and once triggered, can travel up to 600 miles an hour on the open ocean.

5)   A land-shoaling tsunami is capable of extraordinary destruction; some tsunami have deposited large boats miles inland, washed out two-foot-thick seawalls, and scattered locomotive trains over long distances.

The best order is

A.   4 1 3 2 5
B.   1 3 4 2 5
C.   5 1 3 2 4
D.   2 4 1 3 5

Group 3

1) Soon, by the 1940's, jazz was the most popular type of music among American intellectuals and college students.

2) In the early days of jazz, it was considered "lowdown" music, or music that was played only in rough, disreputable bars and taverns.

3) However, jazz didn't take long to develop from early ragtime melodies into more complex, sophisticated forms, such as Charlie Parker's "bebop" style of jazz.

4) After charismatic band leaders such as Duke Ellington and Count Basie brought jazz to a larger audience, and jazz continued to evolve into more complicated forms, white audiences began to accept and even to enjoy the new American art form.

5) Many white Americans, who then dictated the tastes of society, were wary of music that was played almost exclusively in black clubs in the poorer sections of cities and towns.

The best order is

A.   5 4 3 2 1
B.   2 5 3 4 1
C.   4 5 3 1 2
D.   1 2 4 3 5

Group 4

1) Then, hanging in a windless place, the magnetized end of the needle would always point to the south.

2) The needle could then be balanced on the rim of a cup, or the edge of a fingernail, but this balancing act was hard to maintain, and the needle often fell off.

3) Other needles would point to the north, and it was important for any traveler finding his way with a compass to remember which kind of magnetized needle he was carrying.

4) To make some of the earliest compasses in recorded history, ancient Chinese "magicians" would rub a needle with a piece of magnetized iron called a lodestone.

5) A more effective method of keeping the needle free to swing with its magnetic pull was to attach a strand of silk to the center of the needle with a tiny piece of wax.

The best order is

A.   4 2 5 1 3
B.   4 3 5 2 1
C.   4 5 2 1 3
D.   4 1 3 5 2

Group 5

1)   The now-famous first mate of the *HMS Bounty*, Fletcher Christian, founded one of the world's most peculiar civilizations in 1790.

2)   The men knew they had just committed a crime for which they could be hanged, so they set sail for Pitcairn, a remote, abandoned island in the far eastern region of the Polynesian archipelago, accompanied by twelve Polynesian women and six men.

3)   In a mutiny that has become legendary, Christian and the others forced Captain Bligh into a lifeboat and set him adrift off the coast of Tonga in April of 1789.

4)   In early 1790, the *Bounty* landed at Pitcairn Island, where the men lived out the rest of their lives and founded an isolated community which to this day includes direct descendants of Christian and the other crewmen.

5)   The *Bounty*, commanded by Captain William Bligh, was in the middle of a global voyage, and Christian and his shipmates had come to the conclusion that Bligh was a reckless madman who would lead them to their deaths unless they took the ship from him.

The best order is

A.   4 5 3 2 1
B.   1 3 5 2 4
C.   1 5 3 2 4
D.   3 1 5 4 2

Group 6

1) But once the vines had been led to make orchids, the flowers had to be carefully hand-pollinated, because unpollinated orchids usually lasted less than a day, wilting and dropping off the vine before it had even become dark.

2) The Totonac farmers discovered that looping a vine back around once it reached a five-foot height on its host tree would cause the vine to flower.

3) Though they knew how to process the fruit pods and extract vanilla's flavoring agent, the Totonacs also knew that a wild vanilla vine did not produce abundant flowers or fruit.

4) Wild vines climbed along the trunks and canopies of trees, and this constant upward growth diverted most of the vine's energy to making leaves instead of the orchid flowers that, once pollinated, would produce the flavorful pods.

5) Hundreds of years before vanilla became a prized food flavoring in Europe and the Western World, the Totonac Indians of the Mexican Gulf Coast were skilled cultivators of the vanilla vine, whose fruit they literally worshipped as a goddess.

The best order is

A.   2 3 4 1 5
B.   2 4 3 1 5
C.   5 3 4 2 1
D.   3 4 1 2 5

Group 7   7. _____

1) Once airborne, the spider is at the mercy of the air currents—usually the spider takes a brief journey, traveling close to the ground, but some have been found in air samples collected as high as 10,000 feet, or been reported landing on ships far out at sea.

2) Once a young spider has hatched, it must leave the environment into which it was born as quickly as possible, in order to avoid competing with its hundreds of brothers and sisters for food.

3) The silk rises into warm air currents, and as soon as the pull feels adequate the spider lets go and drifts up into the air, suspended from the silk strand in the same way that a person might parasail.

4) To help young spiders do this, many species have adapted a practice known as "aerial dispersal," or, in common speech, "ballooning."

5) A spider that wants to leave its surroundings quickly will climb to the top of a grass stem or twig, face into the wind, and aim its back end into the air, releasing a long stream of silk from the glands near the tip of its abdomen.

The best order is

A.   5 4 2 3 1
B.   5 2 4 1 3
C.   2 5 4 3 1
D.   2 4 5 3 1

Group 8

1)   For about a year, Tycho worked at a castle in Prague with a scientist named Johannes Kepler, but their association was cut short by another argument that drove Kepler out of the castle, to later develop, on his own, the theory of planetary orbits.

2)   Tycho found life without a nose embarrassing, so he made a new nose for himself out of silver, which reportedly remained glued to his face for the rest of his life.

3)   Tycho Brahe, the 17th-century Danish astronomer, is today more famous for his odd and arrogant personality than for any contribution he has made to our knowledge of the stars and planets.

4)   Early in his career, as a student at Rostock University, Tycho got into an argument with the another student about who was the better mathematician, and the two became so angry that the argument turned into a sword fight, during which Tycho's nose was sliced off.

5)   Later in his life, Tycho's arrogance may have kept him from playing a part in one of the greatest astronomical discoveries in history: the elliptical orbits of the solar system's planets.

The best order is

A.   1 4 2 3 5
B.   4 2 3 5 1
C.   4 2 1 3 5
D.   3 4 2 5 1

Group 9

1)   The processionaries are so used to this routine that if a person picks up the end of a silk line and brings it back to the origin—creating a closed circle—the caterpillars may travel around and around for days, sometimes starving ar freezing, without changing course.

2)   Rather than relying on sight or sound, the other caterpillars, who are lined up end-to-end behind the leader, travel to and from their nests by walking on this silk line, and each will reinforce it by laying down its own marking line as it passes over.

3)   In order to insure the safety of individuals, the processionary caterpillar nests in a tree with dozens of other caterpillars, and at night, when it is safest, they all leave together in search of food.

4)   The processionary caterpillar of the European continent is a perfect illustration of how much some insect species rely on instinct in their daily routines.

5)   As they leave their nests, the processionaries form a single-file line behind a leader who spins and lays out a silk line to mark the chosen path.

The best order is

A.   4 3 5 2 1
B.   3 5 4 2 1
C.   3 5 2 1 4
D.   4 5 3 1 2

Group 10

1)   Often, the child is also given a handcrafted walker or push cart, to provide support for its first upright explorations.

2)   In traditional Indian families, a child's first steps are celebrated as a ceremonial event, rooted in ancient myth.

3)   These carts are often intricately designed to resemble the chariot of Krishna, an important figure in Indian mythology.

4)   The sound of these anklet bells is intended to mimic the footsteps of the legendary child Rama, who is celebrated in devotional songs throughout India.

5)   When the child's parents see that the child is ready to begin walking, they will fit it with specially designed ankle bracelets, adorned with gently ringing bells.

The best order is

A.   2 3 4 1 5
B.   2 5 3 1 4
C.   5 4 1 3 2
D.   5 3 2 1 4

Group 11

1)   The settlers planted Osage orange all across Middle America, and today long lines and rectangles of Osage orange trees can still be seen on the prairies, running along the former boundaries of farms that no longer exist.

2)   After trying sod walls and water-filled ditches with no success, American farmers began to look for a plant that was adaptable to prairie weather, and that could be trimmed into a hedge that was "pig-tight, horse-high, and bull-strong."

3)   The tree, so named because it bore a large (but inedible) fruit the size of an orange, was among the sturdiest and hardiest of American trees, and was prized among Native Americans for the strength and flexibility of bows which were made from its wood.

4)   The first people to practice agriculture on the American flatlands were faced with an important problem: what would they use to fence their land in a place that was almost entirely without trees or rocks?

5)   Finally, an Illinois farmer brought the settlers a tree that was native to the land between the Red and Arkansas rivers, a tree called the Osage orange.

The best order is

A.   2 1 5 3 4
B.   1 2 3 4 5
C.   4 2 5 3 1
D.   4 2 1 3 5

Group 12

1) After about ten minutes of such spirited and complicated activity, the head dancer is free to make up his or her own movements while maintaining the interest of the New Year's crowd.

2) The dancer will then perform a series of leg kicks, while at the same time operating the lion's mouth with his own hand and moving the ears and eyes by means of a string which is attached to the dancer's own mouth.

3) The most difficult role of this dance belongs to the one who controls the lion's head; this person must lead all the other "parts" of the lion through the choreographed segments of the dance.

4) The head dancer begins with a complex series of steps, alternately stepping forward with the head raised, and then retreating a few steps while lowering the head, a movement that is intended to create the impression that the lion is keeping a watchful eye for anything evil.

5) When performing a traditional Chinese New Year's lion dance, several performers must fit themselves inside a large lion costume and work together to enact different parts of the dance.

The best order is

A.   5 3 4 2 1
B.   3 4 2 5 1
C.   3 1 5 4 2
D.   4 2 3 5 1

Group 13

1) For many years the shell of the chambered nautilus was treasured in Europe for its beauty and intricacy, but collectors were unaware that they were in possession of the structure that marked a "missing link" in the evolution of marine mollusks.

2) The nautilus, however, evolved a series of enclosed chambers in its shell, and invented a new use for the structure: the shell began to serve as a buoyancy device.

3) Equipped with this new flotation device, the nautilus did not need the single, muscular foot of its predecessors, but instead developed flaps, tentacles, and a gentle form of jet propulsion that transformed it into the first mollusk able to take command of its own destiny and explore a three-dimensional world.

4) By pumping and adjusting air pressure into the chambers, the nautilus could spend the day resting on the bottom, and then rise toward the surface at night in search of food.

5) The nautilus shell looks like a large snail shell, similar to those of its ancestors, who used their shells as protective coverings while they were anchored to the sea floor.

The best order is

A.   5 2 4 1 3
B.   5 1 2 3 4
C.   1 2 5 3 4
D.   1 5 2 4 3

Group 14

1)   While France and England battled for control of the region, the Acadiens prospered on the fertile farmland, which was finally secured by England in 1713.

2)   Early in the 17th century, settlers from western France founded a colony called Acadie in what is now the Canadian province of Nova Scotia.

3)   At this time, English officials feared the presence of spies among the Acadiens who might be loyal to their French homeland, and the Acadiens were deported to spots along the Atlantic and Caribbean shores of America.

4)   The French settlers remained on this land, under English rule, for around forty years, until the beginning of the French and Indian War, another conflict between France and England.

5)   As the Acadien refugees drifted toward a final home in southern Louisiana, neighbors shortened their name to "'Cadien," and finally "Cajun," the name which the descendants of early Acadiens still call themselves.

The best order is

A.   1 4 2 3 5
B.   2 1 3 5 4
C.   2 1 4 3 5
D.   5 2 3 4 1

Group 15

1)   Traditional households in the Eastern and Western regions of Africa serve two meals a day—one at around noon, and the other in the evening.

2)   The starch is then used in the way that Americans might use a spoon, to scoop up a portion of the main dish on the person's plate.

3)   The reason for the starch's inclusion in every meal has to do with taste as well as nutrition; African food can be very spicy, and the starch is known to cool the burning effect of the main dish.

4)   When serving these meals, the main dish is usually served on individual plates, and the starch is served on a communal plate, from which diners break off a piece of bread or scoop rice or fufu in their fingers.

5)   The typical meals usually consist of a thick stew or soup as the main course, and an accompanying starch—either bread, rice, or *fufu*, a starchy grain paste similar in consistency to mashed potatoes.

The best order is

A.   5 2 3 4 1
B.   5 1 4 3 2
C.   1 4 5 3 2
D.   1 5 4 2 3

Group 16

1) In the early days of the American Midwest, Indiana settlers sometimes came together to hold an event called an apple peeling, where neighboring settlers gathered at the homestead of a host family to help prepare the hosts' apple crop for cooking, canning, and making apple butter.

2) At the beginning of the event, each peeler sat down in front of a ten- or twenty-gallon stone jar and was given a crock of apples and a paring knife.

3) Once a peeler had finished with a crock, another was placed next to him; if the peeler was an unmarried man, he kept a strict count of the number of apples he had peeled, because the winner was allowed to kiss the girl of his choice.

4) The peeling usually ended by 9:30 in the evening, when the neighbors gathered in the host family's parlor for a dance social.

5) The apples were peeled, cored, and quartered, and then placed into the jar.

The best order is

A.   1 5 3 4 2
B.   2 5 3 4 1
C.   1 2 5 3 4
D.   2 1 5 4 3

Group 17

1)   If your pet turtle is a land turtle and is native to temperate climates, it will stop eating some time in October, which should be your cue to prepare the turtle for hibernation.

2)   The box should then be covered with a wire screen, which will protect the turtle from any rodents or predators that might want to take advantage of a motionless and helpless animal.

3)   When your turtle hasn't eaten for a while and appears ready to hibernate, it should be moved to its winter quarters, most likely a cellar or garage, where the temperature should range between 40° and 45°F.

4)   Instead of feeding the turtle, you should bathe it every day in warm water, to encourage the turtle to empty its intestines in preparation for its long winter sleep.

5)   Here the turtle should be placed in a well-ventilated box whose bottom is covered with a moisture-absorbing layer of clay beads, and then filled three-fourths full with almost dry peat moss or wood chips, into which the turtle will burrow and sleep for several months.

The best order is

A.   1 4 3 5 2
B.   3 4 2 5 1
C.   3 2 4 1 5
D.   4 5 2 3 1

Group 18

1)   Once he has reached the nest, the hunter uses two sturdy bamboo poles like huge chopsticks to pull the nest away from the mountainside, into a large basket that will be lowered to people waiting below.

2)   The world's largest honeybees colonize the Nepalese mountainsides, building honeycombs as large as a person on sheer rock faces that are often hundreds of feet high.

3)   In the remote mountain country of Nepal, a small band of "honey hunt-ers" carry out a tradition so ancient that 10,000 year-old drawings of the practice have been found in the caves of Nepal.

4)   To harvest the honey and beeswax from these combs, a honey hunter climbs above the nests, lowers a long bamboo-fiber ladder over the cliff, and then climbs down.

5)   Throughout this dangerous practice, the hunter is stung repeatedly, and only the veterans, with skin that has been toughened over the years, are able to return from a hunt without the painful swelling caused by stings.

The best order is

A.   2 4 3 5 1
B.   2 4 1 5 3
C.   5 3 2 4 1
D.   3 2 4 1 5

Group 19   19. _____

1)   After the Romans left Britain, there were relentless attacks on the islands from the barbarian tribes of northern Germany—the Angles, Saxons, and Jutes.

2)   As the empire weakened, Roman soldiers withdrew from Britain, leaving behind a country that continued to practice the Christian religion that had been introduced by the Romans.

3)   Early Latin writings tell of a Christian warrior named Arturius (Arthur, in English) who led the British citizens to defeat these barbarian invaders, and brought an extended period of peace to the lands of Britain.

4)   Long ago, the British Isles were part of the far-flung Roman Empire that extended across most of Europe and into Africa and Asia.

5)   The romantic legend of King Arthur and his knights of the Round Table, one of the most popular and widespread stories of all time, appears to have some foundation in history.
The best order is

A.   5 4 3 2 1
B.   5 4 2 1 3
C.   4 5 2 3 1
D.   4 3 2 1 5

Group 20

1)   The cylinder was allowed to cool until it sould stand on its own, and then it was cut from the tube and split down the side with a single straight cut.

2)   Nineteenth-century glassmakers, who had not yet discovered the glazier's modern techniques for making panes of glass, had to create a method for converting their blown glass into flat sheets.

3)   The bubble was then pierced at the end to make a hole that opened up while the glassmaker gently spun it, creating a cylinder of glass.

4)   Turned on its side and laid on a conveyor belt, the cylinder was strengthened, or tempered, by being heated again and cooled very slowly, eventually flattening out into a single rectangular piece of glass.

5)   To do this, the glassmaker dipped the end of a long tube into melted glass and blew into the other end of the tube, creating an expanding bubble of glass.

The best order is

A.   2 5 3 4 1
B.   2 4 5 3 1
C.   3 5 2 4 1
D.   3 1 4 5 2

Group 21

1) The splints are almost always hidden, but horses are occasionally born whose splinted toes project from the leg on either side, just above the hoof.

2) The second and fourth toes remained, but shrank to thin splints of bone that fused invisibly to the horse's leg bone.

3) Horses are unique among mammals, having evolved feet that each end in what is essentially a single toe, capped by a large, sturdy hoof.

4) Julius Caesar, an emperor of ancient Rome, was said to have owned one of these three-toed horses, and considered it so special that he would not permit anyone else to ride it.

5) Though the horse's earlier ancestors possessed the traditional mammalian set of five toes on each foot, the horse has retained only its third toe; its first and fifth toes disappeared completely as the horse evolved.

The best order is

A.   3 5 2 1 4
B.   5 3 2 4 1
C.   3 2 5 1 4
D.   5 2 3 1 4

Group 22

1)   The new building materials—some of which are twenty feet long, and weigh nearly six tons—were transported to Pohnpei on rafts, and were brought into their present position by using hibiscus fiber ropes and leverage to move the stone columns upward along the inclined trunks of coconut palm trees.

2)   The ancestors built great fires to heat the stone, and then poured cool seawater on the columns, which caused the stone to contract and split along natural fracture lines.

3)   The now-abandoned enclave of Nan Madol, a group of 92 man-made islands off the shore of the Micronesian island of Pohnpei, is estimated to have been built around the year 500 A.D.

4)   The islanders say their ancestors quarried stone columns from a nearby island, where large basalt columns were formed by the cooling of molten lava.

5)   The structures of Nan Madol are remarkable for the sheer size of some of the stone "logs" or columns that were used to create the walls of the off-shore community, and today anthropologists can only rely on the information of existing local people for clues about how Nan Madol was built.

The best order is

A.   5 4 3 2 1
B.   5 3 1 4 2
C.   3 5 4 2 1
D.   3 1 4 2 5

Group 23

23. _____

1) One of the most easily manipulated substances on earth, glass can be made into ceramic tiles that are composed of over 90% air.

2) NASA's space shuttles are the first spacecraft ever designed to leave and re-enter the earth's atmosphere while remaining intact.

3) These ceramic tiles are such effective insulators that when a tile emerges from the oven in which it was fired, it can be held safely in a person's hand by the edges while its interior still glows at a temperature well over 2000° F.

4) Eventually, the engineers were led to a material that is as old as our most ancient civilizations—glass.

5) Because the temperature during atmospheric re-entry is so incredibly hot, it took NASA's engineers some time to find a substance capable of protecting the shuttles.

The best order is

A.   5 2 1 3 4
B.   2 5 4 1 3
C.   2 3 1 2 5
D.   5 4 3 1 2

Group 24

1)   The secret to teaching any parakeet to talk is patience, and the understanding that when a bird "talks," it is simply imitating what it hears, rather than putting ideas into words.

2)   You should stay just out of sight of the bird and repeat the phrase you want it to learn, for at least fifteen minutes every morning and evening.

3)   It is important to leave the bird without any words of encouragement or farewell; otherwise it might combine stray remarks or phrases, such as "Good night," with the phrase you are trying to teach it.

4)   For this reason, to train your bird to imitate your words you should keep it free of any distractions, especially other noises, while you are giving it "lessons."

5)   After your repetition, you should quietly leave the bird alone for a while, to think over what it has just heard.

The best order is

A.   1 4 2 5 3
B.   1 2 4 3 5
C.   3 2 1 5 4
D.   3 1 5 4 2

Group 25

● **1)** As a school approaches, fishermen from neighboring communities join their fishing boats together as a fleet, and string their gill nets together to make a huge fence that is held up by cork floats.

2) At a signal from the party leaders, or *nakura*, the family members pound the sides of the boats or beat the water with long poles, creating a sudden and deafening noise.

3) The fishermen work together to drag the trap into a half-circle that may reach 300 yards in diameter, and then the families move their boats to form the other half of the circle around the school of fish.

4) The school of fish flee from the commotion into the awaiting trap, where a final wall of net is thrown over the open end of the half-circle, securing the day's haul.

5) Indonesian people from the area around the Sulu islands live on the sea, in floating villages made of lashed-together or stilted homes, and make much of their living by fishing their home waters for migrating schools of snapper, scad, and other fish.

The best order is

A. 1 5 3 4 2
B. 1 2 4 3 5
C. 5 1 2 3 4
D. 5 1 3 2 4

KEY (CORRECT ANSWERS)

1. D
2. D
3. B
4. A
5. C

6. C
7. D
8. D
9. A
10. B

11. C
12. A
13. D
14. C
15. D

16. C
17. A
18. D
19. B
20. A

21. A
22. C
23. B
24. A
25. D

EXAMINATION SECTION
TEST 1

DIRECTIONS: Each question or incomplete statement is followed by several suggested answers or completions. Select the one that BEST answers the question or completes the statement. *PRINT THE LETTER OF THE CORRECT ANSWER IN THE SPACE AT THE RIGHT.*

1. The MOST important reason for a supervisor to encourage his staff to make suggestions for improving the work of the unit is that such suggestions may   1.____

    A. indicate who is the most efficient employee in the unit
    B. increase the productivity of the unit
    C. raise the morale of the employees who make the suggestions
    D. reduce the amount of supervision necessary to perform the work of the unit

2. The PRIMARY purpose of a probationary period for a new employee is to   2.____

    A. thoroughly train the new employee in his job duties
    B. permit the new employee to become adjusted to his duties
    C. determine the fitness of the new employee for the job
    D. acquaint the new employee fully with the objectives of his agency

3. A unit supervisor finds that he is spending too much time on routine tasks, and not enough time on coordinating the work of his employees.
It would be MOST advisable for this supervisor to   3.____

    A. delegate the task of work coordination to a capable subordinate
    B. eliminate some of the routine tasks that the unit is required to perform
    C. assign some of the routine tasks to his subordinates
    D. postpone the performance of routine tasks until he has achieved proper coordination of his employees' work

4. Of the following, the MOST important reason for having an office manual in looseleaf form rather than in permanent binding is that the looseleaf form   4.____

    A. facilitates the addition of new material and the removal of obsolete material
    B. permits several people to use different sections of the manual at the same time
    C. is less expensive to prepare than permanent binding
    D. is more durable than permanent binding

5. In his first discussion with an employee newly appointed to the title of Clerk in an agency, the LEAST important of the following topics for a supervisor of a clerical unit to include is the   5.____

    A. duties the subordinate is expected to perform on the job
    B. functions of the unit
    C. methods of determining standards of clerical performance
    D. nature and duration of the training the subordinate will receive on the job

6. Assume that you have been assigned to organize the files so that all the records now located in the various units in your bureau will be centrally located in a separate files unit. In setting up this system of centrally located files, you should be concerned LEAST with making certain that 6.____

    A. the material stored in the files has been checked for accuracy of content
    B. the filing system will be flexible enough to allow for possible future expansion
    C. material stored in the files can be located readily when needed
    D. the filing system will be readily understood by employees assigned to maintaining the files

7. A supervisor of a unit in a city department has just been told by a subordinate, Mr. Jones, that another employee, Mr. Smith, deliberately disobeyed an important rule of the department by taking home some confidential departmental material.
Of the following courses of action, it would be MOST advisable for the supervisor first to 7.____

    A. discuss the matter privately with both Mr. Jones and Mr. Smith at the same time
    B. call a meeting of the entire unit and discuss the matter generally without mentioning any employee by name
    C. arrange to supervise Mr. Smith's activities more closely
    D. discuss the matter privately with Mr. Smith

8. A clerk who has the choice of sending a business letter either by certified mail or by registered mail should realize that 8.____

    A. it is less expensive to send letters by certified mail than by registered mail
    B. it is safer to send letters by certified mail than by registered mail
    C. letters sent by certified mail reach their destinations faster than those sent by registered mail
    D. the person to whom a certified letter is sent is not asked to acknowledge receipt of the letter

9. If the management of a public agency wishes to retain the elasticity of youth among employees who have been with the agency for a long time, it must furnish variety and novelty of work.
To carry out the above recommendation, the BEST course of action for an agency to take is to 9.____

    A. encourage older employees to retire at the minimum retirement age
    B. vary its employees' assignments from time to time
    C. assign the routine tasks to newer and younger employees
    D. provide its employees with varied recreational activities

10. The one of the following actions which would be MOST efficient and economical for a supervisor to take to minimize the effect of seasonal fluctuations in the work load of his unit is to 10.____

    A. increase his permanent staff until it is large enough to handle the work of the busy season
    B. request the purchase of time and labor saving equipment to be used primarily during the busy season

C. lower, temporarily, the standards for quality of work performance during peak loads
D. schedule for the slow season work that it is not essential to perform during the busy season

11. A clerk in an agency should realize that each letter he sends out in response to a letter of inquiry from the public represents an expenditure of time and money by his agency. The one of the following which is the MOST valid implication of this statement is that such a clerk should

    11.____

    A. use the telephone to answer letters of inquiry directly and promptly
    B. answer mail inquiries with lengthy letters to eliminate the need for further corre-spondence
    C. prevent the accumulation of a large number of similar inquiries by answering each of these letters promptly
    D. use simple, concise language in answer to letters of inquiry

12. The forms and methods of discipline used in public agencies are as varied as the offenses which prompt disciplinary action, and range in severity from a frown of disap-proval to dismissal from the service and even to prosecution in the courts.
On the basis of this sentence, the MOST accurate of the following statements is that

    12.____

    A. the severity of disciplinary measures varies directly with the seriousness of the offenses
    B. dismissal from the service is the most severe action that can be taken by a public agency
    C. public agencies use a variety of disciplinary measures to cope with offenses
    D. public agencies sometimes administer excessive punishments

13. A well-planned training program can assist new employees to acquire the information they need to work effectively. Of the following, the information that a newly-appointed clerk would need LEAST in order to perform his work effectively is knowledge of the

    13.____

    A. acceptable ways of taking and recording telephone messages
    B. techniques of evaluating the effectiveness of office forms used in the agency
    C. methods of filing papers used in his bureau
    D. proper manner of handling visitors to the agency

14. A supervisor of a unit who is not specific when making assignments creates a dangerous source of friction, misunderstanding, and inefficiency.
The MOST valid implication of this statement is that

    14.____

    A. supervisors are usually unaware that they are creating sources of friction
    B. it is often difficult to remove sources of friction and misunderstanding
    C. a competent supervisor attempts to find a solution to each problem facing him
    D. employees will perform more efficiently if their duties are defined clearly

15. The employees' interest in the subject matter of a training course must be fully aroused if they are to derive the maximum benefits from the training.
Of the following, the LEAST effective method of arousing such interest is to

    15.____

    A. state to the employees that the subject matter of the training course will be of inter-est to mature, responsible workers
    B. point out to the employees that the training course may help them to win promotion

C. explain to the employees how the training course will help them to perform their work better
D. relate the training course to the employees' interests and previous experiences

16. The control of clerical work in a public agency appears impossible if the clerical work is regarded merely as a series of duties unrelated to the functions of the agency. However, this control becomes feasible when it is realized that clerical work links and coordinates the functions of the agency.
On the basis of this statement, the MOST accurate of the following statements is that the

    A. complexity of clerical work may not be fully understood by those assigned to control it
    B. clerical work can be readily controlled if it is coordinated by other work of the agency
    C. number of clerical tasks may be reduced by regarding coordination as the function of clerical work
    D. purposes of clerical work must be understood to make possible its proper control

16.____

17. Assume that as supervisor of a unit you are to prepare a vacation schedule for the employees in your unit.
Of the following, the factor which is LEAST important for you to consider in setting up this schedule is

    A. the vacation preferences of each employee in the unit
    B. the anticipated work load in the unit during the vacation period
    C. how well each employee has performed his work
    D. how essential a specific employee's services will be during the vacation period

17.____

18. In order to promote efficiency and economy in an agency, it is advisable for the management to systematize and standardize procedures and relationships insofar as this can be done; however, excessive routinizing which does not permit individual contributions or achievements should be avoided.
On the basis of this statement, it is MOST accurate to state that

    A. systematized procedures should be designed mainly to encourage individual achievements
    B. standardized procedures should allow for individual accomplishments
    C. systematization of procedures may not be possible in organizations which have a large variety of functions
    D. individual employees of an organization must fully accept standardized procedures if the procedures are to be effective

18.____

19. Trained employees work most efficiently and with a minimum expenditure of time and energy. Suitable equipment and definite, well-developed procedures are effective only when employees know how to use the equipment and procedures. This statement means MOST NEARLY that

    A. employees can be trained most efficiently when suitable equipment and definite procedures are used
    B. training of employees is a costly but worthwhile investment

19.____

C. suitable equipment and definite procedures are of greatest value when employees have been properly trained to use them

D. the cost of suitable equipment and definite procedures is negligible when the saving in time and energy that they bring is considered

20. Assume that your supervisor has asked you to present to him comprehensive, periodic reports on the progress that your unit is making in meeting its work goals.
For you to give your superior oral reports rather than written ones is   20._____

   A. *desirable*; it will be easier for him to transmit your oral report to his superiors
   B. *undesirable*; the oral reports will provide no permanent record to which he may refer
   C. *undesirable;* there will be less opportunity for you to discuss the oral reports with him than the written ones
   D. *desirable;* the oral reports will require little time and effort to prepare

21. Assume that an employee under your supervision complains to you that your evaluation of his work is too low.
The MOST appropriate action for you to take FIRST is to   21._____

   A. explain how you arrived at the evaluation of his work
   B. encourage him to improve the quality of his work by pointing out specifically how he can do so
   C. suggest that he appeal to an impartial higher authority if he disagrees with your evaluation
   D. point out to him specific instances in which his work has been unsatisfactory

22. The nature of the experience and education that are made a prerequisite to employment determines in large degree the training job to be done after employment begins.
On the basis of this statement, it is MOST accurate to state that   22._____

   A. the more comprehensive the experience and education required for employment the more extensive the training that is usually given after appointment
   B. the training that is given to employees depends upon the experience and education required of them before appointment
   C. employees who possess the experience and education required for employment should need little additional training after appointment
   D. the nature of the work that employees are expected to perform determines the training that they will need

23. Assume that you are preparing a report evaluating the work of a clerk who was transferred to your unit from another unit in the agency about a year ago.
Of the following, the method that would probably be MOST helpful to you in making this evaluation is to   23._____

   A. consult the evaluations this employee received from his former supervisors
   B. observe this employee at his work for a week shortly before you prepare the report
   C. examine the employee's production records and compare them with the standards set for the position
   D. obtain tactfully from his fellow employees their frank opinions of his work

24. Of the following, the CHIEF value of a flow-of-work chart to the management of an organization is its usefulness in

    A. locating the causes of delay in carrying out an operation
    B. training new employees in the performance of their duties
    C. determining the effectiveness of the employees in the organization
    D. determining the accuracy of its organization chart

24.___

25. Assume that a procedure for handling certain office forms has just been extensively revised. As supervisor of a small unit, you are to instruct your subordinates in the use of the new procedure, which is rather complicated.
Of the following, it would be LEAST helpful to your subordinates for you to

    A. compare the revised procedure with the one it has replaced
    B. state that you believe the revised procedure to be better than the one it has replaced
    C. tell them that they will probably find it difficult to learn the new procedure
    D. give only a general outline of the revised procedure at first and then follow with more detailed instructions

25.___

26. A supervisor may make assignments to his subordinates in the form of a command, a request, or a call for volunteers. It is LEAST desirable for a supervisor to make an assignment in the form of a command when

    A. a serious emergency has risen
    B. an employee objects to carrying out an assignment
    C. the assignment must be completed immediately
    D. the assignment is an unpleasant one

26.___

27. For an office supervisor to confer periodically with his subordinates in order to anticipate job problems which are likely to arise is desirable MAINLY because

    A. there will be fewer problems for which hasty decisions will have to be made
    B. some problems which are anticipated may not arise
    C. his subordinates will learn to refer the problems arising in the unit to him
    D. constant anticipation of future problems tends to raise additional problems

27.___

28. A methods improvement program might be called a war against habit.
The MOST accurate implication of this statement is that

    A. routine handling of routine office assignments should be discouraged
    B. standardization of office procedures may encourage employees to form inefficient work habits
    C. employees tend to continue the use of existing procedures, even when such procedures are inefficient
    D. procedures should be changed constantly to prevent them from becoming habits

28.___

29. An office supervisor may give either a written or an oral order to his subordinates when making an assignment.
Of the following, it would be MOST appropriate for a supervisor to issue an order in writing when

    A. a large number of two-page reports must be stapled together before the end of the day
    B. the assignment is to be completed within two hours after it is issued to his subordinates

29.___

C. his subordinates have completed an identical assignment the day before
D. several entries must be made on a form at varying intervals of time by different clerks

30. A supervisor should always remember that the instruction or training of new employees is most effective if it is given when and where it is needed.
On the basis of this statement, it is MOST appropriate to conclude that

    A. the new employee should be trained to handle any aspect of his work at the time he starts his job
    B. the new employee should be given the training essential to get him started and additional training when he requires it
    C. an employee who has received excessive training will be just as ineffective as one who has received inadequate training
    D. a new employee is trained most effectively by his own supervisor

30._____

31. Some employees see an agency training program as a threat. Of the following, the MOST likely reason for such an employee attitude toward training is that the employees involved feel that

    A. some trainers are incompetent
    B. training rarely solves real work-a-day problems
    C. training may attempt to change comfortable behavior patterns
    D. training sessions are boring

31._____

32. Of the following, the CHIEF characteristic which distinguishes a good supervisor from a poor supervisor is the good supervisor's

    A. ability to favorably impress others
    B. unwillingness to accept monotony or routine
    C. ability to deal constructively with problem situations
    D. strong drive to overcome opposition

32._____

33. Of the following, the MAIN disadvantage of on-the-job training is that, generally,

    A. special equipment may be needed
    B. production may be slowed down
    C. the instructor must maintain an individual relationship with the trainee
    D. the on-the-job instructor must be better qualified than the classroom instructor

33._____

34. All of the following are correct methods for a supervisor to use in connection with employee discipline EXCEPT:

    A. Trying not to be too lenient or too harsh
    B. Informing employees of the rules and the penalties for violations of the rules
    C. Imposing discipline immediately after the violation is discovered
    D. Making sure, when you apply discipline, that the employee understands that you do not want to do it

34._____

35. Of the following, the MAIN reason for a supervisor to establish standard procedures for his unit is to

    A. increase the motivation of his subordinates
    B. make it easier for the subordinates to submit to authority

35._____

C. reduce the number of times that his subordinates have to consult him
D. reduce the number of mistakes that his subordinates will make

36. When delegating responsibility for an assignment to a subordinate, it is MOST important that you   36.___

    A. retain all authority necessary to complete the assignment
    B. make yourself generally available for consultation with the subordinate
    C. inform your superiors that you are no longer responsible for the assignment
    D. decrease the number of subordinates whom you have to supervise

37. You, as a unit head, have been asked to submit budget estimates of staff, equipment, and supplies in terms of programs for your unit for the coming fiscal year.
In addition to their use in planning, such unit budget estimates can be BEST used to   37.___

    A. reveal excessive costs in operations
    B. justify increases in the debt limit
    C. analyze employee salary adjustments
    D. predict the success of future programs

38. Because higher status is important to many employees, they will often make an effort to achieve it as an end in itself.
Of the following, the BEST course of action for the supervisor to take on the basis of the preceding statement is to   38.___

    A. attach higher status to that behavior of subordinates which is directed toward reaching the goals of the organization
    B. avoid showing sympathy toward subordinates' wishes for increased wages, improved working conditions, or other benefits
    C. foster interpersonal competitiveness among subordinates so that personal friendliness is replaced by the desire to protect individual status
    D. reprimand subordinates whenever their work is in some way unsatisfactory in order to adjust their status accordingly

39. Assume that a large office in a certain organization operates long hours and is thus on two shifts with a slight overlap. Those employees, including supervisors, who are most productive are given their choice of shifts. The earlier shift is considered preferable by most employees.
As a result of this method of assignment, which of the following is MOST likely to result?   39.___

    A. Most non-supervisory employees will be assigned to the late shift; most supervisors will be assigned to the early shift.
    B. Most supervisors will be assigned to the late shift; most non-supervisory employees will be assigned to the early shift.
    C. The early shift will be more productive than the late shift.
    D. The late shift will be more productive than the early shift.

40. Assume that a supervisor of a unit in which the employees are of average friendliness tells a newly hired employee on her first day that her co-workers are very friendly. The other employees hear his remarks to the new employee. Which of the following is the MOST likely result of this action of the supervisor? The   40.___

A. newly hired employee will tend to feel less friendly than if the supervisor had said nothing
B. newly hired employee will tend to believe that her co-workers are very friendly
C. other employees will tend to feel less friendly toward one another
D. other employees will tend to see the newly hired employee as insincerely friendly

41. A recent study of employee absenteeism showed that, although unscheduled absence for part of a week is relatively high for young employees, unscheduled absence for a full week is low. However, although full-week unscheduled absence is least frequent for the youngest employees, the frequency of such absence increases as the age of employees increases.
Which of the following statements is the MOST logical explanation for the greater full-week absenteeism among older employees?

    A. Older employees are more likely to be males.
    B. Older employees are more likely to have more relatively serious illnesses.
    C. Younger employees are more likely to take longer vacations.
    D. Younger employees are more likely to be newly hired.

41.____

42. An employee can be motivated to fulfill his needs as he sees them. He is not motivated by what others think he ought to have, but what he himself wants.
Which of the following statements follows MOST logically from the foregoing viewpoint?

    A. A person's different traits may be separately classified, but they are all part of one system comprising a whole person.
    B. Every job, however simple, entitles the person who does it to proper respect and recognition of his unique aspirations and abilities.
    C. No matter what equipment and facilities an organization has, they cannot be put to use except by people who have been motivated.
    D. To an observer, a person's needs may be unrealistic, but they are still controlling.

42.____

43. Assume that you are a supervisor of a unit which is about to start work on an urgent job. One of your subordinates starts to talk to you about the urgent job but seems not to be saying what is really on his mind.
What is the BEST thing for you to say under these circumstances?

    A. I'm not sure I understand. Can you explain that?
    B. Please come to the point. We haven't got all day.
    C. What is it? Can't you see I'm busy?
    D. Haven't you got work to do? What do you want?

43.____

44. Assume that you have recently been assigned to a new subordinate. You have explained to this subordinate how to fill out certain forms which will constitute the major portion of her job. After the first day, you find that she has filled out the forms correctly but has not completed as many as most other workers normally complete in a day.
Of the following, the MOST appropriate action for you to take is to

    A. tell the subordinate how many forms she is expected to complete
    B. instruct the subordinate in the correct method of filling out the forms
    C. monitor the subordinate's production to see if she improves
    D. reassign the job of filling out the forms to a more experienced worker in the unit

44.____

45. One of the problems commonly met by the supervisor is the *touchy* employee who imag-   45.___
ines slights when none is intended.
Of the following, the BEST way to deal with such an employee is to

    A.   ignore him until he sees the error of his behavior
    B.   frequently reassure him of his value as a person
    C.   advise him that oversensitive people rarely get promoted
    D.   issue written instructions to him to avoid misinterpretation

46. The understanding supervisor should recognize that a certain amount of anxiety is com-   46.___
mon to all newly hired employees.
If you are a supervisor of a unit and a newly-hired employee has been assigned to you,
you can usually assume that the LEAST likely worry that the new employee has is
worry about

    A.   the job and the standards required in the job
    B.   his acceptance by the other people in your unit
    C.   the difficulty of advancing to top positions in the agency
    D.   your fairness in evaluating his work

47. In assigning work to subordinates, it is often desirable for you to tell them the overall or   47.___
ultimate objective of the assignment.
Of the following, the BEST reason for telling them the objective is that it will

    A.   assure them that you know what you are doing
    B.   eliminate most of the possible complaints about the assignment
    C.   give them confidence in their ability to do the assignment
    D.   help them to make decisions consistent with the objective

48. Assume that the regular 8-hour working day of a laborer is from 8 A.M. to 5 P.M., with an   48.___
hour off for lunch. He earns a regular hourly rate of pay for these 8 hours and is paid at
the rate of time-and-a-half for each hour worked after his regular working day.
If, on a certain day, he works from 8 A.M. to 6 P.M., with an hour off for lunch, and
earns $99.76, his regular hourly rate of pay is

    A. $8.50   B. $9.00   C. $10.50   D. $11.50

49. Two clerical units, X and Y, each having a different number of clerks, are assigned to file   49.___
registration cards. It takes Unit X, which contains 8 clerks, 21 days to file the same number of cards that Unit Y can file, in 28 days. It is also a fact that Unit X can file 174,528
cards in 72 days.
Assuming that all the clerks in both units work at the same rate of speed, the number
of cards which can be filed by Unit Y in 144 days, if 4 more clerks are added to the staff
of Unit Y, is MOST NEARLY

    A. 349,000   B. 436,000   C. 523,000   D. 669,000

50. Each side of a square room which is being used as an office measures 66 feet. The floor 50.____
of the room is divided by six traffic aisles, each aisle being six feet wide. Three of the
aisles run parallel to the east and west sides of the room and the other three run parallel
to the north and south sides of the room, so that the remaining floor space is divided into
16 equal sections.
If all of the floor space which is not being used for traffic aisles is occupied by desk and
chair sets, and each set takes up 24 square feet of floor space, the number of desk
and chair sets in the room is

   A. 80   B. 64   C. 36   D. 96

KEY (CORRECT ANSWERS)

1. B	11. D	21. A	31. C	41. B
2. C	12. C	22. B	32. C	42. D
3. C	13. B	23. C	33. B	43. A
4. A	14. D	24. A	34. D	44. C
5. C	15. A	25. C	35. C	45. B
6. A	16. B	26. D	36. B	46. C
7. D	17. C	27. A	37. A	47. D
8. A	18. B	28. C	38. A	48. C
9. B	19. C	29. D	39. C	49. B
10. D	20. B	30. B	40. B	50. D

TEST 2

DIRECTIONS: Each question or incomplete statement is followed by several suggested answers or completions. Select the one that BEST answers the question or completes the statement. *PRINT THE LETTER OF THE CORRECT ANSWER IN THE SPACE AT THE RIGHT.*

Questions 1-6.

DIRECTIONS: Each of Questions 1 through 6 consists of statements which contains one word that is incorrectly used because it is not in keeping with the meaning that the statement is evidently intended to convey. For each of these questions, you are to select the incorrectly used word and substitute for it one of the words lettered A, B, C, D, or E, which helps BEST to convey the meaning of the quotation. In the space at the right, write the letter preceding the word which should be substituted for the incorrectly used word.

1. The determination of the value of the employees in an organization is fundamental not only as a guide to the administration of salary schedules, promotion, demotion, and transfer, but also as a means of keeping the working force on its toes and of checking the originality of selection methods.

    A. effectiveness   B. initiation   C. increasing
    D. system   E. none of these

1.____

2. No training course can operate to full advantage without job descriptions which indicate training requirements so that those parts of the job requiring the most training can be carefully analyzed before the training course is completed.

    A. improved   B. started   C. least
    D. meet   E. predict

2.____

3. The criticism that supervisors are discriminatory in their treatment of subordinates is to some extent untrue, for the subjective nature of many supervisory decisions makes it probable that many employees who have not progressed will attribute their lack of success to supervisory favoritism.

    A. knowledge   B. unavoidable   C. detrimental
    D. deny   E. indifferent

3.____

4. Some demands of employees will, if satisfied, result in a decrease in production. Some supervisors largely ignore such demands on the part of their subordinates, and instead, concentrate on the direction and production of work; others yield to such requests and thereby emphasize the production goals and objectives set by higher levels of authority.

    A. responsibility   B. increase   C. neglect
    D. value   E. morale

4.____

5. It is generally accepted that when a supervisor is at least as well informed about the work of his unit as are his subordinates, he will fail to win their approval, which is essential to him if he is to supervise the unit effectively.

    A. unimportant   B. preferable   C. unless
    D. attention   E. poorly

5.____

6. The laws of almost every state permit certain classes of persons to vote despite their absence from home at election time. Sometimes this privilege is given only to members of the armed forces of the United States, though more commonly it is extended to all voters whose occupations make absence preventable.

    6.____

    A. prohibition   B. sanction   C. intangible
    D. avoidable   E. necessary

Questions 7-25.

DIRECTIONS: Each of Questions 7 through 25 consists of a word in capitals followed by four suggested meanings of the word. Print in the space at the right the number preceding the word which means MOST NEARLY the same as the word in capitals.

7. ALLEVIATE   7.____

    A. soothe   B. make difficult
    C. introduce gradually   D. complicate

8. OSTENSIBLE   8.____

    A. intelligent   B. successful
    C. necessary   D. apparent

9. REDUNDANT   9.____

    A. excessive   B. sufficient
    C. logical   D. unpopular

10. TANTAMOUNT   10.____

    A. superior   B. opposed
    C. equivalent   D. disturbing

11. EXPUNGE   11.____

    A. leap over   B. erase
    C. exploit   D. concede fully

12. VESTIGE   12.____

    A. ancestor   B. basis   C. choice   D. remnant

13. CONTENTION   13.____

    A. modification   B. controversy
    C. cooperation   D. sight

14. PROSCRIBE   14.____

    A. recommend   B. avoid   C. provide   D. prohibit

15. URBANE   15.____

    A. polite   B. adjacent to a city
    C. modern   D. common

16. INADVERTENT   16.____

    A. unknown   B. public
    C. deliberate   D. unintentional

17. EVINCE   17.____

    A. enlarge   B. conceal   C. display   D. evade

18. SIMULATE   18.____

    A. attempt   B. imitate   C. elude   D. arouse

19. PRECLUDE   19.____

    A. prevent   B. contribute generously
    C. simplify   D. prepare gradually

20. REMISS   20.____

    A. careless   B. absent   C. guilty   D. thorough

21. CONTRIVE   21.____

    A. contract   B. restrict   C. scheme   D. contribute

22. MALIGN   22.____

    A. mislead deliberately   B. slander
    C. flatter excessively   D. disturb

23. CONTINGENT   23.____

    A. loose   B. intentional
    C. dependent   D. forceful

24. SPORADIC   24.____

    A. quick   B. alert   C. destroyed   D. scattered

25. COALESCE   25.____

    A. unite   B. reveal   C. abate   D. freeze

Questions 26-33.

DIRECTIONS: Each of Questions 26 through 33 consists of three sentences lettered A, B, and C. In each of these questions, one of the sentences may contain an error in grammar, sentence structure, or punctuation, or all three sentences may be correct. If one of the sentences in a question contains an error in grammar, sentence structure, or punctuation, write in the space at the right, the letter preceding the sentence which contains the error. If all three sentences are correct, write the letter D.

26. A. Mr. Smith appears to be less competent than I in performing these duties.   26.____
     B. The supervisor spoke to the employee, who had made the error, but did not reprimand him.
     C. When he found the book lying on the table, he immediately notified the owner.

27. A. Being locked in the desk, we were certain that the papers would not be taken.   27.____
     B. It wasn't I who dictated the telegram; I believe it was Eleanor.
     C. You should interview whoever comes to the office today.

28. A. The clerk was instructed to set the machine on the table before summoning the   28.____
        manager.
     B. He said that he was not familiar with those kind of activities.
     C. A box of pencils, in addition to erasers and blotters, was included in the shipment
        of supplies.

29. A. The supervisor remarked, "Assigning an employee to the proper type of work is not   29.____
        always easy."
     B. The employer found that each of the applicants were qualified to perform the
        duties of the position.
     C. Any competent student is permitted to take this course if he obtains the consent
        of the instructor.

30. A. The prize was awarded to the employee whom the judges believed to be most   30.____
        deserving.
     B. Since the instructor believes this book is the better of the two, he is recommend-
        ing it for use in the school.
     C. It was obvious to the employees that the completion of the task by the scheduled
        date would require their working overtime.

31. A. These reports have been typed by employees who were trained by a capable   31.____
        supervisor.
     B. This employee is as old, if not older, than any other employee in the department.
     C. Running rapidly down the street, the manager soon reached the office.

32. A. It is believed, that if these terms are accepted, the building can be constructed at a   32.____
        reasonable cost.
     B. The typists are seated in the large office; the stenographers, in the small office.
     C. Either the operators or the machines are at fault.

33. A. Mr. Jones, who is the head of the agency, will come today to discuss the plans for   33.____
        the new training program.
     B. The reason the report is not finished is that the supply of paper is exhausted.
     C. It is now obvious that neither of the two employees is able to handle this type of
        assignment.

Questions 34-40.

DIRECTIONS: Each of Questions 34 through 40 consists of four words. In each question, one
              of the words may be spelled incorrectly or all four words may be spelled cor-
              rectly. If one of the words in a question is spelled incorrectly, print in the space
              at the right the letter preceding the word which is spelled incorrectly. If all four
              words are spelled correctly, print the letter E.

34. A. guarantee   B. committment   34.____
     C. mitigate   D. publicly

35. A. prerogative   B. apprise   35.____
     C. extrordinary   D. continual

36. A. arrogant   B. handicapped   36.____
     C. judicious   D. perennial

37. A. permissable   B. deceive   37.____
     C. innumerable   D. retrieve

38. A. notable   B. allegiance   38.____
     C. reimburse   D. illegal

39. A. interceed   B. benefited   39.____
     C. analogous   D. altogether

40. A. seizure   B. irrelevant   40.____
     C. inordinate   D. dissapproved

Questions 41-50.

DIRECTIONS: Questions 41 through 50 are based on the Production Record table shown on the following page for the Information Unit in Agency X for the work week ended Friday, December 6. The table shows, for each employee, the quantity of each type of work performed and the percentage of the work week spent in performing each type of work.

NOTE: Assume that each employee works 7 hours a day and 5 days a week, making a total of 35 hours for the work week.

PRODUCTION RECORD - INFORMATION UNIT IN AGENCY X
(For the work week ended Friday, December 6)

Number of

	Papers Filed	Sheets Proofread	Visitors Received	Envelopes Addressed
Miss Agar	3120	33	178	752
Mr. Brun	1565	59	252	724
Miss Case	2142	62	214	426
Mr. Dale	4259	29	144	1132
Miss Earl	2054	58	212	878
Mr. Farr	1610	69	245	621
Miss Glen	2390	57	230	790
Mr. Hope	3425	32	176	805
Miss Iver	3736	56	148	650
Mr. Joad	3212	55	181	495

Percentage of Work Week Spent On

	Filing Papers	Proof-reading	Receiving Visitors	Addressing Envelopes	Performing Miscellaneous Work
Miss Agar	30%	9%	34%	11%	16%
Mr . Brun	13%	15%	52%	10%	10%
Miss Case	23%	18%	38%	6%	15%
Mr. Dale	50%	7%	17%	16%	10%
Miss Earl	24%	14%	37%	14%	11%
Mr. Farr	16%	19%	48%	8%	9%
Miss Glen	27%	12%	42%	12%	7%
Mr . Hope	38%	8%	32%	13%	9%
Miss Iver	43%	13%	24%	9%	11%
Mr. Joad	33%	11%	36%	7%	13%

41. For the week, the average amount of time which the employees spent in proofreading was MOST NEARLY _____ hours.   41._____

    A. 3.1   B. 3.6   C. 4.4   D. 5.1

42. The average number of visitors received daily by an employee was MOST NEARLY   42._____

    A. 40   B. 57   C. 198   D. 395

43. Of the following employees, the one who addressed envelopes at the FASTEST rate was   43._____

    A. Miss Agar   B. Mr. Brun
    C. Miss Case   D. Mr. Dale

44. Mr. Farr's rate of filing papers was MOST NEARLY _____ pages per minute.   44._____

    A. 2   B. 1.7   C. 5   D. 12

45. The average number of hours that Mr. Brun spent daily on receiving visitors exceeded the average number of hours that Miss Iver spent daily on the same type of work by MOST NEARLY _____ hours.   45._____

    A. 2   B. 3   C. 4   D. 5

46. Miss Earl worked at a faster rate than Miss Glen in   46._____

    A. filing papers   B. proofreading sheets
    C. receiving visitors   D. addressing envelopes

47. Mr. Joad's rate of filing papers _____ Miss Iver's rate of filing papers by approximately _____%.   47._____

    A. was less than; 10   B. exceeded; 33
    C. C. was less than; 16   D. exceeded; 12

48. Assume that in the following week, Miss Case is instructed to increase the percentage of   48.____
her time spent in filing papers to 35%.
If she continued to file papers at the same rate as she did for the week ended December 6, the number of additional papers that she filed the following week was MOST NEARLY

   A. 3260   B. 5400   C. 250   D. 1120

49. Assume that in the following week, Mr. Hope increased his weekly total of envelopes   49.____
addressed to 1092.
If he continued to spend the same amount of time on this assignment as he did for the week ended December 6, the increase in his rate of addressing envelopes the following week was MOST NEARLY _____ envelopes per hour.

   A. 15   B. 65   C. 155   D. 240

50. Assume that in the following week, Miss Agar and Mr. Dale spent 3 and 9 hours less,   50.____
respectively, on filing papers than they had spent for the week ended December 6, without changing their rates of work.
The total number of papers filed during the following week by both Miss Agar and Mr. Dale was MOST NEARLY

   A. 4235   B. 4295   C. 4315   D. 4370

KEY (CORRECT ANSWERS)

1.	A	11.	B	21.	C	31.	B	41.	C
2.	B	12.	D	22.	B	32.	A	42.	A
3.	B	13.	B	23.	C	33.	D	43.	B
4.	C	14.	D	24.	D	34.	B	44.	C
5.	C	15.	A	25.	A	35.	C	45.	A
6.	E	16.	D	26.	B	36.	E	46.	C
7.	A	17.	C	27.	A	37.	A	47.	D
8.	D	18.	B	28.	B	38.	E	48.	D
9.	A	19.	A	29.	B	39.	A	49.	B
10.	C	20.	A	30.	D	40.	D	50.	B

EXAMINATION SECTION
TEST 1

DIRECTIONS: Each question or incomplete statement is followed by several suggested answers or completions. Select the one that BEST answers the question or completes the statement. *PRINT THE LETTER OF THE CORRECT ANSWER IN THE SPACE AT THE RIGHT.*

1. As head of the filing unit in your department, you have been receiving complaints that material which should be in the files cannot be located. On investigating this matter, you find that one of your new clerks has been careless in placing material in the files. The BEST of the following actions which you might take FIRST is to

    A. admonish this clerk and tell him that he will be given a below-average service rating if his carelessness continues
    B. remind this clerk that he is a probationary employee and that his services may be terminated at the end of his probationary period if his carelessness continues
    C. call the attention of this clerk to the effects of filing and impress upon him the necessity for accuracy in filing
    D. give this clerk another assignment in the unit where accuracy is less essential

1.____

2. The GREATEST amount of improvement in the efficiency and morale of a unit will be brought about by the supervisor who

    A. reminds his employees constantly that they must follow departmental regulations
    B. frequently praises an employee in the presence of the other employees in the unit
    C. invariably gives mild reproof and constructive criticism to subordinates when he discovers that they have made a mistake
    D. assigns duties to employees in conformance with their abilities and interests as far as practicable

2.____

3. Assume that you are the supervisor of a unit which performs routine clerical work. For you to encourage your subordinates to make suggestions for increasing the efficiency of the unit is

    A. *undesirable;* employees who perform routine work may resent having additional duties and responsibilities assigned to them
    B. *desirable;* by presenting criticism of each other's work, the employees may develop a competitive spirit and in this way increase their efficiency
    C. *undesirable*; the employees may conclude that the supervisor is not capable of efficiently supervising the work of the unit
    D. *desirable*; increased interest in their assignment may be acquired by the employees, and the work of the unit may be performed more efficiently

3.____

4. The MOST accurate of the following statements regarding the chief purpose for maintaining a perpetual inventory of office supplies is that it

    A. eliminates the necessity for making a physical inventory of office supplies
    B. makes available at all times a record of the balance of office supplies on hand
    C. reduces the amount of clerical work required in distributing supplies
    D. reduces the amount of paper work involved in requisitioning supplies

4.____

5. Of the following, a centralized filing system is LEAST suitable for filing   5.___

    A. material which is confidential in nature
    B. routine correspondence
    C. periodic reports of the divisions of the department
    D. material used by several divisions of the department

6. Form letters should be used mainly when   6.___

    A. an office has to reply to a great many similar inquiries
    B. the type of correspondence varies widely
    C. it is necessary to have letters which are well-phrased and grammatically correct
    D. letters of inquiry have to be answered as soon as possible after they are received

7. Assume that you have recommended that one of your subordinates be given a below-average service rating. The subordinate disagreed with your recommendation and requests that you discuss the service rating report with him.
In taking up this matter with the employee, the BEST of the following procedures for you to follow is to   7.___

    A. discuss the general standards of evaluation you have used, rather than his specific deficiencies
    B. tell him that it would be too time-consuming to discuss his report with him, but inform him that objective standards were used in evaluating all employees and that the reports will be reviewed by an impartial board which will make any changes it deems necessary
    C. explain the standards of evaluation you have used and discuss this subordinate's work with him in relation to these standards
    D. point out to your subordinate that you are in a better position than he to compare his work with that of the other employees in your unit

8. Suppose that you are assigned to prepare a form from which certain information will be posted in a ledger. It would be MOST helpful to the person posting the information in the ledger if, in designing the form, you were to   8.___

    A. use the same color paper for both the form and the ledger
    B. make the form the same size as the pages of the ledger
    C. have the information on the form in the same order as that used in the ledger
    D. include in the form a box which is to be initialed when the data on the form have been posted in the ledger

9. A misplaced record is a lost record.
Of the following, the MOST valid implication of this statement in regard to office work is that   9.___

    A. all records in an office should be filed in strict alphabetical order
    B. accuracy in filing is essential
    C. only one method of filing should be used throughout the office
    D. files should be locked when not in use

10. John Smith is applying for a provisional appointment as a clerk in your department. He   10.____
presents a letter of recommendation from a former employer stating: *John Smith was
rarely late or absents he has a very pleasing manner, and never got into an argument
with his fellow employees.*
The above information concerning this applicant

    A. proves clearly that he produces more work than the average employee
    B. indicates that he was probably attempting to conceal his inefficiency from his
former employer
    C. presents no conclusive evidence of his ability to do clerical work
    D. indicates clearly that with additional training he will make a good supervisor

11. It is not possible to draw a hard and fast line between training courses for greater effi-   11.____
ciency on the present job.
This statement means MOST NEARLY that

    A. to be worthwhile, a training course should prepare the employee for promotion as
well as for greater efficiency on the present job
    B. training courses should be designed only to increase employee efficiency on the
present job
    C. training courses should be given only to employees who are competing for promo-
tion
    D. by attending a training course for promotion, employees may become more effi-
cient in their present work

12. Approximate figures serve as well as exact figures to indicate trends and make compari-   12.____
sons.
Of the following, the MOST accurate statement on the basis of this statement is that

    A. it takes less time to obtain approximate figures than exact figures
    B. exact figures are rarely used as they require too much computation
    C. for certain purposes, approximate figures are as revealing as exact figures
    D. approximate figures can usually be used in place of exact figures

13. Suppose that you are placed in charge of a unit in your department. You find that many of   13.____
the employees have been disregarding the staff regulation requiring employees to be at
their desks at 9:05 A.M.
Of the following, the LEAST desirable course of action for you to take would be to

    A. call a meeting of the staff and explain why it is essential that all employees be at
their desks at 9:05 A.M.
    B. post conspicuously on the bulletin board a notice calling the employees' attention
to the frequent violation of this regulation and requesting them to observe this regulation
    C. recommend an above-average service rating for all employees who consistently
comply with this regulation, provided their work is satisfactory
    D. summon the offenders and explain to them how their violation of this regulation
results in decreasing the efficiency of the unit

14. Suppose that certain office responsibilities require you to be frequently absent from the unit you supervise. You have, therefore, decided to designate one of your staff members to act as unit head in your absence.
Of the following factors, the one which is MOST important in selecting the employee best fitted for this assignment is his

    A. manner and personal appearance
    B. estimated ability to perform work of a supervisory nature
    C. ability to perform his present duties
    D. relative seniority in the service

15. One of the assignments in the unit you supervise is the checking of a list of 500 unalphabetized names against an alphabetical 5x8 card index containing several thousand names. The clerk performing this task is to make sure that there is a card in the file for each name on the list.
The one of the following which you should suggest as the BEST procedure for the clerk to follow is for him to

    A. rewrite the names on the list in alphabetical order, look for the corresponding card in the file, and place a check mark next to each name on the list for which he finds a card
    B. take each name on the list in turn, look for the corresponding card in the file, and place a check mark in the corner of each card he finds
    C. go through all the cards in the file in consecutive order and place a check mark next to each name on the list for which he finds a card
    D. take each name on the list in turn, look for the corresponding card in the file, and place a check mark next to each name on the list for which he finds a card

16. Suppose that you are in charge of a unit which maintains a rather intricate filing system. A new file clerk has been added to your staff.
Of the following assignments that may be given to this clerk, the one which requires the LEAST amount of knowledge of the filing system is

    A. placing material in the files
    B. removing papers from the files
    C. classifying and coding material for filing
    D. keeping a record of material taken from, and returned to, the files

17. In undertaking to improve the method of performing a certain job or operation, the new office manager should first ascertain the

    A. present method of performing the job
    B. purpose of the job
    C. number and titles of employees assigned to the job
    D. methods used by other agencies to perform the same kind of job

18. The proofreading of a large number of papers has been assigned to two clerks. These clerks have been instructed to indicate all necessary corrections on a slip of paper, attach this correction slip to the papers, and send them to the typist for correction.
Of the following additional steps that might be taken before sending the papers to the xerox operator, the BEST one is that the

A. clerks should proofread each paper in its entirety after the corrections have been made on it
B. typist should make the necessary corrections and return the correction slip and the corrected papers to the clerks; the clerks should then examine the papers to see that all the requested corrections have been made properly
C. typist should make the necessary corrections, placing a check mark opposite each correction noted on the correction slip; she should then review the correction slip to make sure that no correction has been omitted
D. typist should make the necessary corrections, place a check mark opposite each correction noted on the correction slip, and return the papers and the correction slip to the clerks; the clerks should then review the correction slip to make sure that a check mark has been placed opposite each item on the correction slip

19. Suppose you are the supervisor of a unit in a department. You notice that a clerk with long service in the department is arguing with a recently appointed clerk regarding the procedure to be followed in performing a certain task. Each is convinced he is right. The argument is disturbing the other employees.
Of the following, the BEST action for you to take in dealing with this problem is to

19._____

A. call the clerks to your desk, discuss the matter with them, and then state which procedure is the correct one
B. support the employee with the longer service, for to do otherwise will impair the morale of the office
C. call the clerks to your desk and tell them to settle their differences without disturbing the others
D. order the clerks to discontinue their argument immediately and to bring the matter up at the next staff conference, where the staff will determine which procedure is the correct one

20. Assume that you devised a new procedure which you expected would result in a substantial reduction in the amount of paper used in performing the work of the unit you supervise. After trying out this new procedure in your unit for several weeks, you find that the quantity of paper saved is considerably less than you anticipated.
Of the following, the BEST action for you to take first is to

20._____

A. inform your staff that they are probably using paper unnecessarily, and that in view of the current paper shortage, you expect them to conserve paper as much as possible
B. suspend the use of this new procedure until you can discover why it has not worked out as you anticipated
C. invite your subordinates to submit suggestions as to how the procedure may be improved
D. analyze the various processes involved in the new procedure to determine whether there are any factors which you may have overlooked

21. Assume that you are the head of the bureau of information in a department. You are faced with the problem of replacing the clerk assigned to the information desk.
Of the following available employees, the one who should be given the assignment is

21._____

A. John Jones, a new clerk who specialized in English at college and recently received a Master of Arts degree; at present, he has no permanent assignment
B. Mary Smith, an excellent stenographer who has had much experience as secretary to one of the bureau heads; she is intelligent, pleasant in manner, and learns quickly
C. Richard Roe, a clerk who has been rated as *tactful, dependable,* and *resourceful* by the various bureau heads who have prepared his service rating reports during the four years that he has been in the department
D. Jane Doe, who is a diligent typist when she works alone but who disturbs the other typists by her constant stream of chatter when she works near them

22. The one of the following which is the MOST accurate statement regarding routine operations in an office is that   22.____

    A. routine assignments should not last more than two or three days each week
    B. methods for performing routine work should be standardized as much as is practicable
    C. routine work performed by one employee should be checked by another employee
    D. changes in the procedures of a unit should not affect the existing routine operations of the unit

23. Modern management realizes the importance of sound personnel practices in business   23.____
administration. It has found that production is largely dependent upon the effective utilization of an employee's interests, capabilities, and skills.
Of the following, the MOST logical implication of the above statement is that

    A. there should be one bureau in each business organization to take charge of both production and personnel administration
    B. production cannot be increased without the utilization of a sound personnel policy
    C. production will increase if the number of persons assigned to work in a business organization is increased
    D. maximum efficiency in an organization cannot be achieved without proper placement of employees

24. One of the stenographers under your supervision has completed all of her assignments,   24.____
and there is no additional typing to be done.
It would be LEAST desirable for you to suggest that she

    A. straighten up the supply cabinet to improve its appearance
    B. check the files for material that is surplus or outdated
    C. read the daily newspaper to keep up with current events
    D. practice shorthand or typing to improve her speed

25. Of the following, the BEST way for a supervisor to determine when further on-the-job   25.____
training in a particular work area is needed is by

    A. evaluating the employees' work performance
    B. asking the employees
    C. determining the ratio of idle time to total work time
    D. classifying the jobs in the work area

Questions 26-30.

DIRECTIONS: Each of Questions 26 through 30 consists of a statement containing five words in capital letters. One of these words in capital letters is not in keeping with the meaning which the statement is evidently intended to carry. The five words in capital letters in each statement are reprinted after the statement. In the space at the right, write the letter preceding the one of the five words which does most to spoil the true meaning of the statement.

26. Within each major DIVISION in a properly set-up public or private organization, provision   26.____
is made so that each NECESSARY activity is CARED for and lines of AUTHORITY and
responsibility are clear-cut and INFINITE.

    A. division   B. necessary   C. cared
    D. authority   E. infinite

27. In public service, the scale of salaries paid must be INCIDENTAL to the services ren-   27.____
dered, with due CONSIDERATION for the attraction of the desired MANPOWER and for
the MAINTENANCE of a standard of living COMMENSURATE with the work to be performed.

    A. incidental   B. consideration   C. manpower
    D. maintenance   E. commensurate

28. An understanding of the AIMS of an organization by the staff will AID greatly in increas-   28.____
ing the DEMAND of the correspondence work of the office, and will to a large extent
DETERMINE the NATURE of the correspondence.

    A. aims   B. aid   C. demand
    D. determine   E. nature

29. BECAUSE the Civil Service Commission strongly feels that the MERIT system is a key   29.____
factor in the MAINTENANCE of democratic government, it has adopted as one of its
major DEFENSES the progressive democratization of its own PROCEDURES in dealing
with candidates for positions in the public service.

    A. Because   B. merit   C. maintenance
    D. defenses   E. procedures

30. Retirement and pensions systems are ESSENTIAL not only to provide employees with a   30.____
means of support in the future, but also to prevent longevity and CHARITABLE
considerations from UPSETTING the PROMOTIONAL opportunities for RETIRED members of the career service.

    A. essential   B. charitable   C. upsetting
    D. promotional   E. retired

31. Suppose that the amount of money spent for supplies in 2005 for a division of a depart-   31.____
ment was $15,650. This represented an increase of 12% over the amount spent for sup-
plies for this division in 2004. The amount of money spent for supplies for this division in
2004 was MOST NEARLY

    A. $13,973   B. $13,772   C. $14,346   D. $13,872

32. Suppose that a group of five clerks have been assigned to insert 24,000 letters into envelopes. The clerks perform this work at the following rates of speed: Clerk A, 1100 letters an hour; Clerk B, 1450 letters an hour; Clerk C, 1200 letters an hour; Clerk D, 1300 letters an hour; Clerk E, 1250 letters an hour. At the end of two hours of work, Clerks C and D are assigned to another task. Fron the time that Clerks C and D were taken off the assignment, the number of hours required for the remaining clerks to complete this assignment is   32.____

 A. less than 3 hours
 B. 3 hours
 C. more than 3 hours, but less than 4 hours
 D. more than 4 hours

33. The employees were SKEPTICAL about the usefulness of the new procedure. The word *skeptical,* as used in this sentence, means MOST NEARLY   33.____

 A. enthusiastic
 C. doubtful
 B. indifferent
 D. misinformed

34. He presented ABSTRUSE reasons in defense of his proposal. The word *abstruse,* as used in this sentence, means MOST NEARLY   34.____

 A. unnecessary under the circumstances
 B. apparently without merit or value
 C. hard to be understood
 D. obviously sound

35. A program of AUSTERITY is in effect in many countries. The word *austerity,* as used in this sentence, means MOST NEARLY   35.____

 A. rigorous self-restraint
 C. rugged individualism
 B. military censorship
 D. self-indulgence

36. The terms of the contract were ABROGATED at the last meeting of the board. The *word abrogated,* as used in this sentence, means MOST NEARLY   36.____

 A. discussed
 C. agreed upon
 B. summarized
 D. annulled

37. The enforcement of STRINGENT regulations is a difficult task. The word *stringent,* as used in this sentence, means MOST NEARLY   37.____

 A. unreasonable
 C. unpopular
 B. strict
 D. obscure

38. You should not DISPARAGE the value of his suggestions. The word *disparage,* as used in this sentence, means MOST NEARLY   38.____

 A. ignore
 C. belittle
 B. exaggerate
 D. reveal

39. The employee's conduct was considered REPREHENSIBLE by his superior. The word *reprehensible,* as used in this sentence, means MOST NEARLY   39.____

A. worthy of reward or honor
B. in accordance with rules and regulations
C. detrimental to efficiency and morale
D. deserving of censure or rebuke

40. He said he would EMULATE the persistence of his co-workers. The word *emulate,* as used in this sentence, means MOST NEARLY

    A. strive to equal
    C. encourage
    B. acknowledge
    D. attach no significance to

40.____

41. The revised regulations on discipline contained several MITIGATING provisions. The word *mitigating,* as used in this sentence, means MOST NEARLY

    A. making more effective
    C. rendering less harsh
    B. containing contradictions
    D. producing much criticism

41.____

42. The arrival of the inspector at the office on that day was FORTUITOUS. The word *fortuitous,* as used in this sentence, means MOST NEARLY

    A. accidental
    C. prearranged
    B. unfortunate
    D. desirable

42.____

43. A clerk who comes across the abbreviation *et.al.* should know that it stands for

    A. for example
    B. and others
    C. disposition pending
    D. and every month thereafter

43.____

Questions 44-50.

DIRECTIONS: Questions 44 through 50 are to be answered SOLELY on the basis of the following information.

Assume that the following regulations were established in your department to compute vacation allowances for services rendered by its employees during the period from June 1, 2007 through May 31, 2008. You are to determine the answer to each of the questions on the basis of these regulations.

<u>VACATION REGULATIONS</u>
(For the Period June 1, 2007 - May 31, 2008)

The vacation allowance for this period is to be taken after May 31, 2008.

Standard Vacation Allowance
    Permanent per annum employees shall be granted 25 days vacation for a full year's service in such status. Employees who have served less than a full year in a permanent per annum status shall receive an allowance of 2 days for each month of such service.
    Per diem employees shall be granted 1 1/2 days vacation for each month of service in such status.
    Temporary employees shall be granted one day of vacation for each month of service in such status.

No vacation credit shall accrue to employees for the time they are on leave of absence.

Additional Allowance for Overtime

One day of vacation allowance shall be granted for each seven hours of accrued overtime. Where there is a balance of less than 7 hours of accrued overtime, one-half day of vacation shall be granted for each 3 1/2 hours of such overtime. In no case shall the additional vacation allowed for accrued overtime exceed 6 days.

Deductions for Excessive Sick Leave

Sick leave allowance for all employees, regardless of length of service, shall be 12 days for the year. Sick leave taken in excess of 12 days shall be deducted from vacation allowance. Any unused sick leave balance will be canceled on May 31, 2008.

Deductions for Excessive Lateness

Deductions for excessive lateness shall be made from vacation allowance in accordance with the following schedule:

No. of Times Late	Deduction from Vacation Allowance
0-50	no deduction
51-60	1/2 day
61-70	1 day
71-80	1 1/2 days
81-90	2 days
91-100	2 1/2 days
101-120	4 days
121-140	6 days
141 or over	penalty to be determined by Secretary of Department

Unused Vacation

Unused vacation allowance earned during the previous year shall be added to the current vacation allowance, up to a maximum of twelve days.

Note that the vacation allowances are for services rendered during the year ending May 31, 2008, and that computations for all employees are to be made as of that date.

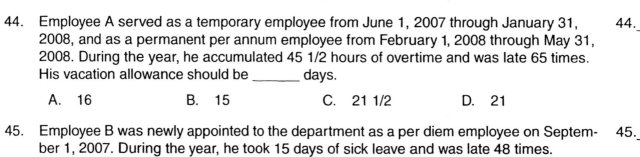

44. Employee A served as a temporary employee from June 1, 2007 through January 31, 2008, and as a permanent per annum employee from February 1, 2008 through May 31, 2008. During the year, he accumulated 45 1/2 hours of overtime and was late 65 times. His vacation allowance should be _____ days. 44.__

   A. 16   B. 15   C. 21 1/2   D. 21

45. Employee B was newly appointed to the department as a per diem employee on September 1, 2007. During the year, he took 15 days of sick leave and was late 48 times. His vacation allowance should be _____ days. 45.__

A. less than 10   B. 10 1/2
C. 15   D. 12 1/2

46. Employee C has been a permanent per annum employee throughout the year. He had 15   46._____
days of vacation due him from the previous year. During the year, he was late 85 times,
he took 10 days of sick leave, and he accumulated 38 1/2 hours of overtime.
His vacation allowance should be _____ days.

   A. 38 1/2   B. 42 1/2
   C. 40 1/2   D. more than 43

47. Employee D was newly appointed to the department as a permanent per annum   47._____
employee on July 1, 2007. He was on leave of absence from December 1, 2007 through
February 28, 2008. During the year, he took 6 days of sick leave, he was late 70 times,
and he accumulated 21 hours of overtime.
His vacation allowance should be _____ days.

   A. 24   B. 18   C. 17 1/2   D. 19 1/2

48. Employee E served as a per diem employee from June 1, 2007 through July 31, 2007,   48._____
and as a permanent per annum employee from August 1, 2007 to May 31, 2008. He had
6 days of vacation due him from the previous year. During the year, he took 13 days of
sick leave, he accumulated 70 hours of overtime, and he was late 132 times.
His vacation allowance should be _____ days.

   A. less than 29   B. 29
   C. 30   D. more than 30

49. The maximum total vacation allowance which a permanent per annum employee can   49._____
have due him by May 31, 2008 is _____ days.

   A. 43   B. 25   C. 31   D. 37

50. An employee who has served as a temporary employee for 6 months and as a perma-   50._____
nent per annum employee for 6 months will earn exactly

   A. two-thirds as much vacation as an employee who has been on a permanent per
      annum basis for the whole year
   B. as much vacation as an employee who has been on a per diem basis for the whole
      year
   C. as much vacation as an employee who has been on a per diem basis for 4 months
      and on a permanent per annum basis for 8 months
   D. as much vacation as an employee who has been on a per diem basis for 8 months
      and on a permanent per annum basis for 5 months

Questions 51-60.

DIRECTIONS: Each of Questions 51 through 60 may be classified under one of the following
              four categories:

              A. faulty because of incorrect grammar or sentence structure
              B. faulty because of incorrect punctuation
              C. faulty because of incorrect spelling
              D. correct

Examine each sentence carefully to determine under which of the above four options it is best classified. Then, in the space at the right, write the letter preceding the option which is the BEST of the four suggested above. Each incorrect sentence contains but one type of error. Consider a sentence to be correct if it contains none of the types of errors mentioned, even though there may be other correct ways of expressing the same thought.

51. Although the department's supply of scratch pads and stationery have diminished considerably, the allotment for our division has not been reduced.   51.____

52. You have not told us whom you wish to designate as your secretary.   52.____

53. Upon reading the minutes of the last meeting, the new proposal was taken up for consideration.   53.____

54. Before beginning the discussion, we locked the door as a precautionery measure.   54.____

55. The supervisor remarked, "Only those clerks, who perform routine work, are permitted to take a rest period."   55.____

56. Not only will this duplicating machine make accurate copies, but it will also produce a quantity of work equal to fifteen transcribing typists.   56.____

57. "Mr. Jones," said the supervisor, "we regret our inability to grant you an extention of your leave of absence."   57.____

58. Although the employees find the work monotonous and fatigueing, they rarely complain.   58.____

59. We completed the tabulation of the receipts on time despite the fact that Miss Smith our fastest operator was absent for over a week.   59.____

60. The reaction of the employees who attended the meeting, as well as the reaction of those who did not attend, indicates clearly that the schedule is satisfactory to everyone concerned.   60.____

KEY (CORRECT ANSWERS)

1.	C	16.	D	31.	A	46.	C
2.	D	17.	B	32.	B	47.	B
3.	D	18.	B	33.	C	48.	A
4.	B	19.	A	34.	C	49.	A
5.	A	20.	D	35.	A	50.	B
6.	A	21.	C	36.	D	51.	A
7.	C	22.	B	37.	B	52.	D
8.	C	23.	D	38.	C	53.	A
9.	B	24.	C	39.	D	54.	C
10.	C	25.	A	40.	A	55.	B
11.	D	26.	E	41.	C	56.	A
12.	C	27.	A	42.	A	57.	C
13.	C	28.	C	43.	B	58.	C
14.	B	29.	D	44.	D	59.	B
15.	D	30.	E	45.	B	60.	D

EXAMINATION SECTION

TEST 1

DIRECTIONS: Each question or incomplete statement is followed by several suggested answers or completions. Select the one that BEST answers the question or completes the statement. *PRINT THE LETTER OF THE CORRECT ANSWER IN THE SPACE AT THE RIGHT.*

1. There is considerable rivalry among employees in a certain   1.___
   department over location of desks. It is the practice of
   the supervisor to assign desks without any predetermined
   plan. The supervisor is reconsidering his procedure.
   In assigning desks, PRIMARY consideration should *ordinarily*
   be given to
      A. past practices
      B. flow of work
      C. employee seniority
      D. social relations among employees

2. Assume that, when you tell some of the workers under your   2.___
   supervision that the jobs they prepare have too many
   errors, they contend that the performance is sufficient
   and that they obtain more satisfaction from their jobs
   if they do not have to be as concerned about errors.
   These workers are
      A. *correct*, because the ultimate objective should be job
         satisfaction
      B. *incorrect*, because every job should be performed
         perfectly
      C. *correct*, because they do not create the jobs themselves
      D. *incorrect*, because their satisfaction is not the only
         consideration

3. Which of the following possible conditions is LEAST likely   3.___
   to represent a hindrance to effective communication?
      A. The importance of a situation may not be apparent.
      B. Words may mean different things to different people.
      C. The recipient of a communication may respond to it,
         sometimes unfavorably.
      D. Communications may affect the self-interest of those
         communicating.

4. You are revising the way in which your unit handles records. 4.___
   One of the BEST ways to make sure that the change will be
   implemented with a minimum of difficulty is to
      A. allow everyone on the staff who is affected by the
         change to have an opportunity to contribute their
         ideas to the new procedures
      B. advise only the key members of your staff in advance
         so that they can help you enforce the new method when
         it is implemented
      C. give the assignment of implementation to the newest
         member of the unit
      D. issue a memorandum announcing the change and stating
         that complaints will not be tolerated

5. One of your assistants is quite obviously having personal   5.___
   problems that are affecting his work performance.
   As a supervisor, it would be MOST appropriate for you to
   A. avoid any inquiry into the nature of the situation
      since this is not one of your responsibilities
   B. avoid any discussion of personal problems on the basis
      that there is nothing you could do about them anyhow
   C. help the employee obtain appropriate help with these
      problems
   D. advise the employee that personal problems cannot be
      considered when evaluating work performance

6. The key to improving communication with your staff and   6.___
   other departments is the development of an awareness of
   the importance of communication.
   Which of the following is NOT a good suggestion for
   developing this awareness?
   A. Be willing to look at your own attitude toward how
      you communicate
   B. Be sensitive and receptive to reactions to what you
      tell people
   C. Make sure all communication is in writing
   D. When giving your subordinates directions, try to put
      yourself in their place and see if your instructions
      still make sense

7. One of the assistants on your staff has neglected to com-   7.___
   plete an important assignment on schedule. You feel that
   a reprimand is necessary.
   When speaking to the employee, it would *usually* be LEAST
   desirable to
   A. display your anger to show the employee how strongly
      you feel about the problem
   B. ask several questions about the reasons for failure
      to complete the assignment
   C. take the employee aside so that nobody else is present
      when you discuss the matter
   D. give the employee as much time as he needs to explain
      exactly what happened

8. One of the techniques of management often used by super-   8.___
   visors is performance appraisal.
   Which of the following is NOT one of the objectives of
   performance appraisal?
   A. Improve staff performance
   B. Determine individual training needs
   C. Improve organizational structure
   D. Set standards and performance criteria for employees

9. An employee can be motivated to fulfill his needs as he   9.___
   sees them. He is not motivated by what others think he
   ought to have, but what he himself wants.
   Which of the following statements follows MOST logically
   from the foregoing viewpoint?
   A. A person's different traits may be separately classi-
      fied, but they are all part of one system comprising
      a whole person.

B. Every job, however simple, entitles the person who
does it to proper respect and recognition of his
unique aspirations and abilities.
C. No matter what equipment and facilities an organization
has, they cannot be put to use except by people who
have been motivated.
D. To an observer, a person's need may be unrealistic
but they are still controlling.

10. When delegating responsibility for an assignment to a sub-   10.___
ordinate, it is MOST important that you
   A. retain all authority necessary to complete the assign-
      ment
   B. make yourself generally available for consultation
      with the subordinate
   C. inform your superiors that you are no longer respon-
      sible for the assignment
   D. decrease the number of subordinates whom you have
      to supervise

11. One of the things that can ruin morale in a work group is   11.___
the failure to exercise judgment in the assignment of over-
time work to your subordinates.
Of the following, the MOST desirable supervisory practice
in assigning overtime work is to
   A. rotate overtime on a uniform basis among all your
      subordinates
   B. assign overtime to those who are *moonlighting* after
      regular work hours
   C. rotate overtime as much as possible among employees
      willing to work additional hours
   D. assign overtime to those employees who take frequent
      long weekend vacations

12. The consistent delegation of authority by you to experi-   12.___
enced and reliable subordinates in your work group is
GENERALLY considered
   A. *undesirable*,because your authority in the group may
      be threatened by an unscrupulous subordinate
   B. *undesirable*,because it demonstrates that you cannot
      handle your own workload
   C. *desirable*,because it shows that you believe that you
      have been accepted by your subordinates
   D. *desirable*,because the development of subordinates
      creates opportunities for assuming broader responsi-
      bilities yourself

13. The MOST effective way for you to deal with a false rumor   13.___
circulating among your subordinates is to
   A. have a trusted subordinate start a counter-rumor
   B. recommend disciplinary action against the *rumor mongers*
   C. point out to your subordinates that rumors degrade
      both listener and initiator
   D. furnish your subordinates with sufficient authentic
      information

14. Two of your subordinates tell you about a mistake they   14.___
    made in a report that has already been sent to top manage-
    ment.
    Which of the following questions is *most likely* to elicit
    the MOST valuable information from your subordinates?
       A. Who is responsible?
       B. How can we explain this to top management?
       C. How did it happen?
       D. Why weren't you more careful?

15. Assume that you are responsible for implementing major   15.___
    changes in work flow patterns and personnel assignments
    in the unit of which you are in charge.
    The one of the following actions which is MOST likely to
    secure the willing cooperation of those persons who will
    have to change their assignment is
       A. having the top administrators of the agency urge their
          cooperation at a group meeting
       B. issuing very detailed and carefully planned instructions
          to the affected employees regarding the changes
       C. integrating employee participation into the planning
          of the changes
       D. reminding the affected employees that career advance-
          ment depends upon compliance with organizational
          objectives

16. Of the following, the BEST reason for using face-to-face   16.___
    communication instead of written communication is that
    face-to-face communication
       A. allows for immediate feedback
       B. is more credible
       C. enables greater use of detail and illustration
       D. is more polite

17. Of the following, the MOST likely disadvantage of giving   17.___
    detailed instructions when assigning a task to a subordinate
    is that such instructions may
       A. conflict with the subordinate's ideas of how the task
          should be done
       B. reduce standardization of work performance
       C. cause confusion in the mind of the subordinate
       D. inhibit the development of new procedures by the
          subordinate

18. Assume that you are a supervisor of a unit consisting of   18.___
    a number of subordinates and that one subordinate, whose
    work is otherwise acceptable, keeps on making errors in
    one particular task assigned to him in rotation. This
    task consists of routine duties which all your subordinates
    should be able to perform.
    Of the following, the BEST way for you to handle this
    situation is to
       A. do the task yourself when the erring employee is
          scheduled to perform it and assign this employee
          other duties

    B. reorganize work assignments so that the task in
       question is no longer performed in rotation but
       assigned full-time to your most capable subordinate
    C. find out why this subordinate keeps on making the
       errors in question and see that he learns how to do
       the task properly
    D. maintain a well-documented record of such errors
       and, when the evidence is overwhelming, recommend
       appropriate disciplinary action

19. It is better for an employee to report and be responsible   19.___
    directly to several supervisors than to report and be
    responsible to only one supervisor.
    This statement directly CONTRADICTS the supervisory prin-
    ciple *generally* known as
    A. span of control   B. unity of command
    C. delegation of authority D. accountability

20. The one of the following which would MOST likely lead to   20.___
    friction among clerks in a unit is for the unit supervisor
    to
    A. defend the actions of his clerks when discussing them
       with his own supervisor
    B. praise each of his clerks *in confidence* as the best
       clerk in the unit
    C. get his men to work together as a team in completing
       the work of the unit
    D. consider the point of view of the rank and file clerks
       when assigning unpleasant tasks

21. You become aware that one of the employees you supervise   21.___
    has failed to follow correct procedure and has been per-
    mitting various reports to be prepared, typed, and trans-
    mitted improperly.
    The BEST action for you to take FIRST in this situation
    is to
    A. order the employee to review all departmental proce-
       dures and reprimand him for having violated them
    B. warn the employee that he must obey regulations
       because uniformity is essential for effective
       departmental operation
    C. confer with the employee both about his failure to
       follow regulations and his reasons for doing so
    D. watch the employee's work very closely in the future
       but say nothing about this violation

22. When routine procedures covering the ordinary work of an   22.___
    office are established, the supervisor of the office tends
    to be relieved of the need to
    A. make repeated decisions on the handling of recurring
       similar situations
    B. check the accuracy of the work completed by his sub-
       ordinates
    C. train his subordinates in new work procedures
    D. plan and schedule the work of his office

23. Of the following, the method which would be LEAST helpful   23.____
to a supervisor in effectively applying the principles of
on-the-job safety to the daily work of his unit is for him
to
   A. initiate corrections of unsafe layouts of equipment
      and unsafe work processes
   B. take charge of operations that are not routine to
      make certain that safety precautions are established
      and observed
   C. continue to *talk safety* and promote safety conscious-
      ness in his subordinates
   D. figure the cost of all accidents which could possibly
      occur on the job

24. A clerk is assigned to serve as receptionist for a large   24.____
and busy office. Although many members of the public
visit this office, the clerk often experiences periods of
time in which he has nothing to do.
In these circumstances, the MOST advisable of the following
actions for the supervisor to take is to
   A. assign a number of relatively low priority clerical
      jobs to the receptionist to do in the slow periods
   B. regularly rotate this assignment so that all of the
      clerks experience this lighter workload
   C. assign the receptionist job as part of the duties of
      a number of clerks whose desks are nearest the
      reception room
   D. overlook the situation since most of the receptionist's
      time is spent in performing a necessary and meaningful
      function

25. For a supervisor to require all workers in a gang to   25.____
produce the same amount of work on a particular day is
   A. *advisable* since it will prove that the supervisor
      plays no favorites
   B. *fair* since all the workers are receiving approximately
      the same salary, their output should be equivalent
   C. *not necessary* since the fast workers will compensate
      for the slow workers
   D. *not realistic* since individual differences in abilities
      and work assignment must be taken into consideration

KEY (CORRECT ANSWERS)

1. B	6. C	11. C	16. A	21. C
2. D	7. A	12. D	17. D	22. A
3. C	8. C	13. D	18. C	23. D
4. A	9. D	14. C	19. B	24. A
5. C	10. B	15. C	20. B	25. D

TEST 2

1. A certain employee has a poor tardiness record and was recently warned by her supervisor that certain disciplinary action would be taken if she were late again.
   If she comes in late again, in private, the supervisor should
     A. speak to her right away and, after listening to her explanation, impose any warranted discipline quietly and impersonally
     B. speak to her during the next afternoon; this will prevent an emotional confrontation and will give her time to fully realize the consequences of her actions
     C. speak to her right away and make an attempt to soften the necessary disciplinary action by apologizing for having to use discipline
     D. speak to her right away and remind her, in no uncertain terms, of the difficulty she has caused him by her continual lateness before imposing any warranted discipline

2. Choosing supervisors strictly from within a particular working section GENERALLY is
     A. *desirable*, primarily because the budgeting necessary for promotion is substantially decreased
     B. *undesirable* because personal preferences will always outweigh merit
     C. *desirable*, primarily because a good worker within that section will be a good supervisor for that section alone
     D. *undesirable*, primarily because the pool of candidates will be severely limited

3. Of the following, a supervisor interested in setting quality standards for work produced by his subordinates PRIMARILY should
     A. consult with supervisors in other organizations to determine the range of acceptable standards
     B. institute a quality improvement program and set standards at the point where quality levels off at desirable levels
     C. establish an ad hoc committee comprised of a representative sample of workers to set firm and exacting standards
     D. consult the QUALITY STANDARDS HANDBOOK which predetermines with mathematical precision the level of quality the work should meet

1.___

2.___

3.___

4. The supervisor who would be MOST likely to have poor   4.___
   control over his subordinates is the one who
       A. goes to unusually great lengths to try to win their
          approval
       B. pitches in with the work they are doing during periods
          of heavy workload when no extra help can be obtained
       C. encourages and helps his subordinates toward advance-
          ment
       D. considers suggestions from his subordinates before
          establishing new work procedures involving them

5. Suppose that a clerk who has been transferred to your   5.___
   office from another division in your agency because of
   difficulties with his supervisor has been placed under
   your supervision.
   The BEST course of action for you to take FIRST is to
       A. instruct the clerk in the duties he will be performing
          in your office and make him feel *wanted* in his new
          position
       B. analyze the clerk's past grievance to determine if
          the transfer was the best solution to the problem
       C. advise him of the difficulties his former supervisor
          had with other employees and encourage him not to feel
          bad about the transfer
       D. warn him that you will not tolerate any nonsense and
          that he will be under continuous surveillance while
          assigned to you

6. A certain office supervisor takes the initiative to   6.___
   represent his employees' interests related to working
   conditions, opportunities for advancement, etc. to his
   own supervisor and the administrative levels of the agency.
   This supervisor's actions will MOST probably have the effect
   of
       A. preventing employees from developing individual
          initiative in their work goals
       B. encouraging employees to compete openly for the
          special attention of their supervisor
       C. depriving employees of the opportunity to be repre-
          sented by persons and/or unions of their own choosing
       D. building employee confidence in their supervisor and
          a spirit of cooperation in their work

7. Suppose that you have been promoted, assigned as a super- 7.___
   visor of a certain unit, and asked to reorganize its functions so that specific routine procedures can be established.
   Before deciding which routines to establish, the FIRST of
   the following steps you should take is to
       A. decide who will perform each task in the routine
       B. determine the purpose to be served by each routine
          procedure
       C. outline the sequence of steps in each routine to be
          established
       D. calculate if more staff will be needed to carry out
          the new procedures

8. The establishment of a centralized typing pool to service   8.___
   the various units in an organization is MOST likely to be
   worthwhile when there is
   A. wide fluctuation from time to time in the needs of
      the various units for typing service
   B. a large volume of typing work to be done in each of
      the units
   C. a need by each unit for different kinds of typing
      service
   D. a training program in operation to develop and main-
      tain typing skills

9. A newly appointed supervisor should learn as much as   9.___
   possible about the backgrounds of his subordinates.
   This statement is GENERALLY correct because
   A. knowing their backgrounds assures they will be treated
      objectively, equally, and without favor
   B. effective handling of subordinates is based upon
      knowledge of their individual differences
   C. subordinates perform more efficiently under one
      supervisor than under another
   D. subordinates have confidence in a supervisor who
      knows all about them

10. The use of electronic computers in modern businesses has   10.___
    produced many changes in office and information management.
    Of the following, it would NOT be correct to state that
    computer utilization
    A. broadens the scope of managerial and supervisory
       authority
    B. establishes uniformity in the processing and reporting
       of information
    C. cuts costs by reducing the personnel needed for
       efficient office operation
    D. supplies management rapidly with up-to-date data to
       facilitate decision-making

11. The CHIEF advantage of having a single, large open office   11.___
    instead of small partitioned ones for a clerical unit is
    that the single, large open office
    A. affords privacy without isolation for all office
       workers not directly dealing with the public
    B. assures the smoother, more continuous inter-office
       flow of work that is essential for efficient work
       production
    C. facilitates the office supervisor's visual control
       over and communication with his subordinates
    D. permits a more decorative and functional arrangement
       of office furniture and machines

12. When a supervisor provides a new employee with the informa- 12.___
    tion necessary for a basic knowledge and a general under-
    standing of practices and procedures of the agency, he is
    applying the type of training GENERALLY known as ____ training.
    A. pre-employment   B. induction
    C. on-the-job   D. supervisory

13. Assume that a large office in a certain organization   13.___
    operates long hours and is thus on two shifts with a
    slight overlap. Those employees, including supervisors,
    who are most productive are given their choice of shifts.
    The earlier shift is considered preferable by most employees.
    As a result of this method of assignment, which of the
    following is MOST likely to result?
     A. Most non-supervisory employees will be assigned to
        the late shift; most supervisors will be assigned to
        the early shift.
     B. Most supervisors will be assigned to the late shift;
        most non-supervisory employees will be assigned to
        the early shift.
     C. The early shift will be more productive than the late
        shift.
     D. The late shift will be more productive than the early
        shift.

14. Assume that a supervisor of a unit in which the employees   14.___
    are of average friendliness tells a newly-hired employee
    on her first day that her co-workers are very friendly.
    The other employees her his remarks to the new employee.
    Which of the following is the MOST likely result of this
    action of the supervisor?
    The
     A. newly-hired employee will tend to feel less friendly
        than if the supervisor had said nothing
     B. newly-hired employee will tend to believe that her
        co-workers are very friendly
     C. other employees will tend to feel less friendly
        toward one another
     D. other employees will tend to see the newly-hired
        employee as insincerely friendly

15. A recent study of employee absenteeism showed that, al-   15.___
    though unscheduled absence for part of a week is relatively
    high for young employees, unscheduled absence for a full
    week is low. However, although full-week unscheduled
    absence is least frequent for the youngest employees, the
    frequency of such absence increases as the age of
    employees increase.
    Which of the following statements is the MOST logical
    explanation for the greater full-week absenteeism among
    older employees?
     A. Older employees are more likely to be males.
     B. Older employees are more likely to have more relatively
        serious illnesses.
     C. Younger employees are more likely to take longer
        vacations.
     D. Younger employees are more likely to be newly-hired.

16. Because higher status is important to many employees, they   16.___
    will often make an effort to achieve it as an end in itself.
    Of the following, the BEST course of action for the super-
    visor to take on the basis of the preceding statement is to
     A. attach higher status to that behavior of subordinates
        which is directed toward reaching the goals of the
        organization

B. avoid showing sympathy toward subordinates' wishes for increased wages, improved working conditions, or other benefits
C. foster interpersonal competitiveness among subordinates so that personal friendliness is replaced by the desire to protect individual status
D. reprimand subordinates whenever their work is in some way unsatisfactory in order to adjust their status accordingly

17. From the viewpoint of an office supervisor, the BEST of the following reasons for distributing the incoming mail before the beginning of the regular work day is that   17.___
    A. distribution can be handled quickly and most efficiently at that time
    B. distribution later in the day may be distracting to or interfere with other employees
    C. the employees who distribute the mail can then perform other tasks during the rest of the day
    D. office activities for the day based on the mail may then be started promptly

18. Suppose you are the head of a unit with 10 staff members who are located in several different rooms.   18.___
    If you want to inform your staff of a minor change in procedure, the BEST and LEAST expensive way of doing so would *usually* be to
    A. send a mimeographed copy to each staff member
    B. call a special staff meeting and announce the change
    C. circulate a memo, having each staff member initial it
    D. have a clerk tell each member of the staff about the change

19. Suppose you are the supervisor of the mailroom of a large city agency where the mail received daily is opened by machine, sorted by hand for delivery, and time-stamped. Letters and any enclosures are removed from envelopes and stapled together before distribution. One of your newest clerks asks you what should be done when a letter makes reference to an enclosure but no enclosure is in the envelope.   19.___
    You should tell him that, in this situation, the BEST procedure is to
    A. make an entry of the sender's name and address in the *missing enclosures* file and forward the letter to its proper destination
    B. return the letter to its sender, attaching a request for the missing enclosure
    C. put the letter aside until a proper investigation may be made concerning the missing enclosure
    D. route the letter to the person for whom it is intended, noting the absence of the enclosure on the letter-margin

20. James Jones is applying for a provisional appointment as a   20.____
clerk in your department. He presents a letter of recom-
mendation from a former employer stating: *James Jones
was rarely late or absent; he has a very pleasing manner
and never got into an argument with his fellow employees.*
The above information concerning this applicant
   A. proves clearly that he produces more work than the
     average employee
   B. indicates that he was probably attempting to conceal
     his inefficiency from his former employer
   C. presents no conclusive evidence of his ability to
     do clerical work
   D. indicates clearly that with additional training he
     will make a good supervisor

21. In the past, Mr. T, one of your subordinates, had been   21.____
generally withdrawn and suspicious of others, but he had
produced acceptable work. However, Mr. T has lately
started to get into arguments with his fellow workers
during which he displays intense rage. Friction between
this subordinate and the others in your unit is mounting,
and the unit's work is suffering.
Of the following, which would be the BEST way for you to
handle this situation?
   A. Rearrange work schedules and assignments so as to
     give Mr. T no cause for complaint
   B. Instruct the other workers to avoid Mr. T and not
     to respond to any abuse
   C. Hold a unit meeting and appeal for harmony and sub-
     mergence of individual differences in the interest
     of work
   D. Maintain a record of incidents and explore with
     Mr. T the possibility of seeking professional help

22. You are responsible for seeing to it that your unit is   22.____
functioning properly in the accomplishment of its
budgeted goals.
Which of the following will provide the LEAST information
on how well you are accomplishing such goals?
   A. Measurement of employee performance
   B. Identification of alternative goals
   C. Detection of employee errors
   D. Preparation of unit reports

23. Some employees see an agency training program as a threat.   23.____
Of the following, the MOST likely reason for such an
employee attitude toward training is that the employees
involved feel that
   A. some trainers are incompetent
   B. training rarely solves real work-a-day problems
   C. training may attempt to change comfortable behavior
     patterns
   D. training sessions are boring

24. All of the following are correct methods for a supervisor   24.___
to use in connection with employee discipline EXCEPT
    A. trying not to be too lenient or too harsh
    B. informing employees of the rules and the penalties
       for violations of the rules
    C. imposing discipline immediately after the violation
       is discovered
    D. making sure, when you apply discipline, that the
       employee understands that you do not want to do it

25. Of the following, the MAIN reason for a supervisor to   25.___
establish standard procedures for his unit is to
    A. increase the motivation of his subordinates
    B. make it easier for the subordinates to submit to
       authority
    C. reduce the number of times that his subordinates
       have to consult him
    D. reduce the number of mistakes that his subordinates
       will make

KEY (CORRECT ANSWERS)

1. A		11. C	
2. D		12. B	
3. B		13. C	
4. A		14. B	
5. A		15. B	
6. D		16. A	
7. B		17. D	
8. A		18. C	
9. B		19. D	
10. A		20. C	

21. D
22. B
23. C
24. D
25. C

PHILOSOPHY, PRINCIPLES, PRACTICES, AND TECHNICS
OF
SUPERVISION, ADMINISTRATION, MANAGEMENT, AND ORGANIZATION

CONTENTS

CONTENTS (cont'd)

PHILOSOPHY, PRINCIPLES, PRACTICES, AND TECHNICS
OF
SUPERVISION, ADMINISTRATION, MANAGEMENT, AND ORGANIZATION

I. MEANING OF SUPERVISION

The extension of the democratic philosophy has been accompanied by an extension in the scope of supervision. Modern leaders and supervisors no longer think of supervision in the narrow sense of being confined chiefly to visiting employees, supplying materials, or rating the staff. They regard supervision as being intimately related to all the concerned agencies of society, they speak of the supervisor's function in terms of "growth", rather than the "improvement," of employees

This modern concept of supervision may be defined as follows:

Supervision is leadership and the development of leadership within groups which are cooperatively engaged in inspection, research, training, guidance and evaluation.

II. THE OLD AND THE NEW SUPERVISION

TRADITIONAL	*MODERN*
1. Inspection	1. Study and analysis
2. Focused on the employee	2. Focused on aims, materials, methods, supervisors, employees, environment
3. Visitation	3. Demonstrations, intervisitation, workshops, directed reading, bulletins, etc.
4. Random and haphazard	4. Definitely organized and planned (scientific)
5. Imposed and authoritarian	5. Cooperative and democratic
6. One person usually	6. Many persons involved (creative)

III. THE EIGHT (8) BASIC PRINCIPLES OF THE NEW SUPERVISION

1. *PRINCIPLE OF RESPONSIBILITY*

   Authority to act and responsibility for acting must be joined.
   a. If you give responsibility, give authority.
   b. Define employee duties clearly.
   c. Protect employees from criticism by others.
   d. Recognize the rights as well as obligations of employees.
   e. Achieve the aims of a democratic society insofar as it is possible within the area of your work.
   f. Establish a situation favorable to training and learning.
   g. Accept ultimate responsibility for everything done in your section, unit, office, division, department.
   h. Good administration and good supervision are inseparable.

2. *PRINCIPLE OF AUTHORITY*

   The success of the supervisor is measured by the extent to which the power of authority is not used.
   a. Exercise simplicity and informality in supervision.
   b. Use the simplest machinery of supervision.
   c. If it is good for the organization as a whole, it is probably justified.
   d. Seldom be arbitrary or authoritative.
   e. Do not base your work on the power of position or of personality.
   f. Permit and encourage the free expression of opinions.

3. *PRINCIPLE OF SELF-GROWTH*

   The success of the supervisor is measured by the extent to which, and the speed with which, he is no longer needed.
   a. Base criticism on principles, not on specifics.
   b. Point out higher activities to employees.

    c. Train for self-thinking by employees,to meet new situations.
    d. Stimulate initiative,self-reliance and individual responsibility.
    e. Concentrate on stimulating the growth of employees rather than on removing defects.

4. *PRINCIPLE OF INDIVIDUAL WORTH*
Respect for the individual is a paramount consideration in supervision.
    a. Be human and sympathetic in dealing with employees.
    b. Don't nag about things to be done.
    c. Recognize the individual differences among employees and seek opportunities to permit best expression of each personality.

5. *PRINCIPLE OF CREATIVE LEADERSHIP*
The best supervision is that which is not apparent to the employee.
    a. Stimulate,don't drive employees to creative action.
    b. Emphasize doing good things.
    c. Encourage employees to do what they do best.
    d. Do not be too greatly concerned with details of subject or method.
    e. Do not be concerned exclusively with immediate problems and activities.
    f. Reveal higher activities and make them both desired and maximally possible.
    g. Determine procedures in the light of each situation but see that these are derived from a sound basic philosophy.
    h. Aid, inspire and lead so as to liberate the creative spirit latent in all good employees.

6. *PRINCIPLE OF SUCCESS AND FAILURE*
There are no unsuccessful employees, only unsuccessful supervisors who have failed to give proper leadership.
    a. Adapt suggestions to the capacities, attitudes, and prejudices of employees.
    b. Be gradual, be progressive, be persistent.
    c. Help the employee find the general principle; have the employee apply his own problem to the general principle.
    d. Give adequate appreciation for good work and honest effort.
    e. Anticipate employee difficulties and help to prevent them.
    f. Encourage employees to do the desirable things they will do anyway.
    g. Judge your supervision by the results it secures.

7. *PRINCIPLE OF SCIENCE*
Successful supervision is scientific,objective,and experimental.
It is based on facts, not on prejudices.
    a. Be cumulative in results.
    b. Never divorce your suggestions from the goals of training.
    c. Don't be impatient of results.
    d. Keep all matters on a professional, not a personal level.
    e. Do not be concerned exclusively with immediate problems and activities.
    f. Use objective means of determining achievement and rating where possible.

8. *PRINCIPLE OF COOPERATION*
Supervision is a cooperative enterprise between supervisor and employee.
    a. Begin with conditions as they are.
    b. Ask opinions of all involved when formulating policies.

c. Organization is as good as its weakest link.
d. Let employees help to determine policies and department programs.
e. Be approachable and accessible - physically and mentally.
f. Develop pleasant social relationships.

IV. WHAT IS ADMINISTRATION?

Administration is concerned with providing the environment, the material facilities, and the operational procedures that will promote the maximum growth and development of supervisors and employees. (Organization is an aspect, and a concomitant, of administration.)

There is no sharp line of demarcation between supervision and administration; these functions are intimately interrelated and, often, overlapping. They are complementary activities.

1. *PRACTICES COMMONLY CLASSED AS "SUPERVISORY"*
    a. Conducting employees conferences
    b. Visiting sections, units, offices, divisions, departments
    c. Arranging for demonstrations
    d. Examining plans
    e. Suggesting professional reading
    f. Interpreting bulletins
    g. Recommending in-service training courses
    h. Encouraging experimentation
    i. Appraising employee morale
    j. Providing for intervisitation

2. *PRACTICES COMMONLY CLASSIFIED AS "ADMINISTRATIVE"*
    a. Management of the office
    b. Arrangement of schedules for extra duties
    c. Assignment of rooms or areas
    d. Distribution of supplies
    e. Keeping records and reports
    f. Care of audio-visual materials
    g. Keeping inventory records
    h. Checking record cards and books
    i. Programming special activities
    j. Checking on the attendance and punctuality of employees

3. *PRACTICES COMMONLY CLASSIFIED AS BOTH "SUPERVISORY" AND "ADMINISTRATIVE"*
    a. Program construction
    b. Testing or evaluating outcomes
    c. Personnel accounting
    d. Ordering instructional materials

V. RESPONSIBILITIES OF THE SUPERVISOR

A person employed in a supervisory capacity must constantly be able to improve his own efficiency and ability. He represents the employer to the employees and only continuous self-examination can make him a capable supervisor.

Leadership and training are the supervisor's responsibility. An efficient working unit is one in which the employees work with the supervisor. It is his job to bring out the best in his employees. He must always be relaxed, courteous and calm in his association with his employees. Their feelings are important, and a harsh attitude does not develop the most efficient employees.

3

VI. COMPETENCIES OF THE SUPERVISOR

1. Complete knowledge of the duties and responsibilities of his position.
2. To be able to organize a job, plan ahead and carry through.
3. To have self-confidence and initiative.
4. To be able to handle the unexpected situation and make quick decisions.
5. To be able to properly train subordinates in the positions they are best suited for.
6. To be able to keep good human relations among his subordinates.
7. To be able to keep good human relations between his subordinates and himself and to earn their respect and trust.

VII. THE PROFESSIONAL SUPERVISOR-EMPLOYEE RELATIONSHIP

There are two kinds of efficiency: one kind is only apparent and is produced in organizations through the exercise of mere discipline; this is but a simulation of the second, or true, efficiency which springs from spontaneous cooperation. If you are a manager, no matter how great or small your responsibility, it is your job, in the final analysis, to create and develop this involuntary cooperation among the people whom you supervise. For, no matter how powerful a combination of money, machines, and materials a company may have, this is a dead and sterile thing without a team of willing, thinking and articulate people to guide it.

The following 21 points are presented as indicative of the exemplary basic relationship that should exist between supervisor and employee:

1. Each person wants to be liked and respected by his fellow employee and wants to be treated with consideration and respect by his superior.
2. The most competent employee will make an error. However, in a unit where good relations exist between the supervisor and his employees, tenseness and fear do not exist. Thus, errors are not hidden or covered up and the efficiency of a unit is not impaired.
3. Subordinates resent rules, regulations, or orders that are unreasonable or unexplained.
4. Subordinates are quick to resent unfairness, harshness, injustices and favoritism.
5. An employee will accept responsibility if he knows that he will be complimented for a job well done, and not too harshly chastized for failure; that his supervisor will check the cause of the failure, and, if it was the supervisor's fault, he will assume the blame therefor. If it was the employee's fault, his supervisor will explain the correct method or means of handling the responsibility.
6. An employee wants to receive credit for a suggestion he has made, that is used. If a suggestion cannot be used, the employee is entitled to an explanation. The supervisor should not say "no" and close the subject.
7. Fear and worry slow up a worker's ability. Poor working environment can impair his physical and mental health. A good supervisor avoids forceful methods, threats and arguments to get a job done.
8. A forceful supervisor is able to train his employees individually and as a team, and is able to motivate them in the proper channels.

9. A mature supervisor is able to properly evaluate his subordinates and to keep them happy and satisfied.
10. A sensitive supervisor will never patronize his subordinates.
11. A worthy supervisor will respect his employees' confidences.
12. Definite and clear-cut responsibilities should be assigned to each executive.
13. Responsibility should always be coupled with corresponding authority.
14. No change should be made in the scope or responsibilities of a position without a definite understanding to that effect on the part of all persons concerned.
15. No executive or employee, occupying a single position in the organization, should be subject to definite orders from more than one source.
16. Orders should never be given to subordinates over the head of a responsible executive. Rather than do this, the officer in question should be supplanted.
17. Criticisms of subordinates should, whever possible, be made privately, and in no case should a subordinate be criticized in the presence of executives or employees of equal or lower rank.
18. No dispute or difference between executives or employees as to authority or responsibilities should be considered too trivial for prompt and careful adjudication.
19. Promotions, wage changes, and disciplinary action should always be approved by the executive immediately superior to the one directly responsible.
20. No executive or employee should ever be required, or expected, to be at the same time an assistant to, and critic of, another.
21. Any executive whose work is subject to regular inspection should, whever practicable, be given the assistance and facilities necessary to enable him to maintain an independent check of the quality of his work.

VIII. MINI-TEXT IN SUPERVISION, ADMINISTRATION, MANAGEMENT, AND ORGANIZATION
A. BRIEF HIGHLIGHTS
Listed concisely and sequentially are major headings and important data in the field for quick recall and review.
1. *LEVELS OF MANAGEMENT*
   Any organization of some size has several levels of management. In terms of a ladder the levels are:

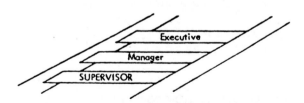

   The first level is very important because it is the beginning point of management leadership.
2. *WHAT THE SUPERVISOR MUST LEARN*
   A supervisor must learn to:
      (1) Deal with people and their differences
      (2) Get the job done through people
      (3) Recognize the problems when they exist
      (4) Overcome obstacles to good performance
      (5) Evaluate the performance of people
      (6) Check his own performance in terms of accomplishment

3. *A DEFINITION OF SUPERVISOR*
    The term supervisor means any individual having authority, in the interests of the employer, to hire, transfer, suspend, lay-off, recall, promote, discharge, assign, reward, or discipline other employees... or responsibility to direct them, or to adjust their grievances, or effectively to recommend such action, if, in connection with the foregoing, exercise of such authority is not of a merely routine or clerical nature but requires the use of independent judgment.

4. *ELEMENTS OF THE TEAM CONCEPT*
    What is involved in teamwork? The component parts are:
    (1) Members   (3) Goals   (5) Cooperation
    (2) A leader   (4) Plans   (6) Spirit

5. *PRINCIPLES OF ORGANIZATION*
    (1) A team member must know what his job is
    (2) Be sure that the nature and scope of a job are understood
    (3) Authority and responsibility should be carefully spelled out
    (4) A supervisor should be permitted to make the maximum number of decisions affecting his employees
    (5) Employees should report to only one supervisor
    (6) A supervisor should direct only as many employees as he can handle effectively
    (7) An organization plan should be flexible
    (8) Inspection and performance of work should be separate
    (9) Organizational problems should receive immediate attention
    (10) Assign work in line with ability and experience

6. *THE FOUR IMPORTANT PARTS OF EVERY JOB*
    (1) Inherent in every job is the *accountability* for results
    (2) A second set of factors in every job are *responsibilities*
    (3) Along with duties and responsibilities one must have the *authority* to act within certain limits without obtaining permission to proceed
    (4) No job exists in a vacuum. The supervisor is surrounded by key *relationships*

7. *PRINCIPLES OF DELEGATION*
    Where work is delegated for the first time, the supervisor should think in terms of these questions:
    (1) Who is best qualified to do this?
    (2) Can an employee improve his abilities by doing this?
    (3) How long should an employee spend on this?
    (4) Are there any special problems for which he will need guidance?
    (5) How broad a delegation can I make?

8. *PRINCIPLES OF EFFECTIVE COMMUNICATIONS*
    (1) Determine the media
    (2) To whom directed?
    (3) Identification and source authority
    (4) Is communication understood?

9. *PRINCIPLES OF WORK IMPROVEMENT*
    (1) Most people usually do only the work which is assigned to them
    (2) Workers are likely to fit assigned work into the time available to perform it
    (3) A good workload usually stimulates output
    (4) People usually do their best work when they know that results will be reviewed or inspected

(5) Employees usually feel that someone else is responsible for conditions of work, workplace layout, job methods, type of tools and equipment, and other such factors

(6) Employees are usually defensive about their job security

(7) Employees have natural resistance to change

(8) Employees can support or destroy a supervisor

(9) A supervisor usually earns the respect of his people through his personal example of diligence and efficiency

10. *AREAS OF JOB IMPROVEMENT*

The *areas* of job improvement are quite numerous, but the most common ones which a supervisor can identify and utilize are:

(1) Departmental layout   (5) Work methods
(2) Flow of work   (6) Materials handling
(3) Workplace layout   (7) Utilization
(4) Utilization of manpower   (8) Motion economy

11. *SEVEN KEY POINTS IN MAKING IMPROVEMENTS*

(1) Select the job to be improved
(2) Study how it is being done now
(3) Question the present method
(4) Determine actions to be taken
(5) Chart proposed method
(6) Get approval and apply
(7) Solicit worker participation

12. *CORRECTIVE TECHNIQUES OF JOB IMPROVEMENT*

Specific Problems	*General Problems*	*Corrective Technique*
(1) Size of workload	(1) Departmental layout	(1) Study with scale model
(2) Inability to meet schedules	(2) Flow of work	(2) Flow chart study
(3) Strain and fatigue	(3) Workplan layout	(3) Motion analysis
(4) Improper use of men and skills	(4) Utilization of manpower	(4) Comparison of units produced to standard allowances
(5) Waste, poor quality, unsafe conditions	(5) Work methods	(5) Methods analysis
(6) Bottleneck conditions that hinder output	(6) Materials handling	(6) Flow chart and equipment study
(7) Poor utilization of equipment and machines	(7) Utilization of equipment	(7) Down time vs. running time
(8) Efficiency and productivity of labor	(8) Motion economy	(8) Motion analysis

13. *A PLANNING CHECKLIST*

(1) Objectives   (8) Equipment
(2) Controls   (9) Supplies and materials
(3) Delegations   (10) Utilization of time
(4) Communications   (11) Safety
(5) Resources   (12) Money
(6) Methods and procedures (13) Work
(7) Manpower   (14) Timing of improvements

14. *FIVE CHARACTERISTICS OF GOOD DIRECTIONS*

In order to get results, directions must be:

(1) Possible of accomplishment   (4) Planned and complete
(2) Agreeable with worker interests (5) Unmistakably clear
(3) Related to mission

15. *TYPES OF DIRECTIONS*
      (1) Demands or direct orders   (3) Suggestion or implication
      (2) Requests   (4) Volunteering
16. *CONTROLS*
    A typical listing of the overall areas in which the supervisor should establish controls might be:
      (1) Manpower   (4) Quantity of work (7) Money
      (2) Materials   (5) Time   (8) Methods
      (3) Quality of work (6) Space
17. *ORIENTING THE NEW EMPLOYEE*
      (1) Prepare for him   (3) Orientation for the job
      (2) Welcome the new employee (4) Follow-up
18. *CHECKLIST FOR ORIENTING NEW EMPLOYEES*

	Yes	No
(1) Do your appreciate the feelings of new employees when they first report for work?	...	...
(2) Are you aware of the fact that the new employee must make a big adjustment to his job?	...	...
(3) Have you given him good reasons for liking the job and the organization?	...	...
(4) Have you prepared for his first day on the job?	...	...
(5) Did you welcome him cordially and make him feel needed?	...	...
(6) Did you establish rapport with him so that he feels free to talk and discuss matters with you?	...	...
(7) Did you explain his job to him and his relationship to you?	...	...
(8) Does he know that his work will be evaluated periodically on a basis that is fair and objective?	...	...
(9) Did you introduce him to his fellow workers in such a way that they are likely to accept him?	...	...
(10) Does he know what employee benefits he will receive?	...	...
(11) Does he understand the importance of being on the job and what to do if he must leave his duty station?	...	...
(12) Has he been impressed with the importance of accident prevention and safe practice?	...	...
(13) Does he generally know his way around the department?	...	...
(14) Is he under the guidance of a sponsor who will teach the right ways of doing things?	...	...
(15) Do you plan to follow-up so that he will continue to adjust successfully to his job?	...	...

19. *PRINCIPLES OF LEARNING*
      (1) Motivation (2) Demonstration or explanation
      (3) Practice
20. *CAUSES OF POOR PERFORMANCE*
      (1) Improper training for job (6) Lack of standards of
      (2) Wrong tools   performance
      (3) Inadequate directions   (7) Wrong work habits
      (4) Lack of supervisory follow-up(8) Low morale
      (5) Poor communications   (9) Other
21. *FOUR MAJOR STEPS IN ON-THE-JOB INSTRUCTION*
      (1) Prepare the worker   (3) Tryout performance
      (2) Present the operation   (4) Follow-up

22. *EMPLOYEES WANT FIVE THINGS*
    (1) Security   (2) Opportunity   (3) Recognition
    (4) Inclusion   (5) Expression
23. *SOME DON'TS IN REGARD TO PRAISE*
    (1) Don't praise a person for something he hasn't done
    (2) Don't praise a person unless you can be sincere
    (3) Don't be sparing in praise just because your superior withholds it from you
    (4) Don't let too much time elapse between good performance and recognition of it
24. *HOW TO GAIN YOUR WORKERS' CONFIDENCE*
    Methods of developing confidence include such things as:
    (1) Knowing the interests, habits, hobbies of employees
    (2) Admitting your own inadequacies
    (3) Sharing and telling of confidence in others
    (4) Supporting people when they are in trouble
    (5) Delegating matters that can be well handled
    (6) Being frank and straightforward about problems and working conditions
    (7) Encouraging others to bring their problems to you
    (8) Taking action on problems which impede worker progress
25. *SOURCES OF EMPLOYEE PROBLEMS*
    On-the-job causes might be such things as:
    (1) A feeling that favoritism is exercised in assignments
    (2) Assignment of overtime
    (3) An undue amount of supervision
    (4) Changing methods or systems
    (5) Stealing of ideas or trade secrets
    (6) Lack of interest in job
    (7) Threat of reduction in force
    (8) Ignorance or lack of communications
    (9) Poor equipment
    (10) Lack of knowing how supervisor feels toward employee
    (11) Shift assignments
    Off-the-job problems might have to do with:
    (1) Health   (2) Finances   (3) Housing   (4) Family
26. *THE SUPERVISOR'S KEY TO DISCIPLINE*
    There are several key points about discipline which the supervisor should keep in mind:
    (1) Job discipline is one of the disciplines of life and is directed by the supervisor.
    (2) It is more important to correct an employee fault than to fix blame for it.
    (3) Employee performance is affected by problems both on the job and off.
    (4) Sudden or abrupt changes in behavior can be indications of important employee problems.
    (5) Problems should be dealt with as soon as possible after they are identified.
    (6) The attitude of the supervisor may have more to do with solving problems than the techniques of problem solving.
    (7) Correction of employee behavior should be resorted to only after the supervisor is sure that training or counseling will not be helpful
    (8) Be sure to document your disciplinary actions.

(9) Make sure that you are disciplining on the basis of facts rather than personal feelings.

(10) Take each disciplinary step in order, being careful not to make snap judgments, or decisions based on impatience.

27. *FIVE IMPORTANT PROCESSES OF MANAGEMENT*
   (1) Planning   (2) Organizing   (3) Scheduling
   (4) Controlling   (5) Motivating

28. *WHEN THE SUPERVISOR FAILS TO PLAN*
   (1) Supervisor creates impression of not knowing his job
   (2) May lead to excessive overtime
   (3) Job runs itself-- supervisor lacks control
   (4) Deadlines and appointments missed
   (5) Parts of the work go undone
   (6) Work interrupted by emergencies
   (7) Sets a bad example
   (8) Uneven workload creates peaks and valleys
   (9) Too much time on minor details at expense of more important tasks

29. *FOURTEEN GENERAL PRINCIPLES OF MANAGEMENT*
   (1) Division of work
   (2) Authority and responsibility
   (3) Discipline
   (4) Unity of command
   (5) Unity of direction
   (6) Subordination of individual interest to general interest
   (7) Remuneration of personnel
   (8) Centralization
   (9) Scalar chain
   (10) Order
   (11) Equity
   (12) Stability of tenure of personnel
   (13) Initiative
   (14) Esprit de corps

30. *CHANGE*

   Bringing about change is perhaps attempted more often, and yet less well understood, than anything else the supervisor does. How do people generally react to change? (People tend to resist change that is imposed upon them by other individuals or circumstances.)

   Change is characteristic of every situation. It is a part of every real endeavor where the efforts of people are concerned.

   A. Why do people resist change?
      People may resist change because of:
         (1) Fear of the unknown
         (2) Implied criticism
         (3) Unpleasant experiences in the past
         (4) Fear of loss of status
         (5) Threat to the ego
         (6) Fear of loss of economic stability

   B. How can we best overcome the resistance to change?
      In initiating change, take these steps:
         (1) Get ready to sell
         (2) identify sources of help
         (3) Anticipate objections
         (4) Sell benefits
         (5) Listen in depth
         (6) Follow up

I. WHO/WHAT IS THE SUPERVISOR?

1. The supervisor is often called the "highest level employee and the lowest level manager."
2. A supervisor is a member of both management and the work group. He acts as a bridge between the two.
3. Most problems in supervision are in the area of human relations, or people problems.
4. Employees expect: Respect, opportunity to learn and to advance, and a sense of belonging, and so forth.
5. Supervisors are responsible for directing people and organizing work. Planning is of paramount importance.
6. A position description is a set of duties and responsibilities inherent to a given position.
7. It is important to keep the position description up-to-date and to provide each employee with his own copy.

II. THE SOCIOLOGY OF WORK

1. People are alike in many ways; however each individual is unique.
2. The supervisor is challenged in getting to know employee differences. Acquiring skills in evaluating individuals is an asset.
3. Maintaining meaningful working relationships in the organization is of great importance.
4. The supervisor has an obligation to help individuals to develop to their fullest potential.
5. Job rotation on a planned basis helps to build versatility and to maintain interest and enthusiasm in work groups.
6. Cross training (job rotation) provides backup skills.
7. The supervisor can help reduce tension by maintaining a sense of humor, providing guidance to employees, and by making reasonable and timely decisions. Employees respond favorably to working under reasonably predictable circumstances.
8. Change is characteristic of all managerial behavior. The supervisor must adjust to changes in procedures, new methods, technological changes, and to a number of new and sometimes challenging situations.
9. To overcome the natural tendency for people to resist change, the supervisor should become more skillful in initiating change.

III. PRINCIPLES AND PRACTICES OF SUPERVISION

1. Employees should be required to answer to only one superior.
2. A supervisor can effectively direct only a limited number of employees, depending upon the complexity, variety, and proximity of the jobs involved.
3. The organizational chart presents the organization in graphic form. It reflects lines of authority and responsibility as well as interrelationships of units within the organization.
4. Distribution of work can be improved through an analysis using the "Work Distribution Chart."
5. The "Work Distribution Chart" reflects the division of work within a unit in understandable form.
6. When related tasks are given to an employee, he has a better chance of increasing his skills through training.
7. The individual who is given the responsibility for tasks must also be given the appropriate authority to insure adequate results.
8. The supervisor should delegate repetitive, routine work. Preparation of recurring reports, maintaining leave and attendance records are some examples.

9. Good discipline is essential to good task performance. Discipline is reflected in the actions of employees on the job in the absence of supervision.
10. Disciplinary action may have to be taken when the positive aspects of discipline have failed. Reprimand, warning, and suspension are examples of disciplinary action.
11. If a situation calls for a reprimand, be sure it is deserved and remember it is to be done in private.

IV. DYNAMIC LEADERSHIP
1. A style is a personal method or manner of exerting influence.
2. Authoritarian leaders often see themselves as the source of power and authority.
3. The democratic leader often perceives the group as the source of authority and power.
4. Supervisors tend to do better when using the pattern of leadership that is most natural for them.
5. Social scientists suggest that the effective supervisor use the leadership style that best fits the problem or circumstances involved.
6. All four styles -- telling, selling, consulting, joining -- have their place. Using one does not preclude using the other at another time.
7. The theory X point of view assumes that the average person dislikes work, will avoid it whenever possible, and must be coerced to achieve organizational objectives.
8. The theory Y point of view assumes that the average person considers work to be as natural as play, and, when the individual is committed, he requires little supervision or direction to accomplish desired objectives.
9. The leader's basic assumptions concerning human behavior and human nature affect his actions, decisions, and other managerial practices.
10. Dissatisfaction among employees is often present, but difficult to isolate. The supervisor should seek to weaken dissatisfaction by keeping promises, being sincere and considerate, keeping employees informed, and so forth.
11. Constructive suggestions should be encouraged during the natural progress of the work.

V. PROCESSES FOR SOLVING PROBLEMS
1. People find their daily tasks more meaningful and satisfying when they can improve them.
2. The causes of problems, or the key factors, are often hidden in the background. Ability to solve problems often involves the ability to isolate them from their backgrounds. There is some substance to the cliché that some persons "can't see the forest for the trees."
3. New procedures are often developed from old ones. Problems should be broken down into manageable parts. New ideas can be adapted from old ones.
4. People think differently in problem-solving situations. Using a logical, patterned approach is often useful. One approach found to be useful includes these steps:
   (a) Define the problem   (d) Weigh and decide
   (b) Establish objectives   (e) Take action
   (c) Get the facts   (f) Evaluate action

VI. TRAINING FOR RESULTS

1. Participants respond best when they feel training is important to them.
2. The supervisor has responsibility for the training and development of those who report to him.
3. When training is delegated to others, great care must be exercised to insure the trainer has knowledge, aptitude, and interest for his work as a trainer.
4. Training (learning) of some type goes on continually. The most successful supervisor makes certain the learning contributes in a productive manner to operational goals.
5. New employees are particularly susceptible to training. Older employees facing new job situations require specific training, as well as having need for development and growth opportunities.
6. Training needs require continuous monitoring.
7. The training officer of an agency is a professional with a responsibility to assist supervisors in solving training problems.
8. Many of the self-development steps important to the supervisor's own growth are equally important to the development of peers and subordinates. Knowledge of these is important when the supervisor consults with others on development and growth opportunities.

VII. HEALTH, SAFETY, AND ACCIDENT PREVENTION

1. Management-minded supervisors take appropriate measures to assist employees in maintaining health and in assuring safe practices in the work environment.
2. Effective safety training and practices help to avoid injury and accidents.
3. Safety should be a management goal. All infractions of safety which are observed should be corrected without exception.
4. Employees' safety attitude, training and instruction, provision of safe tools and equipment, supervision, and leadership are considered highly important factors which contribute to safety and which can be influenced directly by supervisors.
5. When accidents do occur they should be investigated promptly for very important reasons, including the fact that information which is gained can be used to prevent accidents in the future.

VIII. EQUAL EMPLOYMENT OPPORTUNITY

1. The supervisor should endeavor to treat all employees fairly, without regard to religion, race, sex, or national origin.
2. Groups tend to reflect the attitude of the leader. Prejudice can be detected even in very subtle form. Supervisors must strive to create a feeling of mutual respect and confidence in every employee.
3. Complete utilization of all human resources is a national goal. Equitable consideration should be accorded women in the work force, minority-group members, the physically and mentally handicapped, and the older employee. The important question is: "Who can do the job?"
4. Training opportunities, recognition for performance, overtime assignments, promotional opportunities, and all other personnel actions are to be handled on an equitable basis.

IX. IMPROVING COMMUNICATIONS

1. Communications is achieving understanding between the sender and the receiver of a message. It also means sharing information -- the creation of understanding.
2. Communication is basic to all human activity. Words are means of conveying meanings; however, real meanings are in people.
3. There are very practical differences in the effectiveness of one-way, impersonal, and two-way communications. Words spoken face-to-face are better understood. Telephone conversations are effective, but lack the rapport of person-to-person exchanges. The whole person communicates.
4. Cooperation and communication in an organization go hand-in-hand. When there is a mutual respect between people, spelling out rules and procedures for communicating is unnecessary.
5. There are several barriers to effective communications. These include failure to listen with respect and understanding, lack of skill in feedback, and misinterpreting the meanings of words used by the speaker. It is also common practice to listen to what we want to hear, and tune out things we do not want to hear.
6. Communication is management's chief problem. The supervisor should accept the challenge to communicate more effectively and to improve interagency and intra-agency communications.
7. The supervisor may often plan for and conduct meetings. The planning phase is critical and may determine the success or the failure of a meeting.
8. Speaking before groups usually requires extra effort. Stage fright may never disappear completely, but it can be controlled.

X. SELF-DEVELOPMENT

1. Every employee is responsible for his own self-development.
2. Toastmaster and toastmistress clubs offer opportunities to improve skills in oral communications.
3. Planning for one's own self-development is of vital importance. Supervisors know their own strengths and limitations better than anyone else.
4. Many opportunities are open to aid the supervisor in his developmental efforts, including job assignments; training opportunities, both governmental and non-governmental -- to include universities and professional conferences and seminars.
5. Programmed instruction offers a means of studying at one's own rate.
6. Where difficulties may arise from a supervisor's being away from his work for training, he may participate in televised home study or correspondence courses to meet his self-development needs.

XI. TEACHING AND TRAINING

A. The Teaching Process

Teaching is encouraging and guiding the learning activities of students toward established goals. In most cases this process consists in five steps: preparation, presentation, summarization, evaluation, and application.

1. Preparation

Preparation is twofold in nature; that of the supervisor and the employee.

Preparation by the supervisor is absolutely essential to success. He must know what, when, where, how, and whom he will teach. Some of the factors that should be considered are:

(1) The objectives
(2) The materials needed
(3) The methods to be used
(4) Employee participation
(5) Employee interest
(6) Training aids
(7) Evaluation
(8) Summarization

Employee preparation consists in preparing the employee to receive the material. Probably the most important single factor in the preparation of the employee is arousing and maintaining his interest. He must know the objectives of the training, why he is there, how the material can be used, and its importance to him.

2. Presentation

In presentation, have a carefully designed plan and follow it. The plan should be accurate and complete, yet flexible enough to meet situations as they arise. The method of presentation will be determined by the particular situation and objectives.

3. Summary

A summary should be made at the end of every training unit and program. In addition, there may be internal summaries depending on the nature of the material being taught. The important thing is that the trainee must always be able to understand how each part of the new material relates to the whole.

4. Application

The supervisor must arrange work so the employee will be given a chance to apply new knowledge or skills while the material is still clear in his mind and interest is high. The trainee does not really know whether he has learned the material until he has been given a chance to apply it. If the material is not applied, it loses most of its value.

5. Evaluation

The purpose of all training is to promote learning. To determine whether the training has been a success or failure, the supervisor must evaluate this learning.

In the broadest sense evaluation includes all the devices, methods, skills, and techniques used by the supervisor to keep himself and the employees informed as to their progress toward the objectives they are pursuing. The extent to which the employee has mastered the knowledge, skills, and abilities, or changed his attitudes, as determined by the program objectives, is the extent to which instruction has succeeded or failed.

Evaluation should not be confined to the end of the lesson, day, or program but should be used continuously. We shall note later the way this relates to the rest of the teaching process.

B. Teaching Methods

A teaching method is a pattern of identifiable student and instructor activity used in presenting training material.

All supervisors are faced with the problem of deciding which method should be used at a given time.

1. Lecture

The lecture is direct oral presentation of material by the supervisor. The present trend is to place less emphasis on the trainer's activity and more on that of the trainee.

2. Discussion

Teaching by discussion or conference involves using questions and other techniques to arouse interest and focus attention upon certain areas, and by doing so creating a learning situation. This can be one of the most valuable methods because it gives the employees an opportunity to express their ideas and pool their knowledge.

3. Demonstration

The demonstration is used to teach how something works or how to do something. It can be used to show a principle or what the results of a series of actions will be. A well-staged demonstration is particularly effective because it shows proper methods of performance in a realistic manner.

4. Performance

Performance is one of the most fundamental of all learning techniques or teaching methods. The trainee may be able to tell how a specific operation should be performed but he cannot be sure he knows how to perform the operation until he has done so.

As with all methods, there are certain advantages and disadvantages to each method.

5. Which Method to Use

Moreover, there are other methods and techniques of teaching. It is difficult to use any method without other methods entering into it. In any learning situation a combination of methods is usually more effective than any one method alone.

Finally, evaluation must be integrated into the other aspects of the teaching-learning process.

It must be used in the motivation of the trainees; it must be used to assist in developing understanding during the training; and it must be related to employee application of the results of training.

This is distinctly the role of the supervisor.

———

GLOSSARY OF LEGAL TERMS

CONTENTS

GLOSSARY OF LEGAL TERMS

A

ACTION - "Action" includes a civil action and a criminal action.

A FORTIORI - A terra meaning you can reason one thing from the existence of certain facts.

A POSTERIORI - From what goes after; from effect to cause.

A PRIORI - From what goes before; from cause to effect.

AB INITIO - From the beginning.

ABATE - To diminish or put an end to.

ABET - To encourage the commission of a crime.

ABEYANCE - Suspension, temporary suppression.

ABIDE - To accept the consequences of.

ABJURE - To renounce; give up.

ABRIDGE - To reduce; contract; diminish.

ABROGATE - To annul, repeal, or destroy.

ABSCOND - To hide or absent oneself to avoid legal action.

ABSTRACT - A summary.

ABUT - To border on, to touch.

ACCESS - Approach; in real property law it means the right of the owner of property to the use of the highway or road next to his land, without obstruction by intervening property owners.

ACCESSORY - In criminal law, it means the person who contributes or aids in the commission of a crime.

ACCOMMODATED PARTY - One to whom credit is extended on the strength of another person signing a commercial paper.

ACCOMMODATION PAPER - A commercial paper to which the accommodating party has put his name.

ACCOMPLICE - In criminal law, it means a person who together with the principal offender commits a crime.

ACCORD - An agreement to accept something different or less than that to which one is entitled, which extinguishes the entire obligation.

ACCOUNT - A statement of mutual demands in the nature of debt and credit between parties.

ACCRETION - The act of adding to a thing; in real property law, it means gradual accumulation of land by natural causes.

ACCRUE - To grow to; to be added to.

ACKNOWLEDGMENT - The act of going before an official authorized to take acknowledgments, and acknowledging an act as one's own.

ACQUIESCENCE - A silent appearance of consent.

ACQUIT - To legally determine the innocence of one charged with a crime.

AD INFINITUM - Indefinitely.

AD LITEM - For the suit.

AD VALOREM - According to value.

ADJECTIVE LAW - Rules of procedure.

ADJUDICATION - The judgment given in a case.

ADMIRALTY - Court having jurisdiction over maritime cases.

ADULT - Sixteen years old or over (in criminal law).

ADVANCE - In commercial law, it means to pay money or render other value before it is due.

ADVERSE - Opposed; contrary.

ADVOCATE - (v.) To speak in favor of;
(n.) One who assists, defends, or pleads for another.

AFFIANT - A person who makes and signs an affidavit.

AFFIDAVIT - A written and sworn to declaration of facts, voluntarily made.

AFFINITY- The relationship between persons through marriage with the kindred of each other; distinguished from consanguinity, which is the relationship by blood.

AFFIRM - To ratify; also when an appellate court affirms a judgment, decree, or order, it means that it is valid and right and must stand as rendered in the lower court.

AFOREMENTIONED; AFORESAID - Before or already said.

AGENT - One who represents and acts for another.

AID AND COMFORT - To help; encourage.

ALIAS - A name not one's true name.

ALIBI - A claim of not being present at a certain place at a certain time.

ALLEGE - To assert.

ALLOTMENT - A share or portion.

AMBIGUITY - Uncertainty; capable of being understood in more than one way.

AMENDMENT - Any language made or proposed as a change in some principal writing.

AMICUS CURIAE - A friend of the court; one who has an interest in a case, although not a party in the case, who volunteers advice upon matters of law to the judge. For example, a brief amicus curiae.

AMORTIZATION - To provide for a gradual extinction of (a future obligation) in advance of maturity, especially, by periodical contributions to a sinking fund which will be adequate to discharge a debt or make a replacement when it becomes necessary.

ANCILLARY - Aiding, auxiliary.

ANNOTATION - A note added by way of comment or explanation.

ANSWER - A written statement made by a defendant setting forth the grounds of his defense.

ANTE - Before.

ANTE MORTEM - Before death.

APPEAL - The removal of a case from a lower court to one of superior jurisdiction for the purpose of obtaining a review.

APPEARANCE - Coming into court as a party to a suit.

APPELLANT - The party who takes an appeal from one court or jurisdiction to another (appellate) court for review.

APPELLEE - The party against whom an appeal is taken.

APPROPRIATE - To make a thing one's own.

APPROPRIATION - Prescribing the destination of a thing; the act of the legislature designating a particular fund, to be applied to some object of government expenditure.

APPURTENANT - Belonging to; accessory or incident to.

ARBITER - One who decides a dispute; a referee.

ARBITRARY - Unreasoned; not governed by any fixed rules or standard.

ARGUENDO - By way of argument.

ARRAIGN - To call the prisoner before the court to answer to a charge.

ASSENT - A declaration of willingness to do something in compliance with a request.

ASSERT - Declare.

ASSESS - To fix the rate or amount.

ASSIGN - To transfer; to appoint; to select for a particular purpose.

ASSIGNEE - One who receives an assignment.

ASSIGNOR - One who makes an assignment.

AT BAR - Before the court.

AT ISSUE - When parties in an action come to a point where one asserts something and the other denies it.

ATTACH - Seize property by court order and sometimes arrest a person.

ATTEST - To witness a will, etc.; act of attestation.

AVERMENT - A positive statement of facts.

B

BAIL - To obtain the release of a person from legal custody by giving security and promising that he shall appear in court; to deliver (goods, etc.) in trust to a person for a special purpose.

BAILEE - One to whom personal property is delivered under a contract of bailment.

BAILMENT - Delivery of personal property to another to be held for a certain purpose and to be returned when the purpose is accomplished.

BAILOR - The party who delivers goods to another, under a contract of bailment.

BANC (OR BANK) - Bench; the place where a court sits permanently or regularly; also the assembly of all the judges of a court.

BANKRUPT - An insolvent person, technically, one declared to be bankrupt after a bankruptcy proceeding.

BAR - The legal profession.

BARRATRY - Exciting groundless judicial proceedings.

BARTER - A contract by which parties exchange goods for other goods.

BATTERY - Illegal interfering with another's person.

BEARER - In commercial law, it means the person in possession of a commercial paper which is payable to the bearer.

BENCH - The court itself or the judge.

BENEFICIARY - A person benefiting under a will, trust, or agreement.

BEST EVIDENCE RULE,THE - Except as otherwise provided by statute, no evidence other than the writing itself is admissible to prove the content of a writing. This section shall be known and may be cited as the best evidence rule.

BEQUEST - A gift of personal property under a will.

BILL - A formal written statement of complaint to a court of justice; also, a draft of an act of the legislature before it becomes a law; also, accounts for goods sold, services rendered, or work done.

BONA FIDE - In or with good faith; honestly.

BOND - An instrument by which the maker promises to pay a sum of money to another, usually providing that upon performances of a certain condition the obligation shall be void.

BOYCOTT - A plan to prevent the carrying on of a business by wrongful means.

BREACH - The breaking or violating of a law, or the failure to carry out a duty.

BRIEF - A written document, prepared by a lawyer to serve as the basis of an argument upon a case in court, usually an appellate court.

BURDEN OF PRODUCING EVIDENCE - The obligation of a party to introduce evidence sufficient to avoid a ruling against him on the issue.

BURDEN OF PROOF - The obligation of a party to establish by evidence a requisite degree of belief concerning a fact in the mind of the trier of fact or the court. The burden of proof may require a party to raise a reasonable doubt concerning the existence of nonexistence of a fact or that he establish the existence or nonexistence of a fact by a preponderance of the evidence, by clear and convincing proof, or by proof beyond a reasonable doubt.

Except as otherwise provided by law, the burden of proof requires proof by a preponderance of the evidence.

BUSINESS, A - Shall include every kind of business, profession, occupation, calling or operation of institutions, whether carried on for profit or not.

BY-LAWS - Regulations, ordinances, or rules enacted by a corporation, association, etc., for its own government.

C

CANON - A doctrine; also, a law or rule, of a church or association in particular.

CAPIAS - An order to arrest.

CAPTION - In a pleading, deposition or other paper connected with a case in court, it is the heading or introductory clause which shows the names of the parties, name of the court, number of the case on the docket or calendar, etc.

CARRIER - A person or corporation undertaking to transport persons or property.

CASE - A general term for an action, cause, suit, or controversy before a judicial body.

CAUSE - A suit, litigation or action before a court.

CAVEAT EMPTOR - Let the buyer beware. This term expresses the rule that the purchaser of an article must examine, judge, and test it for himself, being bound to discover any obvious defects or imperfections.

CERTIFICATE - A written representation that some legal formality has been complied with.

CERTIORARI - To be informed of; the name of a writ issued by a superior court directing the lower court to send up to the former the record and proceedings of a case.

CHANGE OF VENUE - To remove place of trial from one place to another.

CHARGE - An obligation or duty; a formal complaint; an instruction of the court to the jury upon a case.

CHARTER - (n.) The authority by virtue of which an organized body acts;
(v.) in mercantile law, it means to hire or lease a vehicle or vessel for transportation.

CHATTEL - An article of personal property.

CHATTEL MORTGAGE - A mortgage on personal property.

CIRCUIT - A division of the country, for the administration of justice; a geographical area served by a court.

CITATION - The act of the court by which a person is summoned or cited; also, a reference to legal authority.

CIVIL (ACTIONS)- It indicates the private rights and remedies of individuals in contrast to the word "criminal" (actions) which relates to prosecution for violation of laws.

CLAIM (n.) - Any demand held or asserted as of right.

CODICIL - An addition to a will.

CODIFY - To arrange the laws of a country into a code.

COGNIZANCE - Notice or knowledge.

COLLATERAL - By the side; accompanying; an article or thing given to secure performance of a promise.

COMITY - Courtesy; the practice by which one court follows the decision of another court on the same question.

COMMIT - To perform, as an act; to perpetrate, as a crime; to send a person to prison.

COMMON LAW - As distinguished from law created by the enactment of the legislature (called statutory law), it relates to those principles and rules of action which derive their authority solely from usages and customs of immemorial antiquity, particularly with reference to the ancient unwritten law of England. The written pronouncements of the common law are found in court decisions.

COMMUTE - Change punishment to one less severe.

COMPLAINANT - One who applies to the court for legal redress.

COMPLAINT - The pleading of a plaintiff in a civil action; or a charge that a person has committed a specified offense.

COMPROMISE - An arrangement for settling a dispute by agreement.

CONCUR - To agree, consent.

CONCURRENT - Running together, at the same time.

CONDEMNATION - Taking private property for public use on payment therefor.

CONDITION - Mode or state of being; a qualification or restriction.

CONDUCT - Active and passive behavior; both verbal and nonverbal.

CONFESSION - Voluntary statement of guilt of crime.

CONFIDENTIAL COMMUNICATION BETWEEN CLIENT AND LAWYER - Information transmitted between a client and his lawyer in the course of that relationship and in confidence by a means which, so far as the client is aware, discloses the information to no third persons other than those who are present to further the interest of the client in the consultation or those to whom disclosure is reasonably necessary for the transmission of the information or the accomplishment of the purpose for which the lawyer is consulted, and includes a legal opinion formed and the advice given by the lawyer in the course of that relationship.

CONFRONTATION - Witness testifying in presence of defendant.

CONSANGUINITY - Blood relationship.

CONSIGN - To give in charge; commit; entrust; to send or transmit goods to a merchant, factor, or agent for sale.

CONSIGNEE - One to whom a consignment is made.

CONSIGNOR - One who sends or makes a consignment.

CONSPIRACY - In criminal law, it means an agreement between two or more persons to commit an unlawful act.

CONSPIRATORS - Persons involved in a conspiracy.

CONSTITUTION - The fundamental law of a nation or state.

CONSTRUCTION OF GENDERS - The masculine gender includes the feminine and neuter.

CONSTRUCTION OF SINGULAR AND PLURAL - The singular number includes the plural; and the plural, the singular.

CONSTRUCTION OF TENSES - The present tense includes the past and future tenses; and the future, the present.

CONSTRUCTIVE - An act or condition assumed from other parts or conditions.

CONSTRUE - To ascertain the meaning of language.

CONSUMMATE - To complete.

CONTIGUOUS - Adjoining; touching; bounded by.

CONTINGENT - Possible, but not assured; dependent upon some condition.

CONTINUANCE - The adjournment or postponement of an action pending in a court.

CONTRA - Against, opposed to; contrary.

CONTRACT - An agreement between two or more persons to do or not to do a particular thing.

CONTROVERT - To dispute, deny.

CONVERSION - Dealing with the personal property of another as if it were one's own, without right.

CONVEYANCE - An instrument transferring title to land.

CONVICTION - Generally, the result of a criminal trial which ends in a judgment or sentence that the defendant is guilty as charged.

COOPERATIVE - A cooperative is a voluntary organization of persons with a common interest, formed and operated along democratic lines for the purpose of supplying services at cost to its members and other patrons, who contribute both capital and business.

CORPUS DELICTI - The body of a crime; the crime itself.

CORROBORATE - To strengthen; to add weight by additional evidence.

COUNTERCLAIM - A claim presented by a defendant in opposition to or deduction from the claim of the plaintiff.

COUNTY - Political subdivision of a state.

COVENANT - Agreement.

CREDIBLE - Worthy of belief.

CREDITOR - A person to whom a debt is owing by another person, called the "debtor."

CRIMINAL ACTION - Includes criminal proceedings.

CRIMINAL INFORMATION - Same as complaint.

CRITERION (sing.)

CRITERIA (plural) - A means or tests for judging; a standard or standards.

CROSS-EXAMINATION - Examination of a witness by a party other than the direct examiner upon a matter that is within the scope of the direct examination of the witness.

CULPABLE - Blamable.

CY-PRES - As near as (possible). The rule of *cy-pres* is a rule for the construction of instruments in equity by which the intention of the party is carried out *as near as may be, when it* would be impossible or illegal to give it literal effect.

D

DAMAGES - A monetary compensation, which may be recovered in the courts by any person who has suffered loss, or injury, whether to his person, property or rights through the unlawful act or omission or negligence of another.

DECLARANT - A person who makes a statement.

DE FACTO - In fact; actually but without legal authority.

DE JURE - Of right; legitimate; lawful.

DE MINIMIS - Very small or trifling.

DE NOVO - Anew; afresh; a second time.

DEBT - A specified sum of money owing to one person from another, including not only the obligation of the debtor to pay, but the right of the creditor to receive and enforce payment.

DECEDENT - A dead person.

DECISION - A judgment or decree pronounced by a court in determination of a case.

DECREE - An order of the court, determining the rights of all parties to a suit.

DEED - A writing containing a contract sealed and delivered; particularly to convey real property.

DEFALCATION - Misappropriation of funds.

DEFAMATION - Injuring one's reputation by false statements.

DEFAULT - The failure to fulfill a duty, observe a promise, discharge an obligation, or perform an agreement.

DEFENDANT - The person defending or denying; the party against whom relief or recovery is sought in an action or suit.

DEFRAUD - To practice fraud; to cheat or trick.

DELEGATE (v.)- To entrust to the care or management of another.

DELICTUS - A crime.

DEMUR (v.) - To dispute the sufficiency in law of the pleading of the other side.

DEMURRAGE - In maritime law, it means, the sum fixed or allowed as remuneration to the owners of a ship for the detention of their vessel beyond the number of days allowed for loading and unloading or for sailing; also used in railroad terminology.

DENIAL - A form of pleading; refusing to admit the truth of a statement, charge, etc.

DEPONENT - One who gives testimony under oath reduced to writing.

DEPOSITION - Testimony given under oath outside of court for use in court or for the purpose of obtaining information in preparation for trial of a case.

DETERIORATION - A degeneration such as from decay, corrosion or disintegration.

DETRIMENT - Any loss or harm to person or property.

DEVIATION - A turning aside.

DEVISE - A gift of real property by the last will and testament of the donor.

DICTUM (sing.)

DICTA (plural) - Any statements made by the court in an opinion concerning some rule of law not necessarily involved nor essential to the determination of the case.

DIRECT EVIDENCE - Evidence that directly proves a fact, without an inference or presumption, and which in itself if true, conclusively establishes that fact.

DIRECT EXAMINATION - The first examination of a witness upon a matter that is not within the scope of a previous examination of the witness.

DISAFFIRM - To repudicate.

DISMISS - In an action or suit, it means to dispose of the case without any further consideration or hearing.

DISSENT - To denote disagreement of one or more judges of a court with the decision passed by the majority upon a case before them.

DOCKET (n.) - A formal record, entered in brief, of the proceedings in a court.

DOCTRINE - A rule, principle, theory of law.

DOMICILE - That place where a man has his true, fixed and permanent home to which whenever he is absent he has the intention of returning.

DRAFT (n.) - A commercial paper ordering payment of money drawn by one person on another.

DRAWEE - The person who is requested to pay the money.

DRAWER - The person who draws the commercial paper and addresses it to the drawee.

DUPLICATE - A counterpart produced by the same impression as the original enlargements and miniatures, or by mechanical or electronic re-recording, or by chemical reproduction, or by other equivalent technique which accurately reproduces the original.

DURESS - Use of force to compel performance or non-performance of an act.

E

EASEMENT - A liberty, privilege, or advantage without profit, in the lands of another.

EGRESS - Act or right of going out or leaving; emergence.

EIUSDEM GENERIS - Of the same kind, class or nature. A rule used in the construction of language in a legal document.

EMBEZZLEMENT - To steal; to appropriate fraudulently to one's own use property entrusted to one's care.

EMBRACERY - Unlawful attempt to influence jurors, etc., but not by offering value.

EMINENT DOMAIN - The right of a state to take private property for public use.

ENACT - To make into a law.

ENDORSEMENT - Act of writing one's name on the back of a note, bill or similar written instrument.

ENJOIN - To require a person, by writ of injunction from a court of equity, to perform or to abstain or desist from some act.

ENTIRETY - The whole; that which the law considers as one whole, and not capable of being divided into parts.

ENTRAPMENT - Inducing one to commit a crime so as to arrest him.

ENUMERATED - Mentioned specifically; designated.

ENURE - To operate or take effect.

EQUITY - In its broadest sense, this term denotes the spirit and the habit of fairness, justness, and right dealing which regulate the conduct of men.

ERROR - A mistake of law, or the false or irregular application of law as will nullify the judicial proceedings.

ESCROW - A deed, bond or other written engagement, delivered to a third person, to be delivered by him only upon the performance or fulfillment of some condition.

ESTATE - The interest which any one has in lands, or in any other subject of property.

ESTOP - To stop, bar, or impede.

ESTOPPEL - A rule of law which prevents a man from alleging or denying a fact, because of his own previous act.

ET AL. (alii) - And others.

ET SEQ. (sequential) - And the following.

ET UX. (uxor) - And wife.

EVIDENCE - Testimony, writings, material objects, or other things presented to the senses that are offered to prove the existence or non-existence of a fact.

      Means from which inferences may be drawn as a basis of proof in duly constituted judicial or fact finding tribunals, and includes testimony in the form of opinion and hearsay.

EX CONTRACTU

EX DELICTO - In law, rights and causes of action are divided into two classes, those arising *ex contractu* (from a contract) and those arising *ex delicto* (from a delict or tort).

EX OFFICIO - From office; by virtue of the office.

EX PARTE - On one side only; by or for one.

EX POST FACTO - After the fact.

EX POST FACTO LAW - A law passed after an act was done which retroactively makes such act a crime.

EX REL. (relations) - Upon relation or information.

EXCEPTION - An objection upon a matter of law to a decision made, either before or after judgment by a court.

EXECUTOR (male)

EXECUTRIX (female) - A person who has been appointed by will to execute the will.

EXECUTORY - That which is yet to be executed or performed.

EXEMPT - To release from some liability to which others are subject.

EXONERATION - The removal of a burden, charge or duty.

EXTRADITION - Surrender of a fugitive from one nation to another.

F

F.A.S.- "Free alongside ship"; delivery at dock for ship named.

F.O.B.- "Free on board"; seller will deliver to car, truck, vessel, or other conveyance by which goods are to be transported, without expense or risk of loss to the buyer or consignee.

FABRICATE - To construct; to invent a false story.

FACSIMILE - An exact or accurate copy of an original instrument.

FACTOR - A commercial agent.

FEASANCE - The doing of an act.

FELONIOUS - Criminal, malicious.

FELONY - Generally, a criminal offense that may be punished by death or imprisonment for more than one year as differentiated from a misdemeanor.

FEME SOLE - A single woman.

FIDUCIARY - A person who is invested with rights and powers to be exercised for the benefit of another person.

FIERI FACIAS - A writ of execution commanding the sheriff to levy and collect the amount of a judgment from the goods and chattels of the judgment debtor.

FINDING OF FACT - Determination from proof or judicial notice of the existence of a fact. A ruling implies a supporting finding of fact; no separate or formal finding is required unless required by a statute of this state.

FISCAL - Relating to accounts or the management of revenue.

FORECLOSURE (sale) - A sale of mortgaged property to obtain satisfaction of the mortgage out of the sale proceeds.

FORFEITURE - A penalty, a fine.

FORGERY - Fabricating or producing falsely, counterfeited.

FORTUITOUS - Accidental.

FORUM - A court of justice; a place of jurisdiction.

FRAUD - Deception; trickery.

FREEHOLDER - One who owns real property.

FUNGIBLE - Of such kind or nature that one specimen or part may be used in the place of another.

G

GARNISHEE - Person garnished.

GARNISHMENT - A legal process to reach the money or effects of a defendant, in the possession or control of a third person.

GRAND JURY - Not less than 16, not more than 23 citizens of a county sworn to inquire into crimes committed or triable in the county.

GRANT - To agree to; convey, especially real property.

GRANTEE - The person to whom a grant is made.

GRANTOR - The person by whom a grant is made.

GRATUITOUS - Given without a return, compensation or consideration.

GRAVAMEN - The grievance complained of or the substantial cause of a criminal action.

GUARANTY (n.) - A promise to answer for the payment of some debt, or the performance of some duty, in case of the failure of another person, who, in the first instance, is liable for such payment or performance.

GUARDIAN - The person, committee, or other representative authorized by law to protect the person or estate or both of an incompetent (or of a *sui juris* person having a guardian) and to act for him in matters affecting his person or property or both. An incompetent is a person under disability imposed by law.

GUILTY - Establishment of the fact that one has committed a breach of conduct; especially, a violation of law.

H

HABEAS CORPUS - You have the body; the name given to a variety of writs, having for their object to bring a party before a court or judge for decision as to whether such person is being lawfully held prisoner.

HABENDUM - In conveyancing; it is the clause in a deed conveying land which defines the extent of ownership to be held by the grantee.

HEARING - A proceeding whereby the arguments of the interested parties are heared.

HEARSAY - A type of testimony given by a witness who relates, not what he knows personally, but what others have told hi, or what he has heard said by others.

HEARSAY RULE, THE - (a) "Hearsay evidence" is evidence of a statement that was made other than by a witness while testifying at the hearing and that is offered to prove the truth of the matter stated; (b) Except as provided by law, hearsay evidence is inadmissible; (c) This section shall be known and may be cited as the hearsay rule.

HEIR - Generally, one who inherits property, real or personal.

HOLDER OF THE PRIVILEGE - (a) The client when he has no guardian or conservator; (b) A guardian or conservator of the client when the client has a guardian or conservator; (c) The personal representative of the client if the client is dead; (d) A successor, assign, trustee in dissolution, or any similar representative of a firm, association, organization, partnership, business trust, corporation, or public entity that is no longer in existence.

HUNG JURY - One so divided that they can't agree on a verdict.

HUSBAND-WIFE PRIVILEGE - An accused in a criminal proceeding has a privilege to prevent his spouse from testifying against him.

HYPOTHECATE - To pledge a thing without delivering it to the pledgee.

HYPOTHESIS - A supposition, assumption, or toehry.

I

I.E. (id est) - That is.

IB., OR IBID.(ibidem) - In the same place; used to refer to a legal reference previously cited to avoid repeating the entire citation.

ILLICIT - Prohibited; unlawful.

ILLUSORY - Deceiving by false appearance.

IMMUNITY - Exemption.

IMPEACH - To accuse, to dispute.

IMPEDIMENTS - Disabilities, or hindrances.

IMPLEAD - To sue or prosecute by due course of law.

IMPUTED - Attributed or charged to.

IN LOCO PARENTIS - In place of parent, a guardian.

IN TOTO - In the whole; completely.

INCHOATE - Imperfect; unfinished.

INCOMMUNICADO - Denial of the right of a prisoner to communicate with friends or relatives.

INCOMPETENT - One who is incapable of caring for his own affairs because he is mentally deficient or undeveloped.

INCRIMINATION - A matter will incriminate a person if it constitutes, or forms an essential part of, or, taken in connection with other matters disclosed, is a basis for a reasonable inference of such a violation of the laws of this State as to subject him to liability to punishment therefor, unless he has become for any reason permanently immune from punishment for such violation.

INCUMBRANCE - Generally a claim, lien, charge or liability attached to and binding real property.

INDEMNIFY - To secure against loss or damage; also, to make reimbursement to one for a loss already incurred by him.

INDEMNITY - An agreement to reimburse another person in case of an anticipated loss falling upon him.

INDICIA - Signs; indications.

INDICTMENT - An accusation in writing found and presented by a grand jury charging that a person has committed a crime.

INDORSE - To write a name on the back of a legal paper or document, generally, a negotiable instrument

INDUCEMENT - Cause or reason why a thing is done or that which incites the person to do the act or commit a crime; the motive for the criminal act.

INFANT - In civil cases one under 21 years of age.

INFORMATION - A formal accusation of crime made by a prosecuting attorney.

INFRA - Below, under; this word occurring by itself in a publication refers the reader to a future part of the publication.

INGRESS - The act of going into.

INJUNCTION - A writ or order by the court requiring a person, generally, to do or to refrain from doing an act.

INSOLVENT - The condition of a person who is unable to pay his debts.

INSTRUCTION - A direction given by the judge to the jury concerning the law of the case.

INTERIM - In the meantime; time intervening.

INTERLOCUTORY - Temporary, not final; something intervening between the commencement and the end of a suit which decides some point or matter, but is not a final decision of the whole controversy.

INTERROGATORIES - A series of formal written questions used in the examination of a party or a witness usually prior to a trial.

INTESTATE - A person who dies without a will.

INURE - To result, to take effect.

IPSO FACTO - By the fact iself; by the mere fact.

ISSUE (n.) The disputed point or question in a case,

J

JEOPARDY - Danger, hazard, peril.

JOINDER - Joining; uniting with another person in some legal steps or proceeding.

JOINT - United; combined.

JUDGE - Member or members or representative or representatives of a court conducting a trial or hearing at which evidence is introduced.

JUDGMENT - The official decision of a court of justice.

JUDICIAL OR JUDICIARY - Relating to or connected with the administration of justice.

JURAT - The clause written at the foot of an affidavit, stating when, where and before whom such affidavit was sworn.

JURISDICTION - The authority to hear and determine controversies between parties.

JURISPRUDENCE - The philosophy of law.

JURY - A body of persons legally selected to inquire into any matter of fact, and to render their verdict according to the evidence.

L

LACHES - The failure to diligently assert a right, which results in a refusal to allow relief.

LANDLORD AND TENANT - A phrase used to denote the legal relation existing between the owner and occupant of real estate.

LARCENY - Stealing personal property belonging to another.

LATENT - Hidden; that which does not appear on the face of a thing.

LAW - Includes constitutional, statutory, and decisional law.

LAWYER-CLIENT PRIVILEGE - (1) A "client" is a person, public officer, or corporation, association, or other organization or entity, either public or private, who is rendered professional legal services by a lawyer, or who consults a lawyer with a view to obtaining professional legal services from him; (2) A "lawyer" is a person authorized, or reasonably believed by the client to be authorized, to practice law in any state or nation; (3) A "representative of the lawyer" is one employed to assist the lawyer in the rendition of professional legal services; (4) A communication is "confidential" if not intended to be disclosed to third persons other than those to whom disclosure is in furtherance of the rendition of professional legal services to the client or those reasonably necessary for the transmission of the communication.

General rule of privilege - A client has a privilege to refuse to disclose and to prevent any other person from disclosing confidential communications made for the purpose of facilitating the rendition of professional legal services to the client, (1) between himself or his representative and his lawyer or his lawyer's representative, or (2) between his lawyer and the lawyer's representative, or (3) by him or his lawyer to a lawyer representing another in a matter of common interest, or (4) between representatives of the client or between the client and a representative of the client, or (5) between lawyers representing the client.

LEADING QUESTION - Question that suggests to the witness the answer that the examining party desires.

LEASE - A contract by which one conveys real estate for a limited time usually for a specified rent; personal property also may be leased.

LEGISLATION - The act of enacting laws.

LEGITIMATE - Lawful.

LESSEE - One to whom a lease is given.

LESSOR - One who grants a lease

LEVY - A collecting or exacting by authority.

LIABLE - Responsible; bound or obligated in law or equity.

LIBEL (v.) - To defame or injure a person's reputation by a published writing.
(n.) - The initial pleading on the part of the plaintiff in an admiralty proceeding.

LIEN - A hold or claim which one person has upon the property of another as a security for some debt or charge.

LIQUIDATED - Fixed; settled.

LIS PENDENS - A pending civil or criminal action.

LITERAL - According to the language.

LITIGANT - A party to a lawsuit.

LITATION - A judicial controversy.

LOCUS - A place.

LOCUS DELICTI - Place of the crime.

LOCUS POENITENTIAE - The abandoning or giving up of one's intention to commit some crime before it is fully completed or abandoning a conspiracy before its purpose is accomplished.

M

MALFEASANCE - To do a wrongful act.

MALICE - The doing of a wrongful act Intentionally without just cause or excuse.

MANDAMUS - The name of a writ issued by a court to enforce the performance of some public duty.

MANDATORY (adj.) Containing a command.

MARITIME - Pertaining to the sea or to commerce thereon.

MARSHALING - Arranging or disposing of in order.

MAXIM - An established principle or proposition.

MINISTERIAL - That which involves obedience to instruction, but demands no special discretion, judgment or skill.

MISAPPROPRIATE - Dealing fraudulently with property entrusted to one.

MISDEMEANOR - A crime less than a felony and punishable by a fine or imprisonment for less than one year.

MISFEASANCE - Improper performance of a lawful act.

MISREPRESENTATION - An untrue representation of facts.

MITIGATE - To make or become less severe, harsh.

MITTIMUS - A warrant of commitment to prison.

MOOT (adj.) Unsettled, undecided, not necessary to be decided.

MORTGAGE - A conveyance of property upon condition, as security for the payment of a debt or the performance of a duty, and to become void upon payment or performance according to the stipulated terms.

MORTGAGEE - A person to whom property is mortgaged.

MORTGAGOR - One who gives a mortgage.

MOTION - In legal proceedings, a "motion" is an application, either written or oral, addressed to the court by a party to an action or a suit requesting the ruling of the court on a matter of law.

MUTUALITY - Reciprocation.

N

NEGLIGENCE - The failure to exercise that degree of care which an ordinarily prudent person would exercise under like circumstances.

NEGOTIABLE (instrument) - Any instrument obligating the payment of money which is transferable from one person to another by endorsement and delivery or by delivery only.

NEGOTIATE - To transact business; to transfer a negotiable instrument; to seek agreement for the amicable disposition of a controversy or case.

NOLLE PROSEQUI - A formal entry upon the record, by the plaintiff in a civil suit or the prosecuting officer in a criminal action, by which he declares that he "will no further prosecute" the case.

NOLO CONTENDERE - The name of a plea in a criminal action, having the same effect as a plea of guilty; but not constituting a direct admission of guilt.

NOMINAL - Not real or substantial.

NOMINAL DAMAGES - Award of a trifling sum where no substantial injury is proved to have been sustained.

NONFEASANCE - Neglect of duty.

NOVATION - The substitution of a new debt or obligation for an existing one.

NUNC PRO TUNC - A phrase applied to acts allowed to be done after the time when they should be done, with a retroactive effect.("Now for then.")

O

OATH - Oath includes affirmation or declaration under penalty of perjury.

OBITER DICTUM - Opinion expressed by a court on a matter not essentially -involved in a case and hence not a decision; also called dicta, if plural.

OBJECT (v.) - To oppose as improper or illegal and referring the question of its propriety or legality to the court.

OBLIGATION - A legal duty, by which a person is bound to do or not to do a certain thing.

OBLIGEE - The person to whom an obligation is owed.

OBLIGOR - The person who is to perform the obligation.

OFFER (v.) - To present for acceptance or rejection.

(n.) - A proposal to do a thing, usually a proposal to make a contract.

OFFICIAL INFORMATION - Information within the custody or control of a department or agency of the government the disclosure of which is shown to be contrary to the public interest.

OFFSET - A deduction.

ONUS PROBANDI - Burden of proof.

OPINION - The statement by a judge of the decision reached in a case, giving the law as applied to the case and giving reasons for the judgment; also a belief or view.

OPTION - The exercise of the power of choice; also a privilege existing in one person, for which he has paid money, which gives him the right to buy or sell real or personal property at a given price within a specified time.

ORDER - A rule or regulation; every direction of a court or judge made or entered in writing but not including a judgment.

ORDINANCE - Generally, a rule established by authority; also commonly used to designate the legislative acts of a municipal corporation.

ORIGINAL - Writing or recording itself or any counterpart intended to have the same effect by a person executing or issuing it. An "original" of a photograph includes the negative or any print therefrom. If data are stored in a computer or similar device, any printout or other output readable by sight, shown to reflect the data accurately, is an "original."

OVERT - Open, manifest.

P

PANEL - A group of jurors selected to serve during a term of the court.

PARENS PATRIAE - Sovereign power of a state to protect or be a guardian over children and incompetents.

PAROL - Oral or verbal.

PAROLE - To release one in prison before the expiration of his sentence, conditionally.

PARITY - Equality in purchasing power between the farmer and other segments of the economy.

PARTITION - A legal division of real or personal property between one or more owners.

PARTNERSHIP - An association of two or more persons to carry on as co-owners a business for profit.

PATENT (adj.) - Evident.

(n.) - A grant of some privilege, property, or authority, made by the government or sovereign of a country to one or more individuals.

PECULATION - Stealing.

PECUNIARY - Monetary.

PENULTIMATE - Next to the last.

PER CURIAM - A phrase used in the report of a decision to distinguish an opinion of the whole court from an opinion written by any one judge.

PER SE - In itself; taken alone.

PERCEIVE - To acquire knowledge through one's senses.

PEREMPTORY - Imperative; absolute.

PERJURY - To lie or state falsely under oath.

PERPETUITY - Perpetual existence; also the quality or condition of an estate limited so that it will not take effect or vest within the period fixed by law.

PERSON - Includes a natural person, firm, association, organization, partnership, business trust, corporation, or public entity.

PERSONAL PROPERTY - Includes money, goods, chattels, things in action, and evidences of debt.

PERSONALTY - Short term for personal property.

PETITION - An application in writing for an order of the court, stating the circumstances upon which it is founded and requesting any order or other relief from a court.

PLAINTIFF - A person who brings a court action.

PLEA - A pleading in a suit or action.

PLEADINGS - Formal allegations made by the parties of their respective claims and defenses, for the judgment of the court.

PLEDGE - A deposit of personal property as a security for the performance of an act.

PLEDGEE - The party to whom goods are delivered in pledge.

PLEDGOR - The party delivering goods in pledge.

PLENARY - Full; complete.

POLICE POWER - Inherent power of the state or its political subdivisions to enact laws within constitutional limits to promote the general welfare of society or the community.

POLLING THE JURY - Call the names of persons on a jury and requiring each juror to declare what his verdict is before it is legally recorded.

POST MORTEM - After death.

POWER OF ATTORNEY - A writing authorizing one to act for another.

PRECEPT - An order, warrant, or writ issued to an officer or body of officers, commanding him or them to do some act within the scope of his or their powers.

PRELIMINARY FACT - Fact upon the existence or nonexistence of which depends the admissibility or inadmissibility of evidence. The phrase "the admissibility or inadmissibility of evidence" includes the qualification or disqualification of a person to be a witness and the existence or non-existence of a privilege.

PREPONDERANCE - Outweighing.

PRESENTMENT - A report by a grand jury on something they have investigated on their own knowledge.

PRESUMPTION - An assumption of fact resulting from a rule of law which requires such fact to be assumed from another fact or group of facts found or otherwise established in the action.

PRIMA FACUE - At first sight.

PRIMA FACIE CASE - A case where the evidence is very patent against the defendant.

PRINCIPAL - The source of authority or rights; a person primarily liable as differentiated from "principle" as a primary or basic doctrine.

PRO AND CON - For and against.

PRO RATA - Proportionally.

PROBATE - Relating to proof, especially to the proof of wills.

PROBATIVE - Tending to prove.

PROCEDURE - In law, this term generally denotes rules which are established by the Federal, State, or local Governments regarding the types of pleading and courtroom practice which must be followed by the parties involved in a criminal or civil case.

PROCLAMATION - A public notice by an official of some order, intended action, or state of facts.

PROFFERED EVIDENCE - The admissibility or inadmissibility of which is dependent upon the existence or nonexistence of a preliminary fact.

PROMISSORY (NOTE) - A promise in writing to pay a specified sum at an expressed time, or on demand, or at sight, to a named person, or to his order, or bearer.

PROOF - The establishment by evidence of a requisite degree of belief concerning a fact in the mind of the trier of fact or the court.

PROPERTY - Includes both real and personal property.

PROPRIETARY (adj.) - Relating or pertaining to ownership; usually a single owner.

PROSECUTE - To carry on an action or other judicial proceeding; to proceed against a person criminally.

PROVISO - A limitation or condition in a legal instrument.

PROXIMATE - Immediate; nearest

PUBLIC EMPLOYEE - An officer, agent, or employee of a public entity.

PUBLIC ENTITY - Includes a national, state, county, city and county, city, district, public authority, public agency, or any other political subdivision or public corporation, whether foreign or domestic.

PUBLIC OFFICIAL - Includes an official of a political dubdivision of such state or territory and of a municipality.

PUNITIVE - Relating to punishment.

Q

QUASH - To make void.

QUASI - As if; as it were.

QUID PRO QUO - Something for something; the giving of one valuable thing for another.

QUITCLAIM (v.) - To release or relinquish claim or title to, especially in deeds to realty.

QUO WARRANTO - A legal procedure to test an official's right to a public office or the right to hold a franchise, or to hold an office in a domestic corporation.

R

RATIFY - To approve and sanction.

REAL PROPERTY - Includes lands, tenements, and hereditaments.

REALTY - A brief term for real property.

REBUT - To contradict; to refute, especially by evidence and arguments.

RECEIVER - A person who is appointed by the court to receive, and hold in trust property in litigation.

RECIDIVIST - Habitual criminal.

RECIPROCAL - Mutual.

RECOUPMENT - To keep back or get something which is due; also, it is the right of a defendant to have a deduction from the amount of the plaintiff's damages because the plaintiff has not fulfilled his part of the same contract.

RECROSS EXAMINATION - Examination of a witness by a cross-examiner subsequent to a redirect examination of the witness.

REDEEM - To release an estate or article from mortgage or pledge by paying the debt for which it stood as security.

REDIRECT EXAMINATION - Examination of a witness by the direct examiner subsequent to the cross-examination of the witness.

REFEREE - A person to whom a cause pending in a court is referred by the court, to take testimony, hear the parties, and report thereon to the court.

REFERENDUM - A method of submitting an important legislative or administrative matter to a direct vote of the people.

RELEVANT EVIDENCE - Evidence including evidence relevant to the credulity of a witness or hearsay declarant, having any tendency in reason to prove or disprove any disputed fact that is of consequence to the determination of the action.

REMAND - To send a case back to the lower court from which it came, for further proceedings.

REPLEVIN - An action to recover goods or chattels wrongfully taken or detained.

REPLY (REPLICATION) - Generally, a reply is what the plaintiff or other person who has instituted proceedings says in answer to the defendant's case.

RE JUDICATA - A thing judicially acted upon or decided.

RES ADJUDICATA - Doctrine that an issue or dispute litigated and determined in a case between the opposing parties is deemed permanently decided between these parties.

RESCIND (RECISSION) - To avoid or cancel a contract.

RESPONDENT - A defendant in a proceeding in chancery or admiralty; also, the person who contends against the appeal in a case.

RESTITUTION - In equity, it is the restoration of both parties to their original condition (when practicable), upon the rescission of a contract for fraud or similar cause.

RETROACTIVE (RETROSPECTIVE) - Looking back; effective as of a prior time.

REVERSED - A term used by appellate courts to indicate that the decision of the lower court in the case before it has been set aside.

REVOKE - To recall or cancel.

RIPARIAN (RIGHTS) - The rights of a person owning land containing or bordering on a water course or other body of water, such as lakes and rivers.

S

SALE - A contract whereby the ownership of property is transferred from one person to another for a sum of money or for any consideration.

SANCTION - A penalty or punishment provided as a means of enforcing obedience to a law; also, an authorization.

SATISFACTION - The discharge of an obligation by paying a party what is due to him; or what is awarded to him by the judgment of a court or otherwise.

SCIENTER - Knowingly; also, it is used in pleading to denote the defendant 's guilty knowledge.

SCINTILLA - A spark; also the least particle.

SECRET OF STATE - Governmental secret relating to the national defense or the international relations of the United States.

SECURITY - Indemnification; the term is applied to an obligation, such as a mortgage or deed of trust, given by a debtor to insure the payment or performance of his debt, by furnishing the creditor with a resource to be used in case of the debtor's failure to fulfill the principal obligation.

SENTENCE - The judgment formally pronounced by the court or judge upon the defendant after his conviction in a criminal prosecution.

SET-OFF - A claim or demand which one party in an action credits against the claim of the opposing party.

SHALL and MAY - "Shall" is mandatory and "may" is permissive.

SITUS - Location.

SOVEREIGN - A person, body or state in which independent and supreme authority is vested.

STARE DECISIS - To follow decided cases.

STATE - "State" means this State, unless applied to the different parts of the United States. In the latter case, it includes any state, district, commonwealth, territory or insular possession of the United States, including the District of Columbia.

STATEMENT - (a) Oral or written verbal expression or (b) nonverbal conduct of a person intended by him as a substitute for oral or written verbal expression.

STATUTE - An act of the legislature. Includes a treaty.

STATUTE OF LIMITATION - A statute limiting the time to bring an action after the right of action has arisen.

STAY - To hold in abeyance an order of a court.

STIPULATION - Any agreement made by opposing attorneys regulating any matter incidental to the proceedings or trial.

SUBORDINATION (AGREEMENT) - An agreement making one's rights inferior to or of a lower rank than another's.

SUBORNATION - The crime of procuring a person to lie or to make false statements to a court.

SUBPOENA - A writ or order directed to a person, and requiring his attendance at a particular time and place to testify as a witness.

SUBPOENA DUCES TECUM - A subpoena used, not only for the purpose of compelling witnesses to attend in court, but also requiring them to bring with them books or documents which may be in their possession, and which may tend to elucidate the subject matter of the trial.

SUBROGATION - The substituting of one for another as a creditor, the new creditor succeeding to the former's rights.

SUBSIDY - A government grant to assist a private enterprise deemed advantageous to the public.

SUI GENERIS - Of the same kind.

SUIT - Any civil proceeding by a person or persons against another or others in a court of justice by which the plaintiff pursues the remedies afforded him by law.

SUMMONS - A notice to a defendant that an action against him has been commenced and requiring him to appear in court and answer the complaint.

SUPRA - Above; this word occurring by itself in a book refers the reader to a previous part of the book.

SURETY - A person who binds himself for the payment of a sum of money, or for the performance of something else, for another.

SURPLUSAGE - Extraneous or unnecessary matter.

SURVIVORSHIP - A term used when a person becomes entitled to property by reason of his having survived another person who had an interest in the property.

SUSPEND SENTENCE - Hold back a sentence pending good behavior of prisoner.

SYLLABUS - A note prefixed to a report, especially a case, giving a brief statement of the court's ruling on different issues of the case.

T

TALESMAN - Person summoned to fill a panel of jurors.

TENANT - One who holds or possesses lands by any kind of right or title; also, one who has the temporary use and occupation of real property owned by another person (landlord), the duration and terms of his tenancy being usually fixed by an instrument called "a lease."

TENDER - An offer of money; an expression of willingness to perform a contract according to its terms.

TERM - When used with reference to a court, it signifies the period of time during which the court holds a session, usually of several weeks or months duration.

TESTAMENTARY - Pertaining to a will or the administration of a will.

TESTATOR (male)

TESTATRIX (female) - One who makes or has made a testament or will.

TESTIFY (TESTIMONY) - To give evidence under oath as a witness.

TO WIT - That is to say; namely.

TORT - Wrong; injury to the person.

TRANSITORY - Passing from place to place.

TRESPASS - Entry into another's ground, illegally.

TRIAL - The examination of a cause, civil or criminal, before a judge who has jurisdiction over it, according to the laws of the land.

TRIER OF FACT - Includes (a) the jury and (b) the court when the court is trying an issue of fact other than one relating to the admissibility of evidence.

TRUST - A right of property, real or personal, held by one party for the benefit of another.

TRUSTEE - One who lawfully holds property in custody for the benefit of another.

U

UNAVAILABLE AS A WITNESS - The declarant is (1) Exempted or precluded on the ground of privilege from testifying concerning the matter to which his statement is relevant; (2) Disqualified from testifying to the matter; (3) Dead or unable to attend or to testify at the hearing because of then existing physical or mental illness or infirmity; (4) Absent from the hearing and the court is unable to compel his attendance by its process; or (5) Absent from the hearing and the proponent of his statement has exercised reasonable diligence but has been unable to procure his attendance by the court's process.

ULTRA VIRES - Acts beyond the scope and power of a corporation, association, etc.

UNILATERAL - One-sided; obligation upon, or act of one party.

USURY - Unlawful interest on a loan.

V

VACATE - To set aside; to move out.

VARIANCE - A discrepancy or disagreement between two instruments or two aspects of the same case, which by law should be consistent.

VENDEE - A purchaser or buyer.

VENDOR - The person who transfers property by sale, particularly real estate; the term "seller" is used more commonly for one who sells personal property.

VENIREMEN - Persons ordered to appear to serve on a jury or composing a panel of jurors.

VENUE - The place at which an action is tried, generally based on locality or judicial district in which an injury occurred or a material fact happened.

VERDICT - The formal decision or finding of a jury.

VERIFY - To confirm or substantiate by oath.

VEST - To accrue to.

VOID - Having no legal force or binding effect.

VOIR DIRE - Preliminary examination of a witness or a juror to test competence, interest, prejudice, etc.

W

WAIVE - To give up a right.

WAIVER - The intentional or voluntary relinquishment of a known right.

WARRANT (WARRANTY) (v.) - To promise that a certain fact or state of facts, in relation to the subject matter, is, or shall be, as it is represented to be.

WARRANT (n.) - A writ issued by a judge, or other competent authority, addressed to a sheriff, or other officer, requiring him to arrest the person therein named, and bring him before the judge or court to answer or be examined regarding the offense with which he is charged.

WRIT - An order or process issued in the name of the sovereign or in the name of a court or judicial officer, commanding the performance or nonperformance of some act.

WRITING - Handwriting, typewriting, printing, photostating, photographing and every other means of recording upon any tangible thing any form of communication or representation, including letters, words, pictures, sounds, or symbols, or combinations thereof.

WRITINGS AND RECORDINGS - Consists of letters, words, or numbers, or their equivalent, set down by handwriting, typewriting, printing, photostating, photographing, magnetic impulse, mechanical or electronic recording, or other form of data compilation.

Y

YEA AND NAY - Yes and no.

YELLOW DOG CONTRACT - A contract by which employer requires employee to sign an instrument promising as condition that he will not join a union during its continuance, and will be discharged if he does join.

Z

ZONING - The division of a city by legislative regulation into districts and the prescription and application in each district of regulations having to do with structural and architectural designs of buildings and of regulations prescribing use to which buildings within designated districts may be put.

ANSWER SHEET

USE THE SPECIAL PENCIL.   MAKE GLOSSY BLACK MARKS.

	A B C D E		A B C D E		A B C D E		A B C D E		A B C D E
1	:: :: :: :: ::	26	:: :: :: :: ::	51	:: :: :: :: ::	76	:: :: :: :: ::	101	:: :: :: :: ::
2	:: :: :: :: ::	27	:: :: :: :: ::	52	:: :: :: :: ::	77	:: :: :: :: ::	102	:: :: :: :: ::
3	:: :: :: :: ::	28	:: :: :: :: ::	53	:: :: :: :: ::	78	:: :: :: :: ::	103	:: :: :: :: ::
4	:: :: :: :: ::	29	:: :: :: :: ::	54	:: :: :: :: ::	79	:: :: :: :: ::	104	:: :: :: :: ::
5	:: :: :: :: ::	30	:: :: :: :: ::	55	:: :: :: :: ::	80	:: :: :: :: ::	105	:: :: :: :: ::
6	:: :: :: :: ::	31	:: :: :: :: ::	56	:: :: :: :: ::	81	:: :: :: :: ::	106	:: :: :: :: ::
7	:: :: :: :: ::	32	:: :: :: :: ::	57	:: :: :: :: ::	82	:: :: :: :: ::	107	:: :: :: :: ::
8	:: :: :: :: ::	33	:: :: :: :: ::	58	:: :: :: :: ::	83	:: :: :: :: ::	108	:: :: :: :: ::
9	:: :: :: :: ::	34	:: :: :: :: ::	59	:: :: :: :: ::	84	:: :: :: :: ::	109	:: :: :: :: ::
10	:: :: :: :: ::	35	:: :: :: :: ::	60	:: :: :: :: ::	85	:: :: :: :: ::	110	:: :: :: :: ::

Make only ONE mark for each answer.   Additional and stray marks may be
counted as mistakes.   In making corrections, erase errors COMPLETELY.

	A B C D E		A B C D E		A B C D E		A B C D E		A B C D E
11	:: :: :: :: ::	36	:: :: :: :: ::	61	:: :: :: :: ::	86	:: :: :: :: ::	111	:: :: :: :: ::
12	:: :: :: :: ::	37	:: :: :: :: ::	62	:: :: :: :: ::	87	:: :: :: :: ::	112	:: :: :: :: ::
13	:: :: :: :: ::	38	:: :: :: :: ::	63	:: :: :: :: ::	88	:: :: :: :: ::	113	:: :: :: :: ::
14	:: :: :: :: ::	39	:: :: :: :: ::	64	:: :: :: :: ::	89	:: :: :: :: ::	114	:: :: :: :: ::
15	:: :: :: :: ::	40	:: :: :: :: ::	65	:: :: :: :: ::	90	:: :: :: :: ::	115	:: :: :: :: ::
16	:: :: :: :: ::	41	:: :: :: :: ::	66	:: :: :: :: ::	91	:: :: :: :: ::	116	:: :: :: :: ::
17	:: :: :: :: ::	42	:: :: :: :: ::	67	:: :: :: :: ::	92	:: :: :: :: ::	117	:: :: :: :: ::
18	:: :: :: :: ::	43	:: :: :: :: ::	68	:: :: :: :: ::	93	:: :: :: :: ::	118	:: :: :: :: ::
19	:: :: :: :: ::	44	:: :: :: :: ::	69	:: :: :: :: ::	94	:: :: :: :: ::	119	:: :: :: :: ::
20	:: :: :: :: ::	45	:: :: :: :: ::	70	:: :: :: :: ::	95	:: :: :: :: ::	120	:: :: :: :: ::
21	:: :: :: :: ::	46	:: :: :: :: ::	71	:: :: :: :: ::	96	:: :: :: :: ::	121	:: :: :: :: ::
22	:: :: :: :: ::	47	:: :: :: :: ::	72	:: :: :: :: ::	97	:: :: :: :: ::	122	:: :: :: :: ::
23	:: :: :: :: ::	48	:: :: :: :: ::	73	:: :: :: :: ::	98	:: :: :: :: ::	123	:: :: :: :: ::
24	:: :: :: :: ::	49	:: :: :: :: ::	74	:: :: :: :: ::	99	:: :: :: :: ::	124	:: :: :: :: ::
25	:: :: :: :: ::	50	:: :: :: :: ::	75	:: :: :: :: ::	100	:: :: :: :: ::	125	:: :: :: :: ::

ANSWER SHEET

TEST NO. _____ PART _____ TITLE OF POSITION _____

AS GIVEN IN EXAMINATION ANNOUNCEMENT - INCLUDE OPTION, IF ANY)

PLACE OF EXAMINATION _____ DATE_____

(CITY OR TOWN)   (STATE)

	RATING

USE THE SPECIAL PENCIL.   MAKE GLOSSY BLACK MARKS.

Make only ONE mark for each answer.   Additional and stray marks may be
counted as mistakes.   In making corrections, erase errors COMPLETELY.